# BUSINESS LAW & PRACTICE

**Professor Nicholas Bourne**
**LLB, LLM (Wales), LLM (Cantab), Barrister**
**Head of Swansea Law School**

Cavendish
Publishing
Limited

First published in Great Britain 1994 by Cavendish Publishing
Limited, The Glass House, Wharton Street, London WC1X 9PX.
Telephone: 071-278 8000     Facsimile: 071-278 8080

British Library Cataloguing in Publication Data

Bourne, Nicholas
Business Law and Practice
I Title
344.10666

ISBN 1-874241-77-5

Printed and bound in Great Britain

# PREFACE

I am indebted to my two research assistants, Jane Watkin and N Nanthabalan, both of whom have performed invaluable 'spade work' for me.

I am also very grateful to Vivien Prais of the London School of Economics for permission to use the draft partnership agreement.

The various company forms reproduced are 'Crown Copyright' and reproduced with the permission of Her Majesty's Stationery Office as are the model memoranda, articles of association, Table A and the Company and Business Names Regulations 1981 (SI 1981/1685).

As ever Maureen Turner has done a marvellous job of deciphering and typing up.

The Finance Bill 1993 referred to throughout the text became the Finance Act 1994 on receiving Royal Assent on 3 May 1994.


Nicholas Bourne

May 1994

# CONTENTS

# CONTENTS

# CONTENTS

# CONTENTS

# CONTENTS

# CONTENTS

# CONTENTS

# CONTENTS

# TABLE OF CASES

# TABLE OF STATUTES

# TABLE OF STATUTORY INSTRUMENTS

# TABLE OF EC LEGISLATION

# CHAPTER 1

# OVERVIEW

In this textbook various objectives are set out. These are:

- To outline some of the considerations that may influence the client in deciding what type of business medium to adopt.
- To consider in outline:

  (a)  sole trader status;

  (b)  partnership status including limited partnership status.

  A specimen partnership agreement is also set out.

This section will also consider the role and liabilities of sole traders and partners as well as the cost of setting up each type of business.

- To examine how the company is set up including an examination of the memorandum of association and the articles of association and how these documents may be changed (models of these will also be set out). This section will also consider the role and liabilities of shareholders, directors and other officers and promoters as well as the cost of setting up a company.
- To consider the taxation implications of setting up as a sole trader/partnership or as a company.
- To consider how a company raises capital and rules on the maintenance of capital in a company.
- To consider how shares may be transferred.
- To consider how company meetings are conducted.
- To consider the role and liability of the auditor in the context of the company.
- To consider the company in trouble - administration, administrative receivership and liquidation.
- To consider an outline of certain key features of the law of contract.
- To consider certain key features of the law of agency.
- To consider certain key features of competition law.

Throughout forms that need to be filed at Companies House are set out.

# CHAPTER 2

# INTRODUCTION

## A COMPANY, A PARTNERSHIP OR SOLE TRADER STATUS

When a businessman decides to start a business, one decision that will need to be made early on is whether to operate as a company as a partnership (or firm as it is sometimes called) or as a sole trader. There are certain advantages, and indeed certain disadvantages, that attach to incorporation. The following are therefore matters which businessmen will need to consider. The essence of the company is that it is a separate person in law, see *Salomon v A Salomon & Co Ltd* (1897)[1] (Chapters 8-11). From this very basic difference between the company on the one hand and the partnership and sole trader on the other hand flow many of the advantages and disadvantages of incorporation. A partnership shares many of its advantages and disadvantages with sole trader status.

The most obvious advantage in incorporation is the access to limited liability. Not all companies are limited companies. Unlimited companies do not need to file accounts so sometimes this is an attraction for businessmen. However, the possibility of limiting the liability of the participators to the amount of the issued shares is an attractive one. Sometimes this advantage is, of course, more apparent than real. If a small private company goes to a bank and asks to borrow a large sum of money, the bank is unlikely to be satisfied with the possibility of recourse against the company's assets. In practice the bank manager will require some collateral security from the company's directors. In a partnership, however, all the partners will have unlimited liability for the business's debts and liabilities. This is the case except in a limited partnership governed by the Limited Partnerships Act 1907. In a limited partnership, however, only sleeping partners may have limited liability and it is not possible to form a partnership made up entirely of limited partners. There must always be somebody who is 'picking up the tab' with no limitation of liability. Similarly sole traders have no limit on their liability. Insuring against obvious risks is a sensible course of action for sole traders and partnerships.

---

1    [1897] AC 22

A further advantage of the company is the possibility of separating ownership from control. In a partnership all of the partners are agents for the firm. In a company, and this is particularly the case in public companies, the ownership and the control are separated. Those people owning the share capital will not generally be the people who are running the business (however, in private companies, the owners and the managers may well be the same).

An attraction of incorporation is what is sometimes termed perpetual succession. This means that the company need never die. Companies do go into liquidation but they need not do so. There is no theoretical reason why a company cannot go on for ever; for example, the Hudson's Bay Company has been running for well over 300 years. In the case of partnerships, however, wherever there is a change of partners, there has to be a drawing up of partnership accounts and a reformation of the partnership. Where a partner or sole trader dies, his estate will pass under the rules of succession. If a partner or sole trader goes into bankruptcy, the rules in the Insolvency Act on bankruptcy apply.

Incorporation is an attractive business medium where the participators wish to be able to transfer their shares at some later stage. In a company, shares are freely transferable, subject to the terms of the articles of association and the memorandum of association (Chapters 8-11). In a partnership, by contrast, a partner's share is not so transferable unless the agreement so provides. The advantage of transferability is seen at its clearest where a company is quoted on the Stock Exchange or the Unlisted Securities Market. At-this stage, there will be a market mechanism for disposing of and purchasing shares. Clearly a sole trader is able to dispose of his business subject to there being a market available.

It is said to be easier to raise finance where a company is formed as opposed to where there is a partnership or sole trader status. Clearly, if a company is quoted, it has access to the Stock Exchange to raise finance by issuing its shares and debentures (collectively called securities) to the public (p 102 et seq). In the case of debentures, these may be secured by a floating charge over all of the company's assets and undertaking (p 211). The device of the floating charge is unique to the company and thus neither a partnership nor a sole trader can take advantage of this means of raising finance.

It is probably the case that there is more prestige attached to the company than to the partnership or sole trader status. There is no reason that this should be the case but probably the trading and investing public sees a company in a more favourable light than a partnership.

A further consideration, although it might not be an advantage for companies, is taxation. Companies will pay corporation tax on their profits. These profits may then be distributed as dividends to members who may be liable to pay tax on the dividend less any ACT (Advance Corporation Tax) that has already been paid by the company. Sole traders will pay income tax. In the case of partnerships, the profits of the partnership business are attributable to the partners of the firm who will pay schedular income tax on those profits. It is not possible to say, in isolation from factors concerning the circumstances of the participators and their other sources of income, whether this is an advantage for the sole trader or partnership or not. It will depend on the circumstances.

The disadvantages that attach to incorporation are not numerous. There are clearly formalities to be complied with. A sole trader has no problems in drawing up a business agreement! A partnership agreement need not be written. Clearly it is desirable to have a written agreement for evidential purposes but there is no legal reason why the agreement should be in writing. In the case of a company, there are various formalities to be complied with. A constitution has to be drafted, made up of a memorandum of association and articles of association (Chapter 7). These documents have to be delivered to the Registrar (at Companies House in Cardiff in the case of English and Welsh companies) together with a statement of capital a statement concerning officers and a declaration of compliance. A certificate of incorporation will then be issued to the company. There are various ongoing formalities for a company including the filing of an annual return, the filing of annual accounts (unless the company is unlimited) and the filing of various forms connected with changes of directors, issue of shares, issue of debentures, change of company secretary etc. Companies also have to comply with formalities regarding the holding of meetings which is not the case in a partnership. Private companies may dispense with the need to hold an annual general meeting by unanimous resolution (p 179).

Together with these formalities, there is the disadvantage of publicity in the case of the company. This is generally seen as a disadvantage as a company has no option but to make certain its affairs are made public. These would include the company's directors, company secretary, the accounts of the company (unless unlimited), the annual return of the company, the company's constitution and various registers that have to be kept at the company's registered office.

Together with formalities and publicity, one may add expense as a disadvantage. However, the expense of setting up a company is not great. There is a charge for the issue of a certificate of incorporation and an annual fee for filing the company's annual return but few other charges are made by the company's registry. The cost of the annual audit may well be a deterrent, however.

Two other disadvantages of incorporation may be mentioned here. These are the rules on the maintenance of capital that apply to companies and which are much stricter than in relation to partnerships and the remaining rules on ultra vires that limit a company's freedom of manoeuvre. Partnerships by contrast are free to do what is legal within the law of the land; sole traders also have this same freedom.

Sections 716-717 of the Companies Act 1985 provide that in general there is a prohibition of partnerships with more than 20 members. However, this is subject to wide-ranging exceptions in favour of solicitors, accountants, stock brokers, architects, actuaries and many other professional partnerships.

# CHAPTER 3

# SETTING UP THE BUSINESS – GENERAL COMMENTS

Many considerations that have to be borne in mind in setting up a business will apply whether the business is as a sole trader or as a partnership or as a company. This chapter looks at some of the major issues affecting the businessman setting up.

A business will very often need to employ people. The employer should bear in mind the provisions of the Sex Discrimination Act 1975 and the Race Relations Act 1976 which prohibit direct and indirect discrimination on the grounds of sex, race or marital status etc in relation to offices of employment. The Trade Union and Labour Relations (Consolidation) Act 1992 also prohibits discrimination on the grounds of trade union membership.

Where a person is offered employment, the employee must within eight weeks of commencing the employment receive a written statement containing details of certain aspects of the employment:

- identification of the employer and employee;
- date of commencement of the employment and whether any previous service with the employer counts as continuous employment;
- the scale or rate of pay;
- the intervals of payment of salary;
- the hours of work;
- holidays and holiday pay;
- arrangements for sick pay;
- provisions on pension and pension schemes and whether a contracting out certificate in relation to SERPS is in force;
- the job title;
- the place or places of work;
- where the employment is not permanent the period for which it is expected to continue;
- any collective agreement affecting the terms and conditions of employment;
- where the employee is expected to work outside the UK, the period of foreign service, the currency to be used for pay and any extra benefits;

- the notice that is required to be given by employer or by the employee;
- details of any disciplinary or grievance procedures.

If there is a change to the terms and conditions, then the employer must give the employee written details of the change within one month.

In practice, the contract of employment will generally give a detailed exposition of the employee's duties. In addition there are certain implied terms in an employment relationship:

- to obey lawful and reasonable orders;
- to perform work with reasonable care and skill;
- to act honestly and provide faithful service.

These are duties of the employee.

The employer owes certain duties to the employee:

- to pay salary;
- to indemnify the employee;
- to take reasonable care for the safety of employees. Indeed, an employer in addition to the common law duty to take reasonable care has statutory responsibilities under the Health and Safety at Work Act 1974. However, the employee has no right to claim damages under the 1974 Act. This imposes criminal sanctions for breach.

The employer is liable to pay tax under the Pay As You Earn scheme by deducting the income tax that is due to the Inland Revenue from the employee's gross pay. The employer should also deduct National Insurance.

# NAME

Whether the business is operated as a sole trader, a partnership or a company, the Business Names Act 1985 will have some impact on the use of a name. The Companies Act 1985 is examined below in relation to company names.

Where a business name is used, there is no index to check to ensure that the name is not already in use. The considerations that need to be borne in mind by businessmen are as follows:

- the possibility of an action in tort for passing off if there is a business with a similar name (p 37);
- the stipulation of certain words of a sensitive nature which require the consent of the Department of Trade and Industry or of a nominated body (pp 36 and 39 et seq);

- If the name that is to be used as a business name also constitutes a trade mark, eg Nintendo, Mr Blobby, then the person who has registered the trademark will have a summary remedy against anybody else using that name (Trade Marks Act 1938).

## INSURANCE

Employers need also to consider the necessity and advisability of insurance. Employers must insure against liability towards an employee injured at work. They must also ensure that there is third party cover in relation to motor insurance. Employers might also consider that other types of insurance are wise, for example public liability insurance.

## VAT THRESHOLD

Once a company reaches a turnover of £45,000 in a period of 12 months, registration for Value Added Tax is necessary (Finance Bill 1994).

## MISCELLANEOUS

You may also need to consider other matters. For example, if the business is to take a lease of premises, then the various Rent Act provisions will need to be considered. These are outside the scope of this work. In addition, it may be that the business needs to consider licences of one type or another, this would be the case for example if the business is to operate an off-licence. It would also be the case if it intended to offer credit facilities to members of the public.

A business might also need to consider registration of trade marks, designs or patents. Once again, the detailed rules are outside the scope of this work.

Whatever type of business is being set up, accounting records to demonstrate the profits of the business must be kept. There are strict rules on time limits in relation to companies which are considered below.

# CHAPTER 4

# SETTING UP AS A SOLE TRADER

Anybody can set up in business on their own without the need for registration of any documents as is necessary for a company. The trader may wish to trade under a business name. There is no register of business names as there is of company names. The law is set out in the Business Names Act 1985. Certain names do need prior approval of a specified body. These are set out in The Company and Business Names Regulations 1981[1]. These restrictions are discussed below in the context of company names (pp 36 and 39 et seq).

Thus, for example, use of the word 'Midwife' needs the consent of the Central Midwives Board or the Central Midwives Board for Scotland. It is an offence to use a name which contains one of the restricted words without the required consent; or to use a name which gives the impression of a connection with Her Majesty's Government or with any local authority without the consent of the Secretary of State[2]. Section 4 of the Business Names Act 1985 provides for disclosure of the name of the individual running the business, together with an address in Great Britain where service of any document relating to the business may be effected, on all business letters, written orders for goods or services to be supplied and the business invoices and receipts issued in the course of the business and written demands for payment of debts arising in the course of the business.

The name and address of the trader should also be exhibited in a prominent place at any business premises to which customers and suppliers have access. Contravention of these requirements without reasonable excuse is a criminal offence. Where a trader seeks to enforce a contract etc where he is in breach of these provisions, if the defendant can show that he has a claim that he has been unable to pursue by reason of the plaintiff's breach or that he has suffered some financial loss in connection with the contract because of the plaintiff's breach of the provisions; then the plaintiff's claim will be dismissed unless the court is satisfied that it is just and equitable to permit the proceedings to continue[3].

---

[1] SI 1981/1685.
[2] Business Names Act 1985, s 2 .
[3] Ibid., s 5.

A sole trader is personally liable to the extent of his assets for the debts and liabilities of his business. There are anti-avoidance provisions in the Insolvency Act 1986 to prevent a trader divesting himself of property in advance of bankruptcy unless it is more than five years before the presentation of a bankruptcy petition[4]. In addition, transactions defrauding creditors may be set aside by court order[5]. There is no time limit on the exercise of this power.

There are no automatic costs associated with setting up in business as a sole trader. Formalities are few and in practice may well be limited to contacting the Inland Revenue, Customs and Excise and the local council in relation to planning permission and licensing as appropriate.

---

4  Ibid., ss 339 and 341.
5  Ibid., s 423.

# CHAPTER 5

# SETTING UP A PARTNERSHIP

## DEFINITION

A partnership is the relation which subsists between persons carrying on a business in common with a view of profit[1]. The Partnership Act 1890 is short in comparison with the Companies Act 1985, the former act has 50 sections and no schedules, the latter act has 747 sections and 25 schedules. The Partnership Act is a codification of the common law principles of agency and other rules affecting partnerships. Essentially partnerships are created by agreement between the parties. Partnerships; other than limited partnerships do not require registration.

## LIABILITIES OF PARTNERS

Every partner in a partnership is jointly liable for all debts and obligations of the firm incurred while he is a partner[2]. This used to mean that where a person elected to sue one partner and failed to recover, he could not then decide to sue the other partners. This rule was overturned by s 3 of the Civil Liability (Contribution) Act 1978. The section provides that 'Judgment recovered against a person liable in respect of any debt or damage shall not be a bar to an action or to the continuance of an action, against any other person who is (apart from any such bar) jointly liable with him in respect of the same debt or damage'. The section ends the difficulty of joint liability. Section 12 of the Partnership Act 1890 provides that liability for tortious wrongs of the firm is joint and several, so that an action against one partner which fails would not debar action against other partners.

The Limited Partnerships Act 1907 permits the formation of limited partnerships consisting of one or more general partners with unlimited liability[3]. Limited partners who contribute capital to the firm but who are otherwise not liable to contribute may not be involved in the

---

1   Partnership Act 1890, s 1.
2   Ibid., s 9.
3   Limited Partnerships Act 1907, s 4(2).

running of the firm. If they are they sacrifice their limitation of liability[4]. During the term of the partnership, a limited partner may not in any way draw out or receive back any part of the contribution he has made. If he does he is liable for the firm's debts and liabilities up to the amount drawn out. The limited partnership is not a popular business vehicle, in March 1992 there were 3,193 of them.

A limited partnership must be registered as provided by the Limited Partnerships Act 1907. Registration is with the registrar of companies. A statement is made signed by all the partners giving the following information:

- the firm's name;
- the general nature of the business;
- the address of the principal place of the business;
- the full name of each partner, listing general and limited partners separately;
- the term if any for which the partnership is entered into;
- the date of its commencement;
- a statement that the partnership is limited and the description of every limited partner as such;
- the sum contributed by each limited partner and whether it has been paid in cash or otherwise.

In relation to the choice of name, the registrar will advise against the use of a name which is the same as or similar to a name already on the register as a company or limited partnership. Limited partnerships are subject to the Business Names Act 1985.

## FORMATION AND EXPENSE

Confusion is sometimes caused by the fact that firms are described as companies. This use of 'company' in the firm name should not blur the distinction between the partnership and the company.

Partnerships can be formed orally. There is no need for a written agreement but this is clearly advisable. Where the agreement, whether oral or written, fails to make provision for a particular matter, the Partnership Act 1890 will fill the gap. A written agreement should be drawn up and this agreement should cover matters such as the termination of the partnership, the duties of the partners, expulsion of partners and capital and revenue shares in the firm. A specimen

---

4   Ibid., s 6(1).

partnership agreement is set out below. This is not in any way intended to be seen as a model but is merely an example of an arrangement made between different partners (see Partnership Agreement).

There are no automatic costs associated with setting up and running a partnership. Indeed except in the case of a limited partnership there are no formalities to be complied with other than those which may apply depending upon the nature of the business and mentioned in the context of the sole trader. However, a written partnership agreement is desirable and legal advice should be sought in drawing up such an agreement. It is likely that the partnership agreement will make provision for the drawing up of annual accounts; and for accounts to be prepared upon the cessation of the partnership. Here obviously there are cost implications.

The rules on business names which apply to sole traders apply in just the same way, *mutatis mutandis* to partnerships.

One factor which may affect the choice of business medium is the size of the membership of the business (p 6).

## PARTICIPANTS IN A PARTNERSHIP

Unlike the company where there is at least in theory a clear division between shareholders who invest in the business and the directors who manage the business, in partnership law there is no such division. In partnership law a person who invests in the firm's business will inevitably find that he is a partner in the firm and fully liable for the firm's debts (unless he is a limited partner within the Limited Partnerships Act 1907) (p 13).

It is possible for the partnership to employ people but of course the partners themselves are not employed by the firm. The two relationships are mutually exclusive. The position of a director, even a sole director, is quite different. He may be employed by the company, see *Lee v Lee's Air Farming* (1961)[5].

Sometimes the position of the salaried partner causes particular difficulty. The position is used most prevalently in professional firms as a 'first step on the ladder'. If a person is represented to the outside world as a partner, then, of course, he may bind the firm by his actions, see *United Bank of Kuwait Ltd v Hammond* (1988)[6]. However, within the partnership itself the position will be affected by the question of whether

---

5   [1961] AC 12.
6   [1988] 1 WLR 1051.

the salaried partner is in reality an employee or a partner, see *Stekel v Ellice* (1973)[7].

---

7    [1973] 1 WLR 191.

THIS PARTNERSHIP AGREEMENT is made the    day of
One thousand nine hundred and ninety
BETWEEN
of


and
of


and
of


(all of whom are hereinafter collectively referred to as 'the Partners' and individually as 'a Partner').

*Whereby it is agreed and confirmed* that with effect on and from the First day of April One thousand nine hundred and ninety.......the parties hereto shall continue in partnership (hereinafter called 'the Partnership') upon the terms hereinafter contained namely:

1   *The* Partnership business shall be that of Civil Structural and Services Engineers and Consultants in continuation of the business of..............................................heretofore carried on and shall be carried on at the.........................................and at................................................... or at such other place or places as the Partners may determine under the same style or firm of '..............................'

2   (1)  *The* Partnership shall continue from the 1st April 199_ for a period of three years and thereafter as may be agreed or during such period as the Partners or any two of them shall be living (whichever is the shorter) and so that in the event of any Partner ceasing to be a Partner by reason of his death or expulsion in accordance with the provisions of this Deed the Partnership shall not determine as regards the surviving or continuing Partners.

      (2)  If at the expiration or sooner determination of the period of this Agreement no further Agreement shall be reached between all of the Partners as to the terms upon which they wish to continue in Partnership but a majority of the Partners shall agree such

terms then those agreeing may continue the business of the Partnership and the Partner or Partners not so agreeing shall be deemed to have given due notice pursuant to Clause 15(1)(a) hereof to expire on the expiration or determination of the Agreement of his or their wish to retire from the Partnership.

3   *The* firm name shall be '.............................' as mentioned above.

4   The Bankers of '.............................' shall be

of............................. in the County of

and/or such other bankers as may be agreed between the Partners and all Partnership monies and securities for monies shall be paid into or deposited to the credit of the appropriate accounts with such Bankers cheques whereof shall be drawn in the firm's name by any of the Partners.

5   (1)  On the First day of April 199  the capital of the Partnership shall be £1,000 contributed as to £680 by............., £300 by.............,and £20 by............. Any further sum advanced by way of capital shall unless otherwise agreed be advanced by the Partners in the same shares in which they shall for the time being be entitled to the super profits of the Partnership.

   (2)  Unless otherwise agreed between the Partners no Partner shall be entitled to interest on the amount of any capital for the time being standing to his credit in the books of the firm.

   (3)  The capital for the time being of the Partnership shall belong to the Partners in the proportions in which it has been contributed by them.

6   (1)  Until at any time or from time to time otherwise agreed the Partners shall be entitled to receive a salary as set out in the Schedule hereto and unless otherwise agreed such salary shall be paid before the division of net profits in accordance with sub-clause (2) hereof. Such division shall only relate to the net profits in excess of any such salary (herein referred to as 'super profits').

   (2)  Subject to sub-clause (1) hereof the Partners shall be entitled to the super profits in the shares following or such other shares as may be agreed by the Partners in writing from time to time and shall bear in the same proportions all losses including capital losses:

      Mr............(68%)

      Mr............(30%)

      Mr............( 2%)

   (3)  In the event that the net profits of the business shall not be sufficient to cover in full the salaries payable in accordance with

sub-clause (1) hereof the Partners shall bear any aggregate shortfall in the proportions which their respective salaries bear to each other.

(4)  The division of the profits or losses in no way confers any control or voting power in the administration or decision making of the Partnership and the allocation of more than one half of the profits or losses to any one partner does not confer a controlling interest.

7  *The* usual books of account shall be properly kept in respect of all transactions affecting the partnership.

8  *Each* Partner shall at all times have access to all books and accounts and papers belonging to the firm and shall be entitled by himself or his agent to make such extracts or copies as he may think fit.

9  *On* the 31 day of March One thousand nine hundred and ninety   and on the 31 day of March of each succeeding year during the continuance of the Partnership accounts shall be taken by a qualified accountant as shall be agreed upon by the Partners of all the capital assets and liabilities for the time being of the Partnership and the balance sheet and profit and loss account shall be prepared by such accountant and a copy thereof furnished to each of the Partners who shall be bound thereby unless some manifest error shall be discovered within three months in which case such error shall be rectified.

10 (1)  The annual accounts of the Partnership shall show in respect of each Partner a provision to cover his share of the income tax assessable on the Partnership at the basic and higher rates for the fiscal year ended during the year to which the accounts relate.

(2)  The expression 'Drawable Balance' shall mean an individual Partner's share of the net profits of the Partnership after deduction of the provisions for income tax applicable thereto.

(3)  The Partners may agree from time to time that each Partner shall make drawings in anticipation of his Drawable Balance to the extent that it exceeds his salary payable in accordance with Clause 6(1).

(4)  If in any year the amount so drawn out by any Partner shall on taking the general account provided for in Clause 9 hereof be found to be in excess of his share of the net profits for the year in question then the excess so drawn out shall forthwith be refunded without interest.

11 *Immediately* after the preparation of such balance sheet and profit and loss account the net profits (if any) shown by such account shall be divided subject to the provisions by way of reserves hereinbefore referred to.

12 *Each* Partner shall at all times duly and punctually pay and discharge his separate debts and engagements and shall at all times keep the other Partners or Partner or their or his representatives and the property of the Partnership indemnified against the same and all actions proceedings costs claims and demands in respect thereof.

13 *Each* Partner shall employ himself diligently in the affairs of the Partnership and use his utmost endeavours to promote the interest thereof which in the case of the aforesaid Mr.................and the aforesaid Mr.............shall be their sole occupation and in the case of Mr................shall be such proportion of his time as is commensurate with his percentage of profits or losses as above.

14 *No* Partner shall without the previous consent in writing of the other Partners or Partner:

(1) employ any monies property or effects belonging to the Partnership or engage any credit thereof or contract any debt on account thereof except in the due and regular course of business and upon the account or for the benefit of the Partnership;

(2) release or discharge any debts of the Partnership without receiving the full amount thereof;

(3) enter into any bond or draw endorse or accept any bill of exchange other than a cheque drawn upon any of the Partnership's bank accounts or promissory note or become bail security or surety or security for any person or persons whomsoever;

(4) do or know or suffer any act or thing to be done whereby the property of the Partnership may be seized attached or taken in execution;

(5) lend any money belonging to or give any credit on behalf of the Partnership in any case in which the other Partners or Partner shall have forbidden him to do so.

15 (1) A Partner shall retire from the Partnership

(a) on the expiry of not less than six months notice in writing given by him to each of the other Partners to expire on the 31 March in any year;

(b)  in the case of each Partner on the 31 March next following his 65 birthday or on such later date as no less than two-thirds in number of the Partners for the time being may request in writing;

(c) if so required by six months notice in writing signed by a majority of not less than two-thirds of the Partners for the time being.

(2)  If any Partner

(a)  shall commit any grave breach of this Agreement, or

(b)  shall commit persistent breaches of this Agreement, or

(c)  shall commit an act of bankruptcy, or

(d)  shall suffer his share in the Partnership to be charged for his separate debt under the Partnership Act 1890, or

(e)  shall become permanently mentally or physically unfit to attend to the business of the Partnership, or

(f)  shall be guilty of any conduct which in the opinion of at least two-thirds in number of the Partners for the time being is likely to have a serious adverse effect upon the Partnership the other Partners for the time being shall be entitled by notice in writing signed by at least two-thirds in number of the Partners for the time being and given to him (or if that shall be impracticable sent by registered or recorded delivery post to his last known address) to expel him from the Partnership.

16  *In* the event of any Partner ceasing to be a Partner (hereinafter referred to as the 'outgoing Partner' which expression shall include where appropriate his personal representatives) by reason of his death or in accordance with Clause 15 hereof then the following provisions contained in this Clause shall take effect:

(1)  An account similar to that prescribed in Clause 9 hereof shall be taken up to the day upon which the outgoing Partner ceases to be a Partner from the date of the last previous account and the assets of the Partnership other than goodwill shall be valued for the purposes of such account.

(2)  The sum which upon taking the said account shall appear to be due to the outgoing Partner in respect of undrawn profits up to the date of his ceasing to be a Partner shall with all convenient speed but in any event within six months of his ceasing to be a Partner be paid to the outgoing Partner.

(3)  The share of the outgoing Partner in the goodwill and future profits of the Partnership business shall accrue to the surviving or continuing Partners without the outgoing Partner or his estate or any person being entitled to any part of the said goodwill or profits, future profits or to any payment in respect thereof.

(4)  The share of the outgoing Partner in the capital and assets of the Partnership business shall accrue to the surviving Partners who shall pay to the outgoing Partner a capital sum therefore in accordance with the provisions of this Clause.

(5) The said capital sum shall be the value of the share of the outgoing Partner in the capital and assets as shown upon taking the said account and shall be paid to the outgoing Partner or his legal representative within (6) six months of his ceasing to be a Partner if the said capital sum is £1,500 or less and if it is more than £1,500 then as to £1,500 thereof within these six months and as to the balance thereof by not more than three equal six monthly instalments (the first of which shall be payable one year after the date upon which the outgoing Partner ceased to be a Partner) together with interest at the rate of six per centum per annum on the unpaid instalments from the date upon which the outgoing Partner ceases to be a Partner the first instalment with interest being paid one year after such date.

(6) The said capital sum shall be ascertained by the Auditors of the Partnership acting as experts and not as Arbitrators and in valuing Work in Progress they shall have regard to the expenses and outgoings charged or to be charged against it and the income tax (if any) payable by reference thereto and to any part thereof and to any part thereof representing bad debts or in respect of which a reduced payment shall be accepted.

(7) The said capital sum shall be taken to have been contributed by the surviving or continuing Partners in the same shares in which they shall be entitled at the time the outgoing Partner ceases to be a Partner to share in super profits.

(8) The share of the outgoing Partner in goodwill and future profits and (unless otherwise expressly agreed in any particular case) the share of the outgoing Partner in capital and other assets of the Partnership shall accrue to the surviving or continuing Partners in the same shares in which at the time when the outgoing Partner ceases to be a Partner they shall be entitled to share in super profits.

(9) If in the event of dissolution an outgoing Partner wishes to purchase Work in Progress Debtors and allied Fee advances the Work in Progress will be valued on an 'Earnings' basis. The value of 'Earnings' shall be cost plus overheads plus accrued profit which will be agreed mutually as at the date of dissolution. Any Tax liability thus created will be debited to the said outgoing Partner.

17 *In* the event of an outgoing Partner ceasing to be a Partner by reason of a majority of the Partners agreeing terms upon which they wish to continue in Partnership and the outgoing Partner being deemed to have retired as provided in Clause 2(2) or by reason of his having retired in the circumstances provided in Clause 15(1)(c) the following provisions shall apply:

(1) the outgoing Partner shall be entitled to be paid by the continuing Partners for a period of three calendar years from the date of his ceasing to be a Partner an annuity equal to either (a) that percentage of the profits of the Partnership business during that period (apportioning on a time basis if the period shall not coincide with the Partnership's periods of account covering that period) as was equal to the percentage at which the outgoing Partner shared in the super profits at the time he ceased being a Partner or (b) such greater annuity as the continuing Partners shall decide;

(2) to the annuity payable under the preceding paragraph (1) for each year there shall be added an amount equal to the annual pension contributions made by the outgoing Partner; and respectively to retirement annuity and pension schemes relating to the outgoing Partner in respect of the last complete fiscal year in which he was a Partner;

(3) paragraphs (1) to (8) of the preceding Clause 16 shall apply as if they were repeated in this Clause;

(4) subject as provided above and except as otherwise specifically agreed each of the Partners shall be responsible for making provision for his retirement out of his own resources.

18 *Upon* the determination of the Partnership in any event not otherwise herein provided for a full and general account shall be taken of the assets, credits, debts and liabilities of the Partnership and of the transactions and dealings thereof and with all convenient speed such assets and credits shall be sold, realised, and go in, and the proceeds applied in paying discharging such debts and liabilities and the expenses of and incidental to the winding up of the Partnership affairs and subject thereto in paying to each Partner the unpaid profits which may be due to him and his share of the capital and the balance (if any) of such proceeds shall be divided between the Partners in the shares in which they are entitled to the super profits of the Partnership at the date of such termination and the Partners respectively shall do or concur in all necessary or proper instruments acts matters and things for effecting or facilitating the sale realisation and getting in of the Partnership assets and credits and the due application and division of the proceeds thereof and for their mutual release or indemnity or otherwise. Upon any such determination as aforesaid of the Partnership the goodwill of the Partnership shall not be sold but shall be divided between the Partners.

19 *In* the event of a Partner retiring or being expelled or in the event of a determination of the Partnership as provided for in Clause 18 hereof the outgoing Partner or each of the Partners in the event of a

determination of the Partnership shall be at liberty to commence and carry on a similar business in his own or in any other name provided that such name shall not include the name of any of the other Partners and to send circulars to the customers of the Partnership announcing the facts of such determination and commencement of business.

20 *Upon* the retirement expulsion or death of any Partner he or his personal representatives shall if so requested by the continuing or surviving Partners or Partner join with them in giving to Her Majesty's Inspector of Taxes a notice under sub-section (2) of s 113 of the Income and Corporation Taxes Act 1988 or any statutory replacement or modification thereof for the time being in force and the Partner so expelled or the personal representatives of such deceased Partner shall be indemnified by the continuing or surviving Partner or Partners against any income tax which may be payable by him or them in excess of the income tax which would have been payable if no such notice has been given as a result of giving such notice or as a result of paragraph (b) or sub-section (3) of s 154 of the said Act.

21 Mr............Mr............and Mr............each of them do mutually release and discharge the other of them his Executors and Administrators from all claims and demands actions and proceedings whatsoever for or in respect of the covenants agreements and provisions contained in the Deed of Partnership dated 7 July 198 as amended on 30 September 198 and 24 July 198 and Heads of Agreement dated 10 July 198 and 15 July 198 30 August 198 which is intended to be wholly superseded by this Agreement.

## SCHEDULE OF SALARIES

£27005

£18721

Nil

# CHAPTER 6

# BANKRUPTCY

## INTRODUCTION

Bankruptcy is the term generally applied to individuals who are unable to pay their debts as they fall due. The term applied to companies is insolvency, although both are governed by the Insolvency Act 1986.

Bankruptcy is governed by Parts IX, X and XI of the Insolvency Act 1986.

Bankruptcy is a judicial process which is commenced by the presentation of a bankruptcy petition under s 264 of the Insolvency Act 1986. It may be presented by a creditor or creditors who are owed at least £750. The creditor or creditors must demonstrate the requisite amount is owing and that the debts are for liquidated sums that are due now or at some certain future time and are unsecured. The debts in question must be ones which the debtor appears to be unable to pay or to have no reasonable prospect of being able to pay and there must be no outstanding application to set aside a statutory demand served upon the debtor in respect of any of the debts[1]. It should be noted that a debtor himself may petition to the court on the ground that he is unable to pay his debts[2].

Where an order is made, a trustee in bankruptcy will take over control of the debtor's property. Between the making of the bankruptcy order and the time that the bankrupt's estate is vested in a trustee under Chapter IV of Part IX of the Insolvency Act 1986 the official receiver acts as the receiver and is the manager of the bankrupt's estate[3].

Section 306 of the Insolvency Act 1986 provides that the bankrupt's estate shall vest in the trustee immediately upon his appointment taking effect or in the case of the official receiver on his becoming trustee. The trustee in bankruptcy is appointed under Chapter III of Part IX of the Insolvency Act 1986[4], although he takes control of the property under Chapter IV of Part IX of the Act. Section 306 as has been mentioned,

---

1    Insolvency Act 1986, s 267.
2    Ibid., s 272.
3    Ibid., s 287.
4    Ibid., s 292.

deals with the vesting of property. Section 307 of the Insolvency Act 1986 provides that after acquired property is also subject to the control of the trustee in bankruptcy. Most of the bankrupt's property vests in the trustee in bankruptcy. This is subject to some exceptions, however. Section 283(2) of the Insolvency Act 1986 provides that certain items are not comprised within a bankrupt's estate. These include tools, books, vehicles and other items of equipment as are necessary to the bankrupt for personal use in his employment, business or vocation and such clothing, bedding, furniture, household equipment and provisions as are necessary for satisfying the basic domestic needs of the bankrupt and his family. In addition, although the bankrupt may keep income after the order has been made, the trustee may apply to the court to make an order (an income payments order) claiming for the estate so much of the income of the bankrupt during the period of the bankruptcy as may be specified in the order[5].

Where a dwelling house is occupied by the bankrupt or by his former spouse and this is included in the estate and the trustee is unable to realise the property, he may apply to the court for an order imposing a charge on the property for the benefit of the bankrupt's estate[6]. It should be noted that the matrimonial home may be subject to a charge under the Matrimonial Homes Act 1983. In such a situation the debtor cannot be evicted from the house and the trustee would need to apply for a court order to sell[7].

# CONDUCT OF THE BANKRUPTCY

Many of the provisions relating to individual bankruptcy are mirrored by provisions relating to corporate insolvency. Thus the trustee in bankruptcy may disclaim onerous property under s 315 of the Insolvency Act 1986. A creditor may apply in writing to the trustee requiring the trustee to decide whether he wishes to disclaim or not under s 316 of the Insolvency Act 1986 (Chapter 24).

---

5    Ibid., s 310.
6    Ibid., s 313.
7    Ibid., ss 336–338.

## PREFERENTIAL DEBTS

Preferential debts are as follows:

- Pay As You Earn contributions and National Insurance contributions due in the preceding 12 months;
- wages due to employees for a maximum of four months up to £800 per employee;
- accrued holiday pay that is owed to employees;
- VAT payments due in the six months previous to the bankruptcy order (p 215).

After preferential creditors have been paid, ordinary unsecured creditors are paid and then postponed creditors are paid. The most important category of postponed creditor is a loan that is due from the debtor to a spouse[8].

## INCREASING THE BANKRUPT'S ESTATE

In a similar way to corporate insolvency, transactions at an undervalue may be set aside under s 339 of the Insolvency Act 1986. In the case of a transaction at an undervalue, the period of five years ending with the day of presentation of the bankruptcy petition is the relevant period for re-opening transactions. It must be shown that the debtor was insolvent at the relevant time. If the transaction at an undervalue occurred within two years of the presentation of the bankruptcy petition, then it does not have to be demonstrated that the debtor was insolvent.

Section 340 of the Insolvency Act 1986 deals with preferences (p 242). If a preference is given within two years of the presentation of the bankruptcy petition to a person who is an associate of the individual, then this may be set aside. It may be set aside within six months if it is in favour of somebody who is not an associate of the debtor.

A preference must in general be a voluntary act of the debtor to prefer the position of a particular creditor.

In addition, under Part XVI of the Insolvency Act 1986, s 423 provides that where a transaction is entered into at an undervalue and a person enters into such a transaction for the purpose of putting assets

---

8    Ibid., ss 328 and 329.

beyond the reach of a person who is making or who may at some future time make a claim against him or otherwise prejudicing the interest of such a person in relation to the claim which he is making or may make, then the court may make an order restoring the position to what it would have been if the transaction had not been entered into and protecting the interests of persons who are victims of the transactions. There is no time limit to this particular procedure.

# DISCHARGE OF BANKRUPTCY

A bankrupt is generally discharged from bankruptcy three years from the commencement of the bankruptcy[9]. Section 281 of the Insolvency Act 1986 provides that where a bankrupt is discharged, this releases him from all bankruptcy debts but has no effect on the functioning of the trustee in bankruptcy.

The consequence of bankruptcy has been seen in other parts of the textbook. Section 33 of the Partnership Act 1890 provides that the bankruptcy of a partner will cause the dissolution of the partnership. In the case of a director of a company, bankruptcy is a bar to a person acting as a director or being concerned in the management of a company (s 11 of the Company Directors Disqualification Act 1986 provides for a bankrupt director to be debarred from office or from being directly or indirectly concerned in the promotion, formation or management of a company except with the leave of the court).

# ALTERNATIVES TO BANKRUPTCY

Individuals may seek to organise voluntary arrangements to avoid bankruptcy orders. Section 252 of the Insolvency Act 1986 deals with this situation. An application should be made to the court where a debtor intends to make a proposal to his creditors for a composition in satisfaction of his debts or a scheme of arrangement of his affairs. The proposal should provide for somebody to act as a nominee in relation to the voluntary arrangement. The nominee must be qualified to act as an insolvency practitioner and must be willing to act in relation to the proposal made. The nominee will report to the court on the proposal of the debtor[10]. If he considers that there is a realistic proposal that is being made, he will advise whether a meeting of the creditors of the person

---

9   Ibid., s 279.
10  Ibid., s 256.

concerned should be called (s 257 provides for the summoning of a creditors' meeting). The creditors' meeting will then decide whether to approve the proposed voluntary arrangement under s 258 of the Insolvency Act 1986. If the proposal is approved the nominee becomes a supervisor (s 263(2) of the Insolvency Act 1986) and the supervisor will then implement the proposals.

It may be that under the voluntary arrangement procedure, creditors will obtain a higher percentage payment of their debts than they would do if the debtor were made insolvent. From the point of view of the debtor, he avoids the adverse publicity and stigma attached to bankruptcy.

(Note: There are provisions for instituting bankruptcy proceedings where it transpires that the voluntary arrangement proposals have been made fraudulently or where there is some other irregularity.)

# CHAPTER 7

# SETTING UP A COMPANY

There are essentially three different ways of forming companies. The company may be chartered, in that it may be set up by a charter granted by the monarch. Historically, this was the first form of incorporation with companies such as the Hudsons Bay Company and the East India Company. Today it is of little economic significance, though chartered companies are still formed from time to time, such as the British Broadcasting Corporation and the Institute of Chartered Accountants of England and Wales. A second way of incorporating a company is by statute; that is to say, a separate statute is passed through parliament incorporating a company. This was common in Victorian England, particularly with utilities and transport companies. Today it is of little practical significance, although the remaining nationalised industries, such as British Railways, are statutory companies. The most common way of forming a company today and where your course will focus is by registration. An act of parliament, today the Companies Act 1985, sets out the procedure that needs to be followed in order to incorporate a company by this means. The Companies Act 1985 is a consolidation measure, bringing together the earlier companies legislation. It has since been amended by the Companies Act 1989.

A registered company may be set up according to s 1 of the Act by any two or more persons associated together for a lawful purpose who subscribe their names to a memorandum of association and who comply with the requirements of the Act. This particular provision has in fact been modified by statutory instrument to bring British law into line with the Twelfth European Community Directive on Company Law[1]. As a result of this statutory instrument, single member companies are possible for private companies limited by shares or guarantee.

## THE DOCUMENTS REQUIRED

In order to set up a registered company, whether private or public, the following documents are required:

---

1    SI 1992 No 1699, the Companies' (Single Member Private Limited Companies) Regulations 1992.

- a memorandum of association (sometimes called the external constitution of the company);
- articles of association (sometimes called the internal constitution of the company);
- the statement of the first directors, company secretary and the situation of the registered office (Form 10, see p 302). This will set out the names and addresses of the first directors and secretary and the dates of birth, nationalities, occupations and details of directorships held in the last five years for directors. Any one or more persons may form a private company. A private company must have at least one director and that same person cannot be sole director and company secretary. A public company needs at least two members and two directors;
- a declaration of compliance (Form 12, see p 306). The statutory declaration of compliance is made by a solicitor engaged in forming the company or by a director or company secretary. It must be signed in the presence of a commissioner for oaths, a notary public, a justice of the peace or a solicitor with the powers conferred on a justice of the peace.

Those setting up the company will need to decide what type of company it is to be. There are various possibilities. The company must be either public or private. It would be appropriate to form a public company if it is desired to raise capital from the public. If the company is to be private, it may be unlimited in which case there will be no need to file annual accounts. It is not possible to have a public unlimited company, nor is it possible to have a company limited by guarantee which is a public company. Companies limited by guarantee are appropriate where it is not necessary to have a fund of capital where corporate status may be desired for some other reason. This often occurs if the company is charitable and particularly if it is educational, eg the London School of Economics. It was possible before the Companies Act 1980 came into effect to have companies limited by guarantee with share capital. It is now no longer possible to create such companies but any existing ones continue and they may have public status.

If a company is a public company, there are certain additional considerations that have to be borne in mind. The public company must have a minimum subscribed share capital of £50,000 which has to be paid up to at least 25% as well as the whole of any premium. The company's name should end with the words 'public limited company' or 'plc' or the Welsh equivalents 'cwmni cyhoeddus cyfyngedig' or 'ccc'. The fact that the company is public will also appear in an additional clause in the company's memorandum. Before a public company can trade, in addition to filing the documents mentioned above at

Companies House, it must also file a statutory declaration to the effect that the requirements in relation to share capital have been complied with. When this statutory declaration is filed, a trading certificate should be issued under s 117 of the Act enabling the company to do business and borrow money, but until this trading certificate is issued, it would be an offence for the company and any officer in default to do business or exercise borrowing powers.

# INCORPORATION DOCUMENTS

The following sections will look at the documents that have to be filed when the company is incorporated, and first, at the memorandum.

## The memorandum

As has been noted, the memorandum of association is sometimes called the external constitution of the company. It sets out certain essential matters which people trading with the company would wish to know. The essential clauses of a company's memorandum are set out in s 2 of the Companies Act 1985. Section 3 of the Act provides that there are certain forms of memorandum set out in regulations. These regulations are made by the Secretary of State. The various forms of memorandum are described below (p 88 et seq).

Section 1(3) and s 2 set out the compulsory clauses as follows:

(a) the name of the company;

(b) if the company is a public limited company;

(c) whether the situate of the registered office is in England and Wales or in Scotland;

(d) the objects of the company;

(e) that the liability of the members is limited;

(f) the amount of the authorised share capital and the way that that authorised share capital is divided into shares.

The memorandum must be signed by each subscriber to the memorandum in the presence of a witness who must attest the signature (in the case of a private company, this subscription may be done by just one member).

# CHAPTER 8

# THE COMPANY NAME

The first compulsory clause of the memorandum should set out the company's name. The statutory provisions relating to corporate names are set out in ss 25-34 of the Companies Act 1985. These sections contain the following rules:

1   The name of a limited company should indicate this at the end of the company name. In the case of a public company the company's name should end with the words ' public limited company' or the recognised abbreviation 'plc' or the Welsh equivalent 'cwmni cyhoeddus cyfyngedig' or 'ccc' as the accepted abbreviation. A private company limited by shares or by guarantee should have 'limited' at the end of its name or the recognised abbreviation 'ltd' or the Welsh equivalent 'cyfyngedig' or 'cyf' as the accepted abbreviation.

On occasion a private company may be permitted to omit the word 'limited' from the end of its name. This was previously the case under the Companies Act 1948 where companies could obtain a licence if their work was for charity or for the public good to omit the word 'limited'. Section 30 of the Companies Act 1985 permits companies to omit the word 'limited' on complying with certain conditions. The company concerned must be a private company and have as its objects the promotion of commerce, art, science, education, religion, charity or a profession, together with a requirement in the constitution that its profits, if there are any, or any other income should be applied to the promotion of these objects, where on a winding up, the company's assets, must be transferred to another body with charitable objects.

If it is desired to claim the exemption on forming the company then a statutory declaration should be made on Form 30(5)(a) (see p 307) and submitted to the companies registry. If the company is registered under Section 680 of the Companies Act 1985 being an old joint stock company, Form 30(5)(b) (see p 309) should be completed and filed. If the claim for exemption is made for a company which already exists, Form 30(5)(c) (see p 311) should be completed and filed.

Once the exemption is granted, then the company's memorandum and articles of association must not be altered to bring them into conflict with the conditions set out in the section.

2    Section 26 of the Companies Act 1985 prohibits the use of certain names. The words 'public limited company' and 'limited' can only be used at the end of the company name. Names which in the opinion of the Secretary of State are offensive or constitute a crime cannot be used. The section goes on to provide in s 26(2)(a) that a company may only be registered with a name giving the impression of any connection with Her Majesty's Government or any local authority with the approval of the Secretary of State.

3    The name must not be the same as a name that already appears on the index of names kept by the registrar of companies under s 714 of the Companies Act 1985. In deciding if a name is the same as a name already on the register, certain matters are ignored. These are:

a)    the occurrence of the definite article at the beginning of the name;

b)    the occurrence of the words 'company' or 'limited' or 'unlimited' or 'public limited company' or any abbreviated or Welsh form of these words;

c)    the typography, word division, accenting or punctuation of the name.

If a name is registered by the registrar and it is subsequently discovered that the name is similar to that of an existing name, the Secretary of State can within twelve months of the registration require the company to change its name[1] (other changes of name are considered below).

4    Certain words and expressions require the prior permission of the Secretary of State or some other specified body[2]. There is a list of words specified in regulations made under s 29 of the Act. These regulations are set out below (p 39 et seq).

Basically, if the name of the company implies some regional, national or international pre-eminence, governmental link or sponsorship or some pre-eminent status, then consent may well be required. Thus, if it is desired to use the word 'university' in the company name, the consent of the Department of Education and Science would be needed. In seeking registration of the company name, it would be appropriate to have copies of the letters sent to the relevant body and the response indicating that there is no objection.

5    The choice of company name is also limited by other considerations. If the name constitutes a registered trade mark, the person who has

---

1    Companies Act 1985, s 28(2).
2    Ibid., s 29.

the trade mark may institute summary proceedings to prevent the use of the name, see the Trade Marks Act 1938.

In using a name of an existing business (whether sole trader, partnership or company) or a name which is similar to that of an existing business such that it appears to the trading public that there is a link between the two, it may be subject to a passing off action in tort involving the issuing of an injunction to prevent further use of the name and an account of profits in respect of the past use of the name.

## REGISTRATION OF THE COMPANY NAME

Applicants should clearly check the company name to ensure that it is not the same as one already on the register of company names. The register may be inspected free of charge in the public search rooms at Cardiff, Edinburgh and London or in satellite offices of the companies registry at Leeds, Manchester, Birmingham and Glasgow (pp 58-59). Assistance may be sought from Companies House by telephone.

The regulations setting out the words which require prior approval of the Secretary of State or specified body are set out as an appendix to this chapter (p 39 et seq).

## CHANGE OF NAME

Section 28 of the Companies Act 1985 provides that a company may change its name by special resolution. The same rules apply on the change of name as apply to an initial choice of name. A company may change its name as often as it likes.

The Secretary of State may require a company within twelve months to alter its original or changed name if he finds that it is similar to another company's name[3], in just the same way as an initial incorporation (see above). If you are asked to advise on the name of a company in relation to incorporation, try to check for similar names; as the company may be required later to change its name if it is similar to an existing name.

A signed copy of the resolution setting out the change of name should be sent to the registrar of companies together with the appropriate fee. Generally, the change is effected within five working days from receipt at Companies House. A premium 'same day service' is

3   Ibid., s 28(2).

available for an extra fee. When the application is processed, the registrar of companies will issue a new certificate of incorporation.

If a company provides misleading information to the registrar on incorporation or change of name, the registrar may order a change within five years[4].

The Secretary of State may require an alteration of name if he believes that it gives a misleading indication of the nature or activities of the company, likely to cause harm to the public. This power may be exercised at any time[5]. The direction must be complied with, within six weeks.

Objections to company names are often made by companies with similar names. Objections should be made in writing to:

The Secretary of State for Trade and Industry
Companies Administration Branch
Companies House
Crown Way
Cardiff
CF4 3UZ

or for companies registered in Scotland:

The Secretary of State for Trade and Industry
Companies House
100-102 George Street
Edinburgh
EH2 3DJ

In considering an objection, the degree of similarity between the names will be a factor. If the Secretary of State feels that there is a danger of confusion between the two companies then factors such as the nature and location of the company's business activities and any evidence of confusion that has arisen will be taken into account.

The powers of the Secretary of State are discretionary. The Secretary of State may ask for further information from the objector. At the same time the Secretary of State will usually advise the other company so that it can answer the case made against it.

---

4    Ibid., s 28(3).
5    Ibid., s 32(1).

# APPENDIX TO CHAPTER 8

## THE COMPANY AND BUSINESS NAMES
## REGULATIONS 1981

*Made on 24 November 1981 by the Secretary of State under ss 31 and 32 of the Companies Act 1981. Operative from 26 February 1982.*

- These regulations may be cited as the Company and Business Names Regulations 1981 and shall come into operation on 26 February 1982.
- In these Regulations, unless the context otherwise requires *the act* means the Companies Act 1981.
- The words and expressions stated in column (1) of the Schedule hereto (together with the plural and possessive forms of those words and expressions) are hereby specified as words and expressions for the registration of which as or as part of a company's corporate name the approval of the Secretary of State is required by section 28(2)(b) of the Act.
- Subject to Regulation 5, each Government department or other body stated in column (2) of the Schedule hereto is hereby specified as the relevant body for the purposes of section 31(2) and (3) of the Act in relation to the word or expression (and the plural and possessive forms of that word or expression) opposite to it in column (1).
- Where the Government departments or other bodies are specified in the alternative in Column (2) of the Schedule hereto the second alternative is to be treated as specified.

    (a)  In the case of the corporate name of a company.

    (i)  if the company has not yet been registered and its principal or only place of business in Great Britain is to be Scotland or, if it will have no place of business in Great Britain, its proposed registered office is in Scotland, and

    (ii)  if the company is already registered and its principal or only place of business in Great Britain is in Scotland or, it if has no place of business in Great Britain, its registered office is in Scotland, and

    (b)  in the case of a business name, if the principal or only place of the business carried on or to be carried on in Great Britain is or is to be in Scotland.

    and the first alternative is to be treated as specified in any other case.

# SCHEDULE - SPECIFICATION OF WORDS, EXPRESSIONS AND RELEVANT BODIES

## Regulations 3, 4 and 5

| Column (1) | Column (2) |
|---|---|
| Word or expression | Relevant body |
| Abortion | Department of Health and Social Security |
| Apothecary | Worshipful Society of Apothecaries of London or Pharmaceutical Society of Great Britain |
| Association | |
| Assurance | |
| Assurer | |
| Authority | |
| Benevolent | |
| Board | |
| Breed | |
| Breeder | Ministry of Agriculture, Fisheries and Food |
| Breeding | |
| British | |
| Chamber of Commerce | |
| Chamber of Industry | |
| Chamber of Trade | |
| Charitable | Charity Commission or Scottish Home and Health Department |
| Charity | |
| Charter | |
| Chartered | |
| Chemist | |
| Chemistry | |
| Contact Lens | General Optical Council |
| Co-operative | |
| Council | |
| Dental | |
| Dentistry | General Dental Council |
| District Nurse | Panel of Assessors in District Nurse Training |
| Duke | Home Office or Scottish Home and Health Department |

English
European
Federation
Friendly Society
Foundation
Fund
Giro
Great Britain
Group
Health Centre
Health Service                          Department of Health and Social
                                        Security
Health Visitor                          Council for the Education and
                                        Training of Health Visitors
Her Majesty                             Home Office or Scottish Home and
His Majesty                             Health Department
Holding
Industrial and Provident
     Society
Institute
Institution
Insurance
Insurer
International
Ireland
Irish
King                                    Home Office or Scottish Home
                                        and Health Department
Midwife                                 Central Midwives or Central
Midwifery                               Midwives Board for Scotland
National
Nurse                                   General Nursing Council for
Nursing                                 England and Wales or General
Nursing Home                            Nursing Council for Scotland
                                        Department of Health and Social
                                        Security
Patent
Patentee
Police                                  Home Office or Scottish Home and
                                        Health Department
Polytechnic                             Department of Education and Science
Post Office
Pregnancy Termination                   Department of Health and Social
                                        Security

| | |
|---|---|
| Prince | |
| Princess | Home Office or Scottish Home and |
| Queen | Health Department |
| Reassurance | |
| Reassurer | |
| Register | |
| Registered | |
| Reinsurance | |
| Reinsurer | |
| Royal | |
| Royale | |
| Royalty | Home Office or Scottish Home and |
| | Health Department |
| Scotland | |
| Scottish | |
| Sheffield | |
| Society | |
| Special School | Department of Education and Science |
| Stock Exchange | |
| Trade Union | |
| Trust | |
| United Kingdom | |
| University | The Privy Council |
| Wales | |
| Welsh | |
| | Home Office or Scottish Home and |
| Windsor | Health Department |

# EXPLANATORY NOTE[1]

These regulations specify those words and expressions for the use of which or as part of a company or business name the approval of the Secretary of State is required pursuant to sections 22(2)(b) or 28(2)(b) of the Companies Act 1981. In the case of certain words or expressions, a Government department or other body is specified as the relevant body which must be requested in writing to indicate whether; and if so why it has any objection to the use of a particular word or expression as; or as part of a name pursuant to section 31(2) or (3) of the Act (a statement that such a request has been made and a copy of any response is required to be submitted to the Secretary of State by s 31(3) of the Act).

---

1    This Note is not part of the Regulations.

# CHAPTER 9

# CHANGE OF STATUS

## PUBLIC LIMITED STATUS

If a company is to be a public limited company, this must be stated in the second clause of the company's memorandum. Only companies limited by shares or limited by guarantee with share capital may have public status[1]. As has been noted above, the name of a public company must end with the words 'public limited company' or 'plc' or the Welsh equivalent 'cwmni cyhoeddus cyfyngedig' or 'ccc'.

A public limited company must have a subscribed share capital of £50,000 which must be paid up to at least 25%[2].

## RE-REGISTRATION OF COMPANIES

Sometimes companies will wish to change their status. Where this is the case, they will re-register as another type of company. The Companies Act sets out various provisions relating to change of status.

### Re-registration of a private company as public[3]

The application to re-register as a public company by a private company is made on Form 43(3) (see p 313).

Where a company wishes to re-register as public, it must pass a special resolution to that effect and make an application together with the necessary documents.

Section 43(3) sets out the documents that are to be delivered. These are as follows:

- a printed copy of the company's memorandum and articles as altered in pursuance of the special resolution (certain matters will clearly change such as the company's name);

---

1   Companies Act 1985, s 1(3).
2   Ibid., ss 117-118 and 101(1).
3   Ibid., ss 43-48.

- a copy of a written statement of the company's auditors that in their opinion the relevant balance sheet shows that at the balance sheet date the amount of the company's net assets was not less than the aggregate of its called up share capital and undistributable reserves;

- a copy of the relevant balance sheet together with an unqualified report by the company's auditors;

- a copy of a valuation report if shares have been issued otherwise than for cash;

- a statutory declaration made by a director or the company secretary that the special resolution has been passed, that any shares allotted otherwise than for cash have been valued and that the company's nominal shares are not less than the authorised minimum (£50,000) and that each of the shares is paid up to no less than 25% plus the whole of any premium. In addition, if shares have been issued in exchange for work or services, the work or services should have been performed, and if for an undertaking that undertaking must be performed within five years of the time of the resolution that has been passed under s 43. In addition, the statutory declaration should state that between the balance sheet date and the application for re-registration there has been no change in the company's financial position that has resulted in the amount of its net assets becoming less than the aggregate of its called up share capital and undistributable reserves[4].

Once the application and accompanying documents have been received by the registrar of companies, the registrar of companies will issue a new certificate of incorporation stating that the company is a public company[5]. However, s 47(3) provides that he shall not issue a certificate if it appears to him that the court has made an order confirming a reduction of the company's capital which has the effect of bringing the nominal value of the company's allotted share capital below the authorised minimum.

When the new certificate of incorporation is issued, the company then becomes a public company and any alterations in the memorandum and articles set out in the resolution take effect accordingly[6].

The certificate of incorporation is conclusive evidence that the conditions of the Companies Act are being complied with in respect of re-registration and that the company is a public company[7].

---

4   *Note*: the statutory declaration of compliance is Form 43(3)(e) (see p 315).
5   Companies Act 1985, s 47(1)(b)
6   Ibid., s 47(4).
7   Ibid., s 47(5).

*Note*: Where a company sets up on initial incorporation as a public company, it must obtain a certificate enabling it to trade under s 117 of the Companies Act 1985. There is no such requirement in relation to a change of status. The certificate issued under s 47 enables the company to trade as all the requirements relating to minimum capital should have been satisfied before this certificate is issued.

If an unlimited private company wishes to re-register as public, there are certain additional requirements that must be satisfied. These are set out in s 48. The company must first become limited and a special resolution must be passed to that effect. Any other alterations that need to be made to the company's memorandum must also be accomplished.

## Re-registration of a public company as private (ss 53-55 of the Companies Act 1985)

Where there is a change of status from public to private, a similar procedure has to be followed as on a change from private to public status.

Before formal application is made to the registrar of companies, a special resolution must be passed that the company should be re-registered as private.

Section 53(2) provides that the special resolution must alter the company's memorandum so that it no longer states that the company is to be public and any other alterations that need to be made in the company's memorandum and articles must be carried out.

Where such a special resolution has been passed, an application may be made to the court for cancellation of the resolution. The application may be made by the holders of not less than 5% of the company's issued share capital or if the company is not limited by shares, by not less than 5% of the company's members or by not less than 50 of the company's members. The application may not be made or supported by a person who has consented to, or voted in favour of the resolution. The application must be made within 28 days of the passing of the resolution.

If such an application is made, the company must give notice of this to the registrar of companies under s 54(4).

The prescribed form for notice of an application to the court for cancellation of a special resolution regarding re-registration as private is Form 54 (see p 323).

The formal application to re-register is made on Form 53 (see p 321). This application must be signed by a director or the company secretary and delivered to the registrar of companies together with a copy of the altered memorandum and articles.

If the registrar of companies is satisfied that the company should be re-registered as private, he should retain the application and supporting documents, and issue the company with a new certificate of incorporation setting out that the company is a private company. The effect of this certificate is that the company then becomes private and the alterations in the memorandum and articles take place accordingly. The certificate is conclusive evidence that the requirements relating to re-registration have been complied with and that the company is a private company.

One special situation should be mentioned. This is where the company has reduced its capital under ss 135-137 and the reduction of capital has taken the company's capital below the authorised minimum. In such a situation, s 139(3) provides that the court may authorise the company to be re-registered as private without the necessity of passing a special resolution under s 53. Where this is the case, the court shall specify in the order relating to the reduction of capital the alterations in the company's memorandum and articles that are to be made in connection with the re-registration.

The company may then be re-registered as private if an application is made in the prescribed form (Form 139) (see p 341) and signed by a director or secretary of the company and delivered to the registrar together with a printed copy of the memorandum and articles as altered by the court's order. When this has happened, the company will then be re-registered as private and a new certificate of incorporation issued provided that the requirements of the Act have been satisfied.

# CHAPTER 10

# OTHER PROVISIONS OF
# THE MEMORANDUM

## SITUATE OF REGISTERED OFFICE

When an application is made to the registrar of companies for the company to be registered; one of the forms submitted, Form 10 (see p 302), must set out the address of the company's registered office. This address is important for service of documents upon the company. It is also important as certain company books and records should be kept at the company's registered office.

In addition, the company's memorandum should state whether the situate of the company's registered office is Scotland, England and Wales, or Wales. If the registered office is said to be in Scotland, documents have to be lodged at Companies House in Edinburgh:

| | |
|---|---|
| Registry for Scotland | Tel: 031 225 5774 |
| Companies House | |
| 100-102 George Street | |
| Edinburgh | |
| EH2 3DJ | |

There is a satellite office in Glasgow:

| | |
|---|---|
| 21 Bothwell Street | Tel: 041 248 3315 |
| Glasgow | |
| G2 6NR | |

If the situate of the office is said to be in England and Wales, documents may be lodged at:

| | |
|---|---|
| Companies House | Tel: 0222 388588 |
| Crown Way | |
| Maindy | |
| Cardiff | |
| CF4 3UZ | |

There are branch offices in:

*London:*

Companies House                    Tel: 071 253 9393
55-71 City Road
London
EC1Y 1BB

*Birmingham:*

Birmingham Central Library         Tel: 021 233 9047
Chamberlain Square
Birmingham
B3 3HQ

*Leeds:*

25 Queen Street                    Tel: 0532 338338
Leeds
LS1 2TW

*Manchester:*

75 Mosley Street                   Tel: 061 236 7500
Manchester
M2 2HR

If the situate of the registered office is said to be in Wales, then the company may lodge documents in Welsh provided that a certified English translation is supplied[1].

It is not possible to alter the situate of a company's registered office from Scotland to England and Wales or vice versa. It is possible, however, for a company whose registered office is stated to be in England and Wales to alter it to state Wales to enable it to lodge documents in Welsh provided that the registered office is in Wales.

# OBJECTS

It was once important to take particular care in drafting a company's objects clause. At common law, if an activity fell outside of the objects clause the agreement was *ultra vires* and void. The common law rule on *ultra vires* was one of the disadvantages of incorporation. Now, in general, *ultra vires* agreements are valid.

---

1    Companies Act 1985, s 21(1).

Section 35(1) of the Companies Act 1985 provides 'The validity of an act done by a company shall not be called into question on the ground of lack of capacity by reason of anything in the company's memorandum' and s 35A(1) provides 'In favour of a person dealing with a company in good faith, the power of the board of directors to bind the company, or authorise others to do so, shall be deemed to be free of any limitation under the company's constitution'.

The effect of the statutory protections means that in general agreements outside of the company's objects clause will not be held to be void; and the disadvantage of the *ultra vires* doctrine in comparing the company with the firm or the sole trader is not great.

However, it is still advisable to take care in drafting objects clauses.

- a member of a company may bring proceedings to restrain the doing of an act which is outside of the company's capacity[2];

- also, it remains the duty of directors to observe limits on their powers so acting outside of the company's capacity would involve them in a breach of their duty[3], although this could be ratified by special resolution and the directors could be relieved of liability by a separate special resolution;

- in addition, companies which are charities are outside the scope of s 35 and s 35A unless *either* the other contracting party gives full consideration in money or money's worth in relation to the act in question *and* does not know that the act is beyond the company's capacity or the directors' powers, or does not know that the company is a charity;

- a further qualification exists to s 35 and s 35A where one party to the agreement is a director of the company or its holding company; or connected with such a director or a company with whom such a director is associated. In such situations, s 322A(2) of the Companies Act 1985 provides that such transactions are voidable at the instance of the company.

There are four reasons, therefore, why the drafting of the objects clause with care and precision may still be a matter of some importance. Since the Companies Act 1989, it has been possible for companies to state that 'the object of the company is to carry on business as a general commercial company'[4]. The effect of this is that the object of the company is to carry on any trade or business whatsoever and the company has power to do all such things as are incidental or conducive

---

2    Ibid., s 35(2).
3    Ibid., s 35(3).
4    Ibid., s 3A.

to the carrying on of any trade or business by it. Where companies adopt such an objects clause or alter their existing objects clause and insert such a provision, problems of *ultra vires* are most unlikely to arise, but many companies have not changed their existing objects clauses and companies continue to adopt long comprehensive lists of objects which may still prove to be a minefield for the unwary.

Where long detailed lists of objects are set out in the company's objects clause it is advisable to employ two drafting devices to provide extra latitude for the managers of the business:

- a rounding-off clause: 'to carry on any other trade or business whatsoever which can, in the opinion of the board of directors be advantageously carried on by the company in connection with or as ancillary to any of the above businesses or the general business of the company' (*Bell Houses Ltd v City Wall Properties Ltd* (1966)[5]);

- a main and independent objects sub-clause: 'Every sub-clause is to be construed as a substantive clause and is not to be limited or restricted by references to any other sub-clause or by the name of the company, and no sub-clause nor the objects specified therein is to be deemed subsidiary or auxiliary merely to the objects mentioned in the first sub-clause' (*Cotman v Brougham* (1918)[6]);

It is possible for a company to alter its objects by special resolution[7] but it is open to a 15% dissentient minority to object to a change of objects within 21 days of the resolution The court has a discretion whether to block the change or not (Form 6) (see p 300).

# LIMITED LIABILITY

One of the chief attractions of incorporation is the possibility of limiting the liability of the participants - the shareholders. As has been seen, this is not possible in a general partnership and a limited partnership does not offer a genuine lifeline to cautious entrepreneurs, as at least one partner must have unlimited liability and those who are active in the business cannot be limited partners. The limited liability company offers a route for the cautious - at least as a shareholder.

As a director of a private company the status of limited liability may well be a chimera. Lenders of finance, suppliers of goods, materials etc may well require some collateral guarantee from the company's

---

5    [1966] 2 QB 656.
6    [1918] AC 514.
7    Companies Act 1985, ss 4-5.

directors. In addition, there are various situations where the veil may be lifted and liability imposed upon the directors of a company. Perhaps the chief hazard here is s 214 of the Insolvency Act 1986 which imposes liability on directors and shadow directors for wrongful trading where the director or shadow director 'ought to have concluded that there was no reasonable prospect that the company would avoid going into insolvent liquidation'. (This area of law will be considered below p 245.)

Companies may be limited by guarantee where the liability of the members (or guarantors) is set out in the memorandum as the amount which they undertake to contribute to the assets of the company in the event of its being wound up. As may be seen, such companies do not raise capital and it is not an appropriate medium for trading companies. It is generally employed by an organisation which wishes for corporate status for some other reason eg the London School of Economics. The memorandum of a company limited by guarantee must state the sum that each member undertakes to contribute to the assets of the company if it should be wound up while he is a member or within one year of his ceasing to be a member.

There are some companies which are limited by guarantee with a share capital. They are rare and no new ones can be created since the Companies Act 1980.

It is possible for a company to be unlimited. Where this is the case, the members obviously do not enjoy limited liability and they may be called upon to contribute additionally in the event of the company going into insolvent liquidation. For this reason the unlimited company is not popular although with few exceptions unlimited companies do not need to deliver accounts and reports to the registrar[8].

Most companies are limited by shares.

It is possible to alter from limited status to unlimited status.


## Re-registration of a limited company as unlimited[9]

A public company cannot be re-registered as unlimited without first changing its status to private[10].

An application to re-register as unlimited must be in the prescribed form and signed by a director or the company secretary. It must be lodged with the registrar of companies together with the necessary supporting documents. These documents are: a form of assent signed by

---

8    Ibid., s 254.

9    Ibid., ss 49 and 50.

10   Ibid., s 49(3).

all of the company's members or on their behalf; and a statutory declaration made by the directors of the company that the persons by whom or on whose behalf the form of assent is subscribed constitute the entire membership of the company, and if any of the members have not subscribed that form themselves, the directors have taken all reasonable steps to satisfy themselves that those signing have lawful authority to do so; a printed copy of the memorandum incorporating the alterations set out in the application; and if articles have been registered, a printed copy of them incorporating the alterations set out in the application (if articles have not been registered, the application must have annexed to it and request the registration of printed articles and these must comply with the requirements of the Act).

Once the registrar of companies has issued a new certificate of incorporation on receipt of the required documents the certificate is conclusive of the change of status of the company and the alterations in the memorandum and articles then take effect.

It is also possible to alter from unlimited status to limited status.

## Unlimited company becoming limited[11]

A company which is registered as unlimited may be re-registered as limited if a special resolution to that effect is passed. The resolution should state whether the company is to be limited by shares or by guarantee, and if it is to be limited by shares must state what the share capital is to be and make provision for alterations in the memorandum and articles as are necessary; if it is to be limited by guarantee, the special resolution must provide for the making of such alterations in the memorandum and articles as are necessary under the Companies Act.

The new memorandum and articles should be lodged with the registrar.

The registrar of companies should issue a new certificate of incorporation to the company where the documents are in order. The certificate of incorporation is conclusive of the new status of the company and the alterations in the memorandum and articles take effect when the new certificate is issued.

There are special provisions relating to the continuing liability of unlimited members where the company subsequently goes into insolvent liquidation.

If the company goes into liquidation within three years of the conversion to a limited company, then anybody who was a member at

---

11   Ibid., ss 51 and 52.

the time of the conversion has unlimited liability for any debts incurred while the company was unlimited[12].

Liability is also placed upon past members of unlimited companies where there are no persons who were members at the time of the conversion and still members at the time that the company goes into liquidation. Anybody who was at that time a past or present member may be liable to contribute to the company's assets in respect of liabilities arising before the time of conversion[13] A past member is not liable to contribute if he has ceased to be a member for one year or more before the commencement of the winding up[14].

## SHARE CAPITAL

The last compulsory clause of the memorandum of a company limited by shares, sets out the amount of the company's authorised share capital and the division of the share capital into shares of a fixed amount. (There is no need for this clause if the company is unlimited.)

The different uses of the term capital are discussed below (Chapter 16).

The company may increase its authorised share capital by ordinary resolution in general meeting (s 121 of the Companies Act 1985 discussed below).

## ADDITIONAL CLAUSES

As well as these compulsory clauses, it is possible to insert additional clauses into the company's memorandum[15]. The effect of doing this is to make those provisions more difficult to alter, than if they were in the company's articles. It is more difficult in that even if a special resolution is passed to alter the provision, a 15% dissentient minority of shareholders or any class of shareholders, or if the company is not limited by shares a 15% dissentient minority of members may object to the court to cancel the alteration within 21 days of the resolution. The court will then hear the objections and decide what should be done.

The memorandum ends with an association clause which sets out the wish of the subscribers to the memorandum to set up the company.

---

12  Insolvency Act 1986, s 77(2).

13  Ibid., s 77(3).

14  Ibid., s 74(2)(a).

15  Companies Act 1985, s 17.

Their names and addresses should be set out and they should sign the document. Their signatures should be attested. In the case of a private company, this may now simply be association by one person.

# CHAPTER 11

# ARTICLES OF ASSOCIATION

Another document which has to be submitted to the registrar of companies before the business can be incorporated is the articles of association. In practice these are annexed to the memorandum of association and the two are submitted together.

In the case of a company limited by guarantee or an unlimited company, articles must be printed, divided into paragraphs and numbered. In the case of a company limited by shares, if individual articles are not registered or if articles are registered but are not comprehensive, then Table A will apply in full or part. There have been various sets of Table A articles, the current ones are set out in the Companies (Tables A to F) Regulations 1985 - SI 1985 No 805. If a company were to register today, the current Table A articles would apply. Companies that registered when other Table A articles were in force would continue to apply eg Table A of First Schedule to Companies Act 1948.

It is usual where a company adopts articles to adopt Table A with modifications as it is likely that a company will wish to deviate from the standard Table A on some points.

(*See the Appendix to Chapter 11 for Table A*)

## ALTERATION OF THE ARTICLES

A company's articles are said to be freely alterable. In fact this is a misleading statement. In general a company may alter its articles by special resolution[1] but this is subject to certain restrictions:

- a company cannot alter its articles to contravene the provisions of the Companies Act. Thus any provision in the articles which would seeks to exempt a director from liability for negligence is void by virtue of s 310. By the same token, a provision which seeks to increase the liability of a member beyond that of his original contract is void by virtue of s 16 of the Act (s 9 of the Act);

---

1    Companies Act 1985, s 9.

- any alteration of the articles which clashes with a provision in the company's memorandum is void. See s 9 and *Guinness v Land Corporation of Ireland* (1882)[2];

- any alteration of the articles which conflicts with an order of the court is, of course, void. Thus an order of the court under s 5 relating to changes of objects or under s 461 relating to the remedy for unfairly prejudicial conduct cannot be overridden by a change of articles;

- if the alteration of articles involves an alteration or abrogation of class rights, then in addition to the special resolution required under s 9, the company must follow the regime appropriate to variation of class rights set out in ss 125-127; (This will be considered below - see variation of class rights.)

- in addition to the statutory restrictions, the power to alter a company's articles is subject to the principle that any alteration must be bona fide for the benefit of the company as a whole. In *Allen v The Gold Reefs of West Africa Ltd* (1900)[3], the company's articles of association gave the company a lien upon all partly paid shares held by a member for any debt owed to the company. A member who held some partly paid shares was also the only holder of fully paid shares in the company. Upon his death, he owed money in relation to the partly paid shares. The company altered its articles by special resolution to provide for a lien over fully paid shares. This alteration was questioned. The Court of Appeal held that the company could alter its articles provided that the alteration was in good faith. Lord Lindley MR said at p 671:

'... the power conferred by it [s 9] must, like all other powers, be exercised subject to those general principles of law and equity which are applicable to all powers conferred on majorities and enabling them to bind minorities. It must be exercised, not only in the manner required by law, but also bona fide for the benefit of the company as a whole, and it must not be exceeded.'

Much of the case law has centred upon a discussion of how it is to be determined whether an alteration is for the benefit of the company as a whole. In *Greenhalgh v Arderne Cinemas Ltd* (1951)[4], it was proposed to delete a provision in the company's articles which gave members a right of pre-emption over shares that a member wanted to sell. It seemed that the majority shareholder, Mr Mallard was prompted not by what was in the company's best interest but out of malice towards a minority

---

2    [1882] 22 Ch D 349.
3    [1900] 1 Ch 656.
4    [1951] Ch 286.

shareholder. The question arose as to whether the alteration was for the benefit of the company as a whole. Lord Evershed MR said at p 291 that 'the phrase "the company as a whole" does not (at any rate in such a case as the present) mean the company as a commercial entity, distinct from the corporators; it means the corporators as a general body. That is to say, the case may be taken of an individual hypothetical member and it may be asked what is proposed, in the honest opinion of those who voted in its favour, for that person's benefit'. In this case, the Court of Appeal held that the alteration was valid.

This analysis does raise difficulties in determining the benefit of the individual hypothetical member. It is clear that hardship to a minority will not of itself invalidate an alteration of articles. In *Sidebottom v Kershaw Leese & Co Ltd* (1920)[5], a minority shareholder in the company carried on a business that was competing with the company. It was proposed to alter the company's articles to insert a clause whereby a shareholder who competed with the company would be required to transfer his shares at a fair value to the directors. It was held that the alteration was valid even though it was carried out specifically against one particular member. The clause in question, of course, could apply in relation to any member.

By contrast, in *Brown v British Abrasive Wheel Co Ltd* (1919)[6] where 98% majority shareholders wished to insert a provision in the articles requiring the minority who were not prepared to invest further capital to sell their shares as a condition of the majority's providing further capital, the alteration was held invalid. It was noted that such a provision could be used to require a minority to sell its shares at the will of the majority.

The cases do appear to be inconsistent. If the question is not what is for the benefit of the company as a separate corporate entity, it is difficult to conjure up a hypothetical shareholder in whose interest the alteration must be. Malevolence did not prevent Mr Mallard succeeding in *Greenhalgh v Arderne Cinemas*; why should the majority's view be overridden in *Brown v British Abrasive Wheel Co Ltd*? A possible interpretation is offered by Lord Evershed MR in the *Greenhalgh* case where he argues that if the effect of the alteration is to discriminate between the majority shareholders and the minority shareholders to give the majority an advantage, then the alteration should not be permitted.

It is now the case that ss 459-461 will provide a possible remedy to a shareholder who has been unfairly prejudiced in the conduct of a company's affairs by the use of majority voting power. In addition

---

5    [1920] 1 Ch 154.
6    [1919] 1 Ch 290.

courts have sometimes been willing to act to protect minority shareholders from the oppressive use of majority voting power. (*Clemens v Clemens Brothers Ltd and Another* (1976)[7]); (*Estmanco (Kilner House) Ltd v Greater London Council* (1982)[8]).

A provision in the company's articles that an article or articles is/are unalterable is ineffective *Peters' American Delicacy Co Ltd v Heath* (1939)[9].

A final point should be noted in relation to alteration of the articles. Notwithstanding that an alteration of the articles may result in a breach of contract by the company, an injunction will not issue to stop the alteration taking place, see *Southern Foundries (1926) Ltd v Shirlaw* (1940)[10] The innocent party will, of course, be able to pursue a remedy in relation to the breach of contract.

# USEFUL ADDRESSES

Information concerning the formation of companies may be obtained from:

New Companies Section
PO Box 717
Companies House
Crown Way
Cardiff
CF4 3YA

for companies being formed in England and Wales, and for companies to be formed in Scotland:

The Registrar of Companies
Companies House
100-102 George Street
Edinburgh
EH2 3DJ

Company forms may be obtained from law stationers or:

---

7    [1976] 1 All ER 268.
8    [1982] 1 WLR 2.
9    [1939] 61 CLR 457.
10   [1940] AC 701.

Companies House
100-102 George Street
Companies House, Edinburgh
EH2 3DJ

or

Stationery Section
PO Box 450,
Crown Way,
Cardiff
CF4 3YA

or for person callers only, from:

London Search Room
Companies House
55-71 City Road
London
EC1Y 1BB

## VARIATION OF CLASS RIGHTS

Sometimes where a change of articles is proposed, this may also involve a variation of class rights. In this situation, special procedures have to be followed. First it must be determined that there is more than one class of share in the company. This may not always be as easy as one would think. On occasion, if particular rights attach to a certain shareholding, this might constitute those shares as a separate class of shares. This was the position in *Cumbrian Newspapers Group Ltd v Cumberland & Westmorland Herald Newspaper & Printing Co Ltd* (1986)[11].

The next question that must be determined is whether there has been a variation of the rights attached to those shares. Once again this is not always as simple as it might at first appear. The approach of the courts has tended to be a restrictive one to the question of whether rights have been varied.

### The procedures

If it is established that there has been a variation of class rights, then the rules for the variation are dependent upon where the rights are set out and what the rights concern:

---

11  [1986] 2 BCC 99, 227.

- if the class rights are set out in the company's memorandum and the memorandum does not set out a variation procedure or if the procedure for variation is set out in the articles of association otherwise than on the company's incorporation, then modification of the rights can only be achieved by a scheme of arrangement under s 425 of the Act or by all of the members of the company agreeing to the variation[12];

- if the class rights and the variation procedure are both set out in the memorandum, then that procedure must be followed[13];

- if the class rights are set out in the memorandum and that prohibits variation of the rights, then no variation can be effected except by a scheme of arrangement under s 425 of the Companies Act 1985[14];

- if the class rights are set out in the memorandum and the variation procedure is set out in the articles on incorporation, then that procedure must be followed[15];

- if the class rights are set out otherwise than in the memorandum, for example in the articles, and the variation procedure is set out in the articles, then that procedure must be followed[16];

- if the class rights are attached to a class of shares other than by the company's memorandum and the company's articles do not contain provision with respect to their alteration, they may be altered by the statutory variation procedure set out in s 125(2) of the Companies Act 1985; whereby either the holders of three quarters in nominal value of the issued shares of the class in question consent, or an extraordinary resolution which sanctions the variation is passed at a separate general meeting of the holders of that class.

There are special rules that apply if the class rights are set out in the memorandum or otherwise and the variation procedure is contained in the memorandum or articles and the rights are connected with the giving, variation, revocation or renewal of an authority for the purposes of s 80 of the Companies Act 1985 (allotment of securities by directors), or with the reduction of share capital under s 135 of the Companies Act 1985. In this situation, whatever procedure is set out, the statutory procedure of s 125(2) must be followed.

If the class rights are varied under a procedure set out in the memorandum or articles of the company, or if the class rights are set out

---

12 Companies Act 1985, s 125(4),(5) and (7).

13 Ibid., s 17(2).

14 Ibid., s 17.

15 Ibid., s 125(4)(a).

16 Ibid., s, 125(4)(b).

otherwise than in the memorandum and the articles are silent on variation, dissentient minorities have special rights to object to the alteration.

They must satisfy certain conditions. The dissenters must hold no less than 15% of the issued shares of the class and must not have voted in favour of the resolution. They may then object to the variation within 21 days of consent being given to the resolution. On occasion their objections may be upheld by the court[17].

---

17　Ibid., s 127.

# APPENDIX TO CHAPTER 11

## THE COMPANIES (TABLES A TO F) REGULATIONS 1985
## (SI 1985 NO 805)

*Made by the Secretary of State for Trade and Industry under s 454(2) of the Companies Act 1948 - ss 3 and 8 of the the Companies Act 1985 - on 22 May 1985. Operative from 1 July 1985.*

1    These Regulations may be cited as the Companies (Tables A to F) Regulations 1985 and shall come into operation on 1 July 1985.

2    The regulations in Table A and the forms in Tables B, C, D, E and F in the Schedule to these Regulations shall be the regulations and forms of memorandum and articles of association for the purposes of ss 3 and 8 of the Companies Act 1985.

3    The Companies (Alteration of Table A etc) Regulations 1984 are hereby revoked.

## SCHEDULE

## TABLE A - REGULATIONS FOR MANAGEMENT OF A COMPANY LIMITED BY SHARES

### *Interpretation*

1    In these regulations -

the Act means the Companies Act 1985 including any statutory modification or re-enactment thereof for the time being in force.

*the articles* means the articles of the company.

*clear days* in relation to the period of a notice means that period excluding the day when the notice is given or deemed to be given, and the day for which it is given or on which it is to take effect.

*executed* includes any mode of execution.

*office* means the registered office of the company

*the holder* in relation to shares means the member whose name is entered in the register of members as the holder of the shares.

*the seal* means the common seal of the company.

*secretary* means the secretary of the company or any other person appointed to perform the duties of the secretary of the company, including a joint, assistant or deputy secretary.

*the United Kingdom* means Great Britain and Northern Ireland.

Unless the context otherwise requires, words or expressions contained in these regulations bear the same meaning as in the Act but excluding any statutory modification thereof not in force when these regulations become binding on the company.

## SHARE CAPITAL

2    Subject to the provisions of the Act and without prejudice to any rights attached to any existing shares, any share may be issued with such rights or restrictions as the company may by ordinary resolution determine.

3    Subject to the provisions of the Act, shares may be issued which are to be redeemed or are to be liable to be redeemed at the option of the company or the holder on such terms and in such manner as may be provided by the articles.

4    The company may exercise the powers of paying commissions, conferred by the Act. Subject to the provisions of the Act, any such commission may be satisfied by the payment of cash or by the allotment of fully or partly paid shares or partly in one way and partly in the other.

5    Except as required by law, no person shall be recognised by the company as holding any share upon any trust and (except as otherwise provided by the articles or by law) the company shall not be bound by or recognise any interest in any share except an absolute right to the entirety thereof in the holder.

## SHARE CERTIFICATES

6    Every member, upon becoming the holder of any shares, shall be entitled without payment to one certificate for all the shares of each class held by him (and, upon transferring a part of his holding of shares of any class, to a certificate for the balance of such holding) or several certificates each for one or more of his shares upon payment for every certificate after the first of such reasonable sum as the directors may determine. Every certificate shall be sealed with the seal and shall specify the number, class and distinguishing numbers (if any) of the shares to which it relates and the amount or respective amounts paid up thereon. The company shall not be bound to issue more than one certificate for shares held jointly by several persons and delivery of a certificate to one joint holder shall be a sufficient delivery to all of them.

7    If a share certificate is defaced, worn-out, lost or destroyed, it may be renewed on such terms (if any) as to evidence and indemnity and payment of the expenses reasonably incurred by the company in investigating evidence as the directors may determine but otherwise free of charge, and (in the case of defacement or wearing-out) on delivery up of the old certificate.

## LIEN

8    The company shall have a first and paramount lien on every share (not being a fully paid share) for all moneys (whether presently payable or not) payable at a fixed time or called in respect of that share. The directors may at any time declare any share to be wholly or in part exempt from the provisions of this regulation. The company's lien on a share shall extend to any amount payable in respect of it.

9    The company may sell in such manner as the directors may determine any shares on which the company has a lien if a sum in respect of which the lien exists is presently payable and is not paid within fourteen clear days after notice has been given to the holder of the share or to the person entitled to it in consequence of the death or bankruptcy of the holder, demanding payment and stating that if the notice is not complied with, the shares may be sold.

10   To give effect to a sale the directors may authorise some person to execute an instrument of transfer of the shares sold to, or in accordance with the directions of, the purchaser. The title of the transferee to the shares shall not be affected by any irregularity in or invalidity of the proceedings in reference to the sale.

11   The net proceeds of the sale, after payment of the costs, shall be applied in payment of so much of the sum for which the lien exists as is presently payable, and any residue shall (upon surrender to the company for cancellation of the certificate for the shares sold and subject to a like lien for any moneys not presently payable as existed upon the shares before the sale) be paid to the person entitled to the shares at the date of the sale.

## CALLS ON SHARES AND FORFEITURE

12   Subject to the terms of allotment, the directors may make calls upon the members in respect of any moneys unpaid on their shares (whether in respect of nominal value or premium) and each member shall (subject to receiving at least fourteen clear days' notice specifying when and where payment is to be made) pay to

the company as required by the notice the amount called on his shares. A call may be required to be paid by instalments. A call may, before receipt by the company of any sum due thereunder, be revoked in whole or part and payment of a call may be postponed in whole or part. A person upon whom a call is made shall remain liable for calls made upon him notwithstanding the subsequent transfer of the shares in respect whereof the call was made.

13   A call shall be deemed to have been made at the time when the resolution of the directors authorising the call was passed.

14   The joint holders of a share shall be jointly and severally liable to pay all calls in respect thereof.

15   If a call remains unpaid after it has become due and payable the person from whom it is due and payable shall pay interest on the amount unpaid from the day it became due and payable until it is paid at the rate fixed by the terms of allotment of the share or in the notice of the call or, if no rate is fixed, at the appropriate rate (as defined by the Act) the directors may waive payment of the interest wholly or in part.

16   An amount payable in respect of a share on allotment or at any fixed date, whether in respect of nominal value or premium or as an instalment of a call, shall be deemed to be a call and if it is not paid the provisions of the articles shall apply as if that amount had become due and payable by virtue of a call.

17   Subject to the terms of the allotment, the directors may make arrangements on the issue of shares for a difference between the holders in the amounts and times of payment of calls on their shares.

18   If a call remains unpaid after it has become due and payable, the directors may give to the person from whom it is due not less than fourteen clear days' notice requiring payment of the amount unpaid together with any interest which may have accrued. The notice shall name the place where payment is to be made and shall state that if the notice is not complied with the shares in respect of which the call was made will be liable to be forfeited.

19   If the notice is not complied with any share in respect of which it was given may, before the payment required by the notice has been made, be forfeited by a resolution of the directors and the forfeiture shall include all dividends or other moneys payable in respect of the forfeited shares and not paid before the forfeiture.

20   Subject to the provisions of the Act, a forfeited share may be sold, re-allotted or otherwise disposed of on such terms and in such manner as the directors determine either to the person who was

before the forfeiture the holder or to any other person and at any time before sale, re-allotment or other disposition, the forfeiture may be cancelled on such terms as the directors think fit. Where for the purposes of its disposal a forfeited share is to be transferred to any person the directors may authorise some person to execute an instrument of transfer of the share to that person.

21 A person any of whose shares have been forfeited shall cease to be a member in respect of them and shall surrender to the company for cancellation the certificate for the shares forfeited but shall remain liable to the company for all moneys which at the date of forfeiture were presently payable by him to the company in respect of those shares with interest at the rate at which interest was payable on those moneys before the forfeiture or, if no interest was so payable, at the appropriate rate (as defined in the Act) from the date of forfeiture until payment but the directors may waive payment wholly or in part or enforce payment without any allowance for the value of the shares at the time of forfeiture or for any consideration received on their disposal.

22 A statutory declaration by a director or the secretary that a share has been forfeited on a specified date shall be conclusive evidence of the fact stated in it as against all persons claiming to be entitled to the share and the declaration shall (subject to the execution of an instrument of transfer if necessary) constitute a good title to the share and the person to whom the share is disposed of shall not be bound to see to the application of the consideration, if any, nor shall his title to the share be affected by any irregularity in or invalidity of the proceedings in reference to the forfeiture or disposal of the share.

## TRANSFER OF SHARES

23 The instrument of transfer of a share may be in any usual form or in any other form which the directors may approve and shall be executed by or on behalf of the transferor and, unless the share is fully paid, by or on behalf of the transferee.

24 The directors may refuse to register the transfer of a share which is not fully paid to a person of whom they do not approve and they may refuse to register the transfer of a share on which the company has a lien. They may also refuse to register a transfer unless:

(a) it is lodged at the office or at such other place as the directors may appoint and is accompanied by the certificate for the shares to which it relates and such other evidence as the directors may reasonably require to show the right of the transferor to make the transfer;

(b) it is in respect of only one class of shares; and

(c) it is in favour of not more than four transferees.

25 If the directors refuse to register a transfer of a share, they shall within two months after the date on which the transfer was lodged with the company send to the transferee notice of the refusal.

26 The registration of transfers of shares or of transfers of any class of shares may be suspended at such times and for such periods (not exceeding thirty days in any year) as the directors may determine.

27 No fee shall be charged for the registration of any instrument of transfer or other document relating to or affecting the title to any share.

28 The company shall be entitled to retain any instrument of transfer which is registered, but any instrument of transfer which the directors refuse to register shall be returned to the person lodging it when notice of the refusal is given.

## TRANSMISSION OF SHARES

29 If a member dies the survivor or survivors where he was a joint holder, and his personal representatives where he was a sole holder or the only survivor of joint holders, shall be the only persons recognised by the company as having any title to his interest; but nothing herein contained shall release the estate of a deceased member from any liability in respect of any share which had been jointly held by him.

30 A person becoming entitled to a share in consequence of the death or bankruptcy of a member may, upon such evidence being produced as the directors may properly require, elect either to become the holder of the share or to have some person nominated by him registered as the transferee. If he elects to become the holder he shall give notice to the company to that effect. If he elects to have another person registered he shall execute an instrument of transfer of the share to that person. All the articles relating to the transfer of shares shall apply to the notice or instrument of transfer as if it were an instrument of transfer executed by the member and the death or bankruptcy of the member had not occurred.

31 A person becoming entitled to a share in consequence of the death or bankruptcy of a member shall have the rights to which he would be entitled if he were the holder of the share, except that he shall not, before being registered as the holder of the share, be entitled in respect of it to attend or vote at any meeting of the company or at any separate meeting of the holders of any class of shares in the company.

## ALTERATION OF SHARE CAPITAL

32  The company may by ordinary resolution:

   (a) increase its share capital by new shares of such amount as the resolution prescribes;

   (b) consolidate and divide all or any of its share capital into shares of larger amount than its existing shares;

   (c) subject to the provisions of the Act, sub-divide its shares, or any of them, into shares of smaller amount and the resolution may determine that, as between the shares resulting from the sub-division, any of them may have any preference or advantage as compared with the others; and

   d) cancel shares which, at the date of the passing of the resolution, have not been taken or agreed to be taken by any person and diminish the amount of its share capital by the amount of the shares so cancelled.

33  Whenever as a result of a consolidation of shares any members would become entitled to fractions of a share, the directors, on behalf of those members, sell the shares representing the fractions for the best price reasonably obtainable to any person (including, subject to the provisions of the Act, the company) and distribute the net proceeds of sale in due proportion among those members, and the directors may authorise some person to execute an instrument of transfer of the shares to, or in accordance with the directions of, the purchaser. The transferee shall not be bound to see to the application of the purchase money nor shall his title to the shares be affected by any irregularity in or invalidity of the proceedings in reference to the sale.

34  Subject to the provisions of the Act, the company may by special resolution reduce its share capital, any capital redemption reserve and any share premium account in any way.

## PURCHASE OF OWN SHARES

35  Subject to the provisions of the Act, the company may purchase its own shares (including any redeemable shares) and, if it is a private company, make a payment in respect of the redemption or purchase of its own shares otherwise than out of distributable profits of the company or the proceeds of a fresh issue of shares.

## GENERAL MEETINGS

36   All general meetings other than annual general meetings shall be called extraordinary general meetings.

37   The directors may call general meetings and, on the requisition of members pursuant to the provisions of the Act, shall forthwith proceed to convene an extraordinary general meeting for a date not later than eight weeks after receipt of the requisition. If there are not within the United Kingdom sufficient directors to call a general meeting, any director or any member of the company may call a general meeting.

## NOTICE OF GENERAL MEETINGS

38   An annual general meeting and an extraordinary general meeting called for the passing of a special resolution or a resolution appointing a person as a director shall be called by at least twenty-one clear days' notice. All other extraordinary general meetings shall be called by at least fourteen clear days' notice but a general meeting may be called by shorter notice if it is so agreed:

(a) in the case of an annual general meeting, by all the members entitled to attend and vote thereat; and

(b) in the case of any other meeting by a majority in number of the members having a right to attend and vote being a majority together holding not less than ninety-five per cent in nominal value of the shares giving that right.

The notice shall specify the time and place of the meeting and the general nature of the business to be transacted and, in the case of an annual general meeting, shall specify the meeting as such.

Subject to the provisions of the articles and to any restrictions imposed on any shares, the notice shall be given to all members, to all persons entitled to a share in consequence of the death or bankruptcy of a member and to the directors and auditors.

39   The accidental omission to give notice of a meeting to, or the non-receipt of notice of a meeting by, any person entitled to receive notice shall not invalidate the proceedings at that meeting.

## PROCEEDINGS AT GENERAL MEETINGS

40   No business shall be transacted at any meeting unless a quorum is present. Two persons entitled to vote upon the business to be transacted, each being a member or a proxy for a member or a duly authorised representative of a corporation, shall be a quorum.

41　If such a quorum is not present within half an hour from the time appointed for the meeting, or if during a meeting such a quorum ceases to be present, the meeting shall stand adjourned to the same day in the next week at the same time and place, or to such time and place as the directors may determine.

42　The chairman, if any, of the board or directors or in his absence some other director nominated by the directors shall preside as chairman of the meeting, but if neither the chairman nor such other director (if any) be present within fifteen minutes after the time appointed for holding the meeting and willing to act, the directors present shall elect one of their number to be chairman and, if there is only one director present and willing to act, he shall be chairman.

43　If no director is willing to act as chairman, or if no director is present within fifteen minutes after the time appointed for holding the meeting, the members present and entitled to vote shall choose one of their number to be chairman.

44　A director shall, notwithstanding that he is not a member, be entitled to attend and speak at any general meeting and at any separate meeting of the holders of any class of shares in the company.

45　The chairman may, with the consent of a meeting at which a quorum is present (and shall if so directed by the meeting), adjourn the meeting from time to time and place to place, but no business shall be transacted at an adjourned meeting other than business which might properly have been transacted at the meeting had the adjournment not taken place. When a meeting is adjourned for fourteen days or more, at least seven clear days' notice shall be given specifying the time and place of the adjourned meeting and the general nature of the business to be transacted. Otherwise it shall not be necessary to give any such notice.

46　A resolution put to the vote of a meeting shall be decided on a show of hands unless before, or on the declaration of the result of, the show of hands a poll is dully demanded. Subject to the provisions of the Act, a poll may be demanded:

(a) by the chairman; or

(b) by at least two members having the right to vote at the meeting; or

(c) by a member or members representing not less than one-tenth of the total voting rights of all the members having the right to vote at the meeting; or

(d) by a member or members holding shares conferring a right to vote at the meeting being shares on which an aggregate sum has been paid up equal to not less than one-tenth of the total sum paid up on all the shares conferring that right; and a demand by a person as proxy for a member shall be the same as a demand by the member.

47  Unless a poll is duty demanded, a declaration by the chairman that a resolution has been carried or carried unanimously, or by a particular majority, or lost, or not carried by a particular majority and an entry to that effect in the minutes of the meeting shall be conclusive evidence of the fact without proof of the number or proportion of the votes recorded in favour of or against the resolution.

48  The demand for a poll may, before the poll is taken, be withdrawn but only with the consent of the chairman and a demand so withdrawn shall not be taken to have invalidated the result of a show of hands declared before the demand was made.

49  A poll shall be taken as the chairman directs and he may appoint scrutineers (who need not be members) and fix a time and place for declaring the result of the poll. The result of the poll shall be deemed to be the resolution of the meeting at which the poll was demanded.

50  In the case of an equality of votes, whether on a show of hands or on a poll, the chairman shall be entitled to a casting vote in addition to any other vote he may have.

51  A poll demanded on the election of a chairman or on a question of adjournment shall be taken forthwith. A poll demanded on any other question shall be taken either forthwith or at such time and place as the chairman directs not being more than thirty days after the poll is demanded. The demand for a poll shall not prevent the continuance of a meeting for the transaction of any business other than the question on which the poll was demanded. If a poll is demanded before the declaration of the result of a show of hands and the demand is duly withdrawn, the meeting shall continue as if the demand had not been made.

52  No notice need be given of a poll not taken forthwith if the time and place at which it is to be taken are announced at the meeting at which it is demanded. In any other case at least seven clear days' notice shall be given specifying the time and place at which the poll is to be taken.

53  A resolution in writing executed by or on behalf of each member who would have been entitled to vote upon it if it had been proposed at a general meeting at which he was present shall be as effectual as if it had been passed at a general meeting duly convened and held and may consist of several instruments in the like form each executed by or on behalf of one or more members.

## VOTES OF MEMBERS

54 Subject to any rights or restrictions attached to any shares, on a show of hands every member who (being an individual) is present in person or (being a corporation) is present by a duly authorised representative, not being himself a member entitled to vote, shall have one vote and on a poll every member shall have one vote for every share of which he is the holder.

55 In the case of joint holders the vote of the senior who tenders a vote, whether in person or by proxy, shall be accepted to the exclusion of the votes of the other joint holders, and seniority shall be determined by the order in which the names of the holders stand in the register of members.

56 A member in respect of whom an order has been made by any court having jurisdiction (whether in the United Kingdom or elsewhere) in matters concerning mental disorder may vote, whether on a show of hands or on a poll, by his receiver, curator bonis or other person authorised in that behalf appointed by that court, and any such receiver, curator bonis or other person may, on a poll, vote by proxy. Evidence to the satisfaction of the directors of the authority of the person claiming to exercise the right to vote shall be deposited at the office, or at such other place as is specified in accordance with the articles for the deposit of instruments of proxy, not less than 48 hours before the time appointed for holding the meeting or adjourned meeting at which the right to vote is to be exercised and in default the right to vote shall not be exercisable.

57 No member shall vote at any general meeting or at any separate meeting of the holders of any class of shares in the company, either in person or by proxy, in respect of any share held by him unless all moneys presently payable by him in respect of that share have been paid.

58 No objection shall be raised to the qualification of any voter except at the meeting or adjourned meeting at which the vote objected to is tendered, and every vote not disallowed at the meeting shall be valid. Any objection made in due time shall be referred to the chairman whose decision shall be final and conclusive.

59 On a poll votes may be given either personally or by proxy. A member may appoint more than one proxy to attend on the same occasion.

60 An instrument appointing a proxy shall be in writing, executed by or on behalf of the appointer and shall be in the following form (or in a form as near thereto as circumstances allow or in any other form which is usual or which the directors may approve):

> '.......................................................PLC/Limited
> I/We..............................,of..............................
> ..................................................., being a
> member/members of the above named com-
> pany, hereby appoint.......................................of
> ..................................,or failing him,.....................
> of..................................,as my/our proxy to vote
> in my/our name(s) and on my/our behalf at
> the annual/extraordinary general meeting of the
> company to be held on..................19...., and at any
> adjournment thereof. Signed on..............19....'

61 Where it is desired to afford members an opportunity of instructing the proxy how he shall act the instrument appointing a proxy shall be in the following form (or in a form as near thereto as circumstances allow or in any other form which is usual or which the directors may approve):

> '.......................................................PLC/Limited
> I/We..............................,of..............................
> ..................................................., being a
> member/members of the above named com-
> pany, hereby appoint.......................................of
> ..................................,or failing him,.....................
> of..................................,as my/our proxy to vote
> in my/our name(s) and on my/our behalf at
> the annual/extraordinary general meeting of the
> company to be held on..................19...., and at any
> adjournment thereof. This form is to be used in
> respect of the resolution below as follows:
>   Resolution No 1 for/against*
>   Resolution No 2 for/against*
>   (*Strike out whichever is not desired)
> Unless otherwise instructed, the proxy may vote
> as he thinks fit or abstain from voting.
> Signed this.......day on..............19....'

62 The instrument appointing a proxy and any authority under which it is executed or a copy of such authority certified notarially or in some other way approved by the directors may:

(a) be deposited at the office or at such other place within the United Kingdom as is specified in the notice convening the meeting or in any instrument of proxy sent out by the company in relation to the meeting not less than 48 hours before the time for holding the meeting or adjourned meeting at which the person named in the instrument proposes to vote: or

b) in the case of a poll taken more than 49 hours after it is demanded, be deposited as aforesaid after the poll has been demanded and not less than 24 hours before the time appointed for the taking of the poll; or

c) where the poll is not taken forthwith but is taken not more than 49 hours after it was demanded, be delivered at the meeting at which the poll was demanded to the chairman or to the secretary or to any director; and an instrument of proxy which is not deposited or delivered in a manner so permitted shall be invalid.

63 A vote given or poll demanded by proxy or by the duly authorised representative of a corporation shall be valid notwithstanding the previous determination of the authority of the person voting or demanding a poll unless notice of the determination was received by the company at the office or at such other place at which the instrument of proxy was duly deposited before the commencement of the meeting or adjourned meeting at which the vote is given or the poll demanded or (in the case of a poll taken otherwise than on the same day as the meeting or adjourned meeting) the time appointed for taking the poll.

## NUMBER OF DIRECTORS

64 Unless otherwise determined by ordinary resolution, the number of directors (other than alternate directors) shall not be subject to any maximum but shall be not less than two.

## ALTERNATE DIRECTORS

65 Any director (other than an alternate director) may appoint any other director, or any other person approved by resolution of the directors and willing to act, to be an alternate director and may remove from office an alternate director so appointed by him.

66 An alternate director shall be entitled to receive notice of all meetings of directors and of all meetings of committees of directors of which his appointor is a member, to attend and vote at any such meeting at which the director appointing him is not personally present, and generally to perform all the functions of his appointor as a director in his absence but shall not be entitled to receive any remuneration from the company for his services as an alternate director. But it shall not be necessary to give notice of such a meeting to an alternate director who is absent from the United Kingdom.

67  An alternate director shall cease to be an alternate director if his appointor ceases to be a director; but, if a director retires by rotation or otherwise but is reappointed or deemed to have been reappointed at the meeting at which he retires, any appointment of an alternate director made by him which was in force immediately prior to his retirement shall continue after his reappointment.

68  Any appointment or removal of an alternate director shall be by notice to the company signed by the director making or revoking the appointment or in any other manner approved by the directors.

69  Save as otherwise provided in the articles, an alternate director shall be deemed for all purposes to be director and shall alone be responsible for his own acts and defaults and he shall not be deemed to be the agent of the director appointing him.

## POWERS OF DIRECTORS

70  Subject to the provisions of the Act, the memorandum and the articles and to any directions given by special resolution, the business of the company shall be managed by the directors who may exercise all the powers of the company. No alteration of the memorandum or articles and no such direction shall invalidate any prior act of the directors which would have been valid if that alteration had not been made or that direction had not been given. The powers given by this regulation shall not be limited by any special power given to the directors by the articles and a meeting of directors at which a quorum is present may exercise all powers exercisable by the directors.

71  The directors may, by power of attorney or otherwise, appoint any person to be the agent of the company for such purpose and on such conditions as they determine, including authority for the agent to delegate all or any of his powers.

## DELEGATION OF DIRECTOR'S POWERS

72  The directors may delegate any of their powers to any committee consisting of one or more directors. They may also delegate to any managing director or any director holding any other executive office such of their powers as they consider desirable to be exercised by him. Any such delegation may be made subject to any conditions the directors may impose, and either collaterally with or to the exclusion of their powers and may be revoked or altered. Subject to any such conditions, the proceedings of a committee with two or more members shall be governed by the articles regulating the proceedings of directors so far as they are capable of applying.

## APPOINTMENT AND RETIREMENT OF DIRECTORS

73 At the first annual general meeting all the directors shall retire from office, and at every subsequent annual general meeting one-third of the directors who are subject to retirement by rotation or, if their number is not three or a multiple of three, the number nearest to one-third shall retire from office; but, if there is only one director who is subject to retirement by rotation, he shall retire.

74 Subject to the provisions of the Act, the directors to retire by rotation shall be those who have been longest in office since their last appointment or reappointment, but as between persons who became or were last reappointed directors on the same day those to retire shall (unless they otherwise agree amongst themselves) be determined by lot.

75 If the company, at the meeting at which a director retires by rotation, does not fill the vacancy the retiring director shall, if willing to act, be deemed to have been reappointed unless at the meeting it is resolved not to fill the vacancy or unless a resolution for the reappointment of the director is put to the meeting and lost.

76 No person other than a director retiring by rotation shall be appointed or reappointed a director at any general meeting unless:

(a) he is recommended by the directors; or

(b) not less than fourteen nor more than thirty-five clear days before the date appointed for the meeting, notice executed by a member qualified to vote at the meeting has been given to the company of the intention to propose that person for appointment or reappointment stating the particulars which would, if he were so appointed or reappointed, be required to be included in the company's register of directors together with notice executed by that person of his willingness to be appointed or reappointed.

77 Not less than seven nor more than twenty-eight clear days before the date appointed for holding a general meeting notice shall be given to all who are entitled to receive notice of the meeting of any person (other than a director retiring by rotation at the meeting) who is recommended by the directors for appointment or reappointment as a director at a meeting or in respect of whom notice has been duly given to the company of the intention to propose him at the meeting for appointment as a director. The notice shall give the particulars of that person which would, if her were so appointed or reappointed, be required to be included in the company's register of directors.

78 Subject as aforesaid, the company may by ordinary resolution appoint a person who is willing to act to be a director either to fill a

vacancy or as an additional director and may also determine the rotation in which any additional directors are to retire.

79 The directors may appoint a person who is willing to act to be a director, either to fill a vacancy or as an additional director, provided that the appointment does not cause the number of directors to exceed any number fixed by or in accordance with the articles as the maximum number of directors. A director so appointed shall hold office only until the next following annual general meeting and shall not be taken into account in determining the directors who are to retire by rotation at the meeting. If not reappointed at such annual general meeting, he shall vacate office at the conclusion thereof.

80 Subject as aforesaid, a director who retires at an annual general meeting may, if willing to act, be reappointed. If he is not reappointed, he shall retain office until the meeting appoints someone in his place, or if it does not do so, until the end of the meeting.

## DISQUALIFICATION AND REMOVAL OF DIRECTORS

81 The office of a director shall be vacated if:

(a) he ceases to be a director by virtue of the Act or he becomes prohibited by law from being a director; or

(b) he becomes bankrupt or makes any arrangement or composition with his creditors generally; or

(c) he is, or may be, suffering from mental disorder and either:

(i) he is admitted to hospital in pursuance of an application for admission for treatment under the Mental Health Act 1983 or, in Scotland, an application for admission under the Mental Health (Scotland) Act 1960; or

(ii) an order is made by a court having jurisdiction (whether in the United Kingdom or elsewhere) in matters concerning mental disorder for his detention of for the appointment of a receiver, curator bonis or other person to exercise powers with respect to his property or affairs; or

(d) he resigns his office by notice to the company; or

(e) he shall for more than six consecutive months have been absent without permission of the directors from meetings of directors held during that period and the directors resolve that his office be vacated.

## REMUNERATION OF DIRECTORS

82 The directors shall be entitled to such remuneration as the company may by ordinary resolution determine and, unless the resolution provides otherwise, the remuneration shall be deemed to accrue from day to day.

## DIRECTORS' EXPENSES

83 The directors may be paid all travelling, hotel, and other expenses properly incurred by them in connection with their attendance at meetings of directors or committees of directors or general meetings or separate meetings of the holders of any class of shares or of debentures of the company or otherwise in connection with the discharge of their duties.

## DIRECTORS' APPOINTMENTS AND INTERESTS

84 Subject to the provisions of the Act, the directors may appoint one or more of their number to the office of managing director or to any other executive office under the company and may enter into an agreement or arrangement with any director for his employment by the company or for the provision by him of any services outside the scope of the ordinary duties of a director. Any such appointment, agreement or arrangement may be made upon such terms as the directors determine and they may remunerate any such director for his services as they think fit. Any appointment of a director to an executive office shall terminate if he ceases to be a director but without prejudice to any claim to damages for breach of the contract of service between the director and the company. A managing director and a director holding any other executive office shall not be subject to retirement by rotation.

85 Subject to the provisions of the Act, and provided that he has disclosed to the directors the nature and extent of any material interest of his, a director notwithstanding his office:

(a) may be a party to, or otherwise interested in, any transaction or arrangement with the company or in which the company is otherwise interested;

(b) may be a director or other officer of, or employed by, or a party to any transaction or arrangement with, or otherwise interested in, any body corporate promoted by the company or in which the company is otherwise interested; and

(c) shall not, by reason of his office, be accountable to the company for any benefit which he derives from any such office or employment or from any such transaction or arrangement or from any interest in any such body corporate and no such transaction or arrangement shall be liable to be avoided on the ground of any such interest or benefit.

86 For the purpose of regulation 85:

(a) a general notice given to the directors that a director is to be regarded as having an interest of the nature and extent specified in the notice in any transaction or arrangement in which a specified person or class of persons is interested shall be deemed to be a disclosure that the director has an interest in any such transaction of the nature and extent so specified; and

(b) an interest of which a director has no knowledge and of which it is unreasonable to expect him to have knowledge shall not be treated as an interest of his.

87 The directors may provide benefits, whether by the payment of gratuities or pensions or by insurance or otherwise, for any director who has held but no longer holds any executive office or employment with the company or with any body corporate which is or has been a subsidiary, and for any member of his family (including a spouse and a former spouse) or any person who is or was dependent on him, and may (as well before as after he ceases to hold such office or employment) contribute to any fund and pay premiums for the purchase or provision of any such benefit.

## PROCEEDINGS OF DIRECTORS

88 Subject to the provisions of the articles, the directors may regulate their proceedings as they think fit. A director may, and the secretary at the request of a director shall, call a meeting of the directors. It shall not be necessary to give notice of a meeting to a director who is absent from the United Kingdom. Questions arising at a meeting shall be decided by a majority of votes. In the case of an equality of votes, the chairman shall have a second or casting vote. A director who is also an alternate director shall be entitled in the absence of his appointor to a separate vote on behalf of his appointor to his own vote.

89 The quorum for the transaction of the business of the directors may be fixed by the directors and unless so fixed at any other number shall be two. A person who holds office only as an alternate director shall, if his appointor is not present, be counted in the quorum.

90 The continuing directors or a sole director may act notwithstanding any vacancies in their number, but, if the number of directors is less than the number fixed as the quorum, the continuing directors or director may act only for the purpose of filling vacancies or of calling a general meeting.

91 The directors may appoint one of their number to be the chairman of the board of directors and may at any time remove him from that office. Unless he is unwilling to do so, the director so appointed shall preside at every meeting of directors at which he is present. But if there is no director holding that office, or if the director holding it is unwilling to preside or is not present within five minutes after the time appointed for the meeting, the directors present may appoint one of their number to be chairman of the meeting.

92 All acts done by a meeting of directors, or of a committee of directors, or by a person acting as a director shall, notwithstanding that it be afterwards discovered that there was a defect in the appointment of any director or that any of them were disqualified from holding office, or had vacated office, or were not entitled to vote, be as valid as if every such person had been duly appointed and was qualified and had continued to be a director and had been entitled to vote.

93 A resolution in writing signed by all the directors entitled to receive notice of a meeting of directors or a committee of directors shall be as valid and effectual as if it had been passed at a meeting of directors or (as the case may be) a committee of directors duly convened and held and may consist of several documents in the like form each signed by one or more directors; but a resolution signed by an alternate director need not also be signed by his appointor and, if it is signed by a director who has appointed an alternate director, it need not be signed by the alternate director in that capacity.

Save as otherwise provided by the articles, a director shall not vote at a meeting of directors or of a committee of directors on any resolution concerning a matter in which he had, directly or indirectly, an interest or duty which is material and which conflicts or may conflict with the interests of the company unless his interest or duty arises only because the case falls within one or more of the following paragraphs:

(a) the resolution relates to the giving to him of a guarantee, security, or indemnity in respect of money lent to, or an obligation incurred by him for the benefit of, the company or any of its subsidiaries;

(b) the resolution relates to the giving to a third party of a guarantee, security, or indemnity in respect of an obligation of the company or any of its subsidiaries for which the director has assumed responsibility in whole or part and whether alone or jointly with others under a guarantee or indemnity or by the giving of security;

(c) his interest arises by virtue of his subscribing or agreeing to subscribe for any shares, debentures or other securities of the company or any of its subsidiaries, or by virtue of his being, or intending to become, a participant in the underwriting or sub-underwriting of an offer of any such shares, debentures, or other securities by the company or any of its subsidiaries for subscription, purchase or exchange;

(d) the resolution relates in any way to a retirement benefits scheme which has been approved, or is conditional upon approval, by the Board of Inland Revenue for taxation purposes.

For the purpose of this regulation, an interest of a person who is, for any purpose of the Act (excluding any statutory modification thereof not in force when this regulation becomes binding on the company), connected with a director shall be treated as an interest of the director and, in relation to an alternate director, an interest of his appointor shall be treated as an interest of the alternate director without prejudice to any interest which the alternate director has otherwise.

95    A director shall not be counted in the quorum at a meeting in relation to a resolution on which he is not entitled to vote.

96    The company may by ordinary resolution suspend or relax to any extent, either generally or in respect of any particular matter, any provision of the articles prohibiting a director from voting at a meeting of directors or of a committee of directors.

97    Where proposals are under consideration concerning the appointment of two or more directors to offices or employments with the company or any body corporate in which the company is interested the proposals may be divided and considered in relation to each director separately and (provided he is not for another reason precluded from voting) each of the directors concerned shall be entitled to vote and be counted in the quorum in respect of each resolution except that concerning his own appointment.

98    If a question arises at a meeting of directors or of a committee of directors as to the right of a director to vote, the question may, before the conclusion of the meeting, be referred to the chairman of the meeting and his ruling in relation to any director other than himself shall be final and conclusive.

## SECRETARY

99 Subject to the provisions of the Act, the secretary shall be appointed by the directors for such term, at such remuneration and upon such conditions as they may think fit; and any secretary so appointed may be removed by them.

## MINUTES

100 The directors shall cause minutes to be made in books kept for the purpose:
   (a) of all appointments of officers made by the directors; and
   (b) of all proceedings at meetings of the company, of the holders of any class of shares in the company, and of the directors, and of committees of directors, including the names of the directors present at each such meeting.

## THE SEAL

101 The seal shall only be used by the authority of the directors or of a committee of directors authorised by the directors. The directors may determine who shall sign any instrument to which the seal is affixed and unless otherwise so determined it shall be signed by a director and by the secretary or by a second director.

## DIVIDENDS

102 Subject to the provisions of the Act, the company may by ordinary resolution declare dividends in accordance with the respective rights of the members, but no dividend shall exceed the amount recommended by the directors.

103 Subject to the provisions of the Act, the directors may pay interim dividends if it appears to them that they are justified by the profits of the company available for distribution. If the share capital is divided into different classes, the directors may pay interim dividends on shares which confer deferred or non-preferred rights with regard to dividends as well as on shares which confer preferential rights with regard to dividend, but no interim dividends shall be paid on shares carrying deferred or non-preferred rights if, at the time of payment, any preferential dividend is in arrear. The directors may also pay at intervals settled by them any dividend payable at a fixed rate if its appears to them that the profits available for distribution justify the payment. Provided the

directors act in good faith they shall not incur any liability to the holders of shares conferring preferred rights for any loss they may suffer by the lawful payment of an interim dividend on any shares having deferred or non-preferred rights.

104 Except as otherwise provided by the rights attached to shares, all dividends shall be declared and paid according to the amounts paid up on the shares on which the dividend is paid. All dividends shall be apportioned and paid proportionately to the amounts paid up on the shares during any portion or portions of the period in respect of which the dividend is paid; but, if any share is issued on terms providing that it shall rank for dividend as from a particular date, that share shall rank for dividend accordingly.

105 A general meeting declaring a dividend may, upon the recommendation of the directors, direct that it shall be satisfied wholly or partly by the distribution of assets and, where any difficulty arises in regard to the distribution, the directors may settle the same and in particular may issue fractional certificates and fix the value for distribution of any assets and may determine that cash shall be paid to any member upon the footing of the value so fixed and in order to adjust the rights of members and may vest any assets in trustees.

106 Any dividend or other moneys payable in respect of a share may be paid by cheque sent by post to the registered address of the person entitled or, if two or more persons are the holders of the share or are jointly entitled to it by reason of the death or bankruptcy of the holder, to the registered address of that one of those persons who is first named in the register of members or to such person and to such address as the person or persons entitled may in writing direct. Every cheque shall be made payable to the order of the person or persons entitled or to such other person as the person or persons entitled may in writing direct and payment of the cheque shall be a good discharge to the company. Any joint holder or other person jointly entitled to a share as aforesaid may give receipts for any dividend or other moneys payable in respect of the share.

107 No dividend or other moneys payable in respect of a share shall bear interest against the company unless otherwise provided by the rights attached to the share.

108 Any dividend which has remained unclaimed for twelve years from the date when it became due for payment shall, if the directors so resolve, be forfeited and cease to remain owing by the company.

## ACCOUNTS

109 No member shall (as such) have any rights of inspecting any accounting records or other book or document of the company except as conferred by statue or authorised by the directors or by ordinary resolution of the company.

## CAPITALISATION OF PROFITS

110 The directors may with the authority of an ordinary resolution of the company:

(a) subject as hereinafter provided, resolve to capitalise any undivided profits of the company not required for paying any preferential dividend (whether or not they are available for distribution) or any sum standing to the credit of the company's share premium account or capital redemption reserve;

(b) appropriate the sum resolved to be capitalised to the members who would have been entitled to it if it were distributed by way of dividend and in the same proportions and apply such sum on their behalf either in or towards paying up the amounts, if any, for the time being unpaid on any shares held by them respectively, or in paying up in full unissued shares or debentures credited as fully paid to those members, or as they may direct, in those proportions, or partly in one way and partly in the other; but the share premium account, the capital redemption reserve, and any profits which are not available for distribution may, for the purposes of this regulation, only be applied in paying up unissued shares to be alloted to members credited as fully paid;

(c) make such provisions by the issue of fractional certificates or by payment in cash or otherwise as they determine in the case of shares or debentures becoming distributable under this regulation in fractions; and

(d) authorise any person to enter on behalf of all the members concerned into an agreement with the company providing for the allotment to them respectively, credited as fully paid, of any shares or debentures to which they are entitled upon such capitalisation, any agreement made under such authority being binding on all such members.

## NOTICES

111  Any notice to be given to or by any person pursuant to the articles shall be in writing except that a notice calling a meeting of the directors need not be in writing.

112  The company may give any notice to a member either personally or by sending it by post in a prepaid envelope addressed to the member at his registered address or by leaving it at that address. In the case of joint holders of a share, all notices shall be given to the joint holder whose name stands first in the register of members in respect of the joint holding and notice so given shall be sufficient notice to all the joint holders. A member whose registered address is not within the United Kingdom and who gives to the company an address within the United Kingdom at which notices may be given to him shall be entitled to have notices given to him at that address, but otherwise no such member shall be entitled to receive any notice from the company.

113  A member present, either in person or by proxy, at any meeting of the company or of the holders of any class of shares in the company shall be deemed to have received notice of the meeting, and where requisite, of the purposes for which it was called.

114  Every person who becomes entitled to a share shall be bound by any notice in respect of that share which, before his name is entered in the register of members, has been duly given to a person from whom he derives his title.

115  Proof that an envelope containing a notice was properly addressed, prepaid and posted shall be conclusive evidence that the notice was given. A notice shall be deemed to be given at the expiration of 48 hours after the envelope containing it was posted.

116  A notice may be given by the company to the persons entitled to a share in consequence of the death or bankruptcy of a member by sending or delivering it, in any manner authorised by the articles for the giving of notice to a member, addressed to them by name, or by the title of representatives of the deceased, or trustee of the bankrupt or by any like description at the address, if any, within the United Kingdom supplied for that purpose by the persons claiming to be so entitled. Until such an address has been supplied, a notice may be given in any manner in which it might have been given if the death or bankruptcy had not occurred.

## WINDING UP

117  If the company is wound up, the liquidator may, with the sanction of an extraordinary resolution of the company and any other

sanction required by the Act, divide among the members in specie the whole or any part of the assets of the company and may, for the purpose, value any assets and determine how the division shall be carried out as between the members or different classes of members. The liquidator may, with the like sanction, invest the whole or any part of the assets in trustees upon such trusts for the benefit of the members as he with the like sanction determines, but no member shall be compelled to accept any assets upon which there is a liability.

## INDEMNITY

118 Subject to the provisions of the Act but without prejudice to any indemnity to which a director may otherwise be entitled, every director or other officer or auditor of the company shall be indemnified out of the assets of the company against any liability incurred by him in defending any proceedings, whether civil or criminal, in which judgement is given in his favour or in which he is acquitted or in connection with any application in which relief is granted to him by the court from liability for negligence, default, breach of duty or breach of trust in relation to the affairs of the company.

# TABLE B - A PRIVATE COMPANY LIMITED BY SHARES

## MEMORANDUM OF ASSOCIATION

1 The company's name is 'The South Wales Motor Transport Company cyfyngedig'.

2 The company's registered office is to be situated in Wales.

3 The company's objects are the carriage of passengers and goods in motor vehicles between such places as the company may from time to time determine and the doing of all such other things as are incidental or conducive to the attainment of that object.

4 The liability of the members is limited.

5 The company's share capital is £50,000 divided into 50,000 shares of £1 each.

We, the subscribers to this memorandum of association, wish to be formed into a company pursuant to this memorandum; and we agree to take the number of shares shown opposite our respective names.

| Names and addresses of subscribers | Number of shares taken by each subscriber |
|---|---|
| Thomas Jones, 138 Mountfield Street, Tredegar | 1 |
| Mary Evans, 19 Merthyr Road, Aberystwyth | 1 |
| **TOTAL SHARES TAKEN** | **2** |
| Dated ...............19..... | |
| Witness to the above signatures, Anne Brown 'Woodlands', Fieldside Road Bryn Mawr | |

# TABLE C - A COMPANY LIMITED BY GUARANTEE AND NOT HAVING A SHARE CAPITAL

## MEMORANDUM OF ASSOCIATION

1 The company's name is 'The Dundee School Association Limited'.

2 The company's registered office is to be situated in Scotland.

3 The company's objects are the carrying on of a school for boys and girls in Dundee and the doing of all such other things as are incidental or conducive to the attainment of that object.

4 The liability of the members is limited.

5 Every member of the company undertakes to contribute such amount as may be required (not exceeding £100) to the company's assets if it should be wound up while he is a member or within one year after he ceases to be a member, for payment of the company's debts and liabilities contracted before he ceases to be a member and of the costs, charges and expenses of winding up, and for the adjustment of the rights of the contributories among themselves.

We, the subscribers to this memorandum of association, wish to be formed into a company pursuant to this memorandum.

Names and Addresses of Subscribers

a)  Kenneth Brodie, 14 Bute Street, Dundee

b)  Ian Davis, 2 Burns Avenue, Dundee

Dated.....................19......

Witness to the above signatures,

Anne Brown 149 Princes Street, Edinburgh

## ARTICLES OF ASSOCIATION

### *PRELIMINARY*

1 Regulations 2 to 35 inclusive, 54, 55, 57, 59 102 to 108 inclusive, 110, 114, 116 and 117 of Table A, shall not apply to the company but the articles hereinafter contained and subject to modifications hereinafter expressed, the remaining regulations of Table A shall constitute the articles of association of the company.

## INTERPRETATION

2 In regulation 1 of Table A, the definition of 'the holder' shall be omitted.

## MEMBERS

3 The subscribers to the memorandum of association of the company and such other persons as are admitted to membership in accordance with the articles shall be members of the company. No person shall be admitted a member of the company unless he is approved by the directors. Every person who wishes to become a member shall deliver to the company an application for membership in such form as the directors require executed by him.

4 A member may at any time withdraw from the company by giving at least seven clear days' notice to the company. Membership shall not be transferable and shall cease on death.

## NOTICE OF GENERAL MEETINGS

5 In regulation 38 of Table A:

(a) in paragraph (b) the words 'of the total voting rights at the meeting of all the members' shall be substituted for 'in nominal value of the shares giving that right'; and

(b) the words 'The notice shall be given to all the members and to the directors and auditors' shall be substituted for the last sentence.

## PROCEEDINGS AT GENERAL MEETINGS

6 The words 'and at any separate meeting of the holders of any class of shares in the company' shall be omitted from regulation 44 of Table A.

7 Paragraph (d) of regulation 146 of Table A shall be omitted.

## VOTES OF MEMBERS

8 On a show of hands every member present in person shall have one vote. On a poll every member present in person or by proxy shall have one vote.

## DIRECTORS' EXPENSES

9 The words 'of any class of shares or' shall be omitted from regulation 83 of Table A.

## *PROCEEDINGS OF DIRECTORS*

10  In paragraph (c) of regulation 94 of Table A the word 'debentures' shall be substituted for the works 'shares, debentures or other securities' in both places where they occur.

## *MINUTES*

11  The words 'of the holders of any class of shares in the company' shall be omitted from regulation 100 of Table A.

## *NOTICES*

12  The second sentence of regulation 112 of Table A shall be omitted.

13  The words 'or of the holders of any class of shares in the company' shall be omitted from regulation 113 of Table A.

# TABLE D

# PART 1 - A PUBLIC COMPANY LIMITED BY GUARANTEE AND HAVING A SHARE CAPITAL

## MEMORANDUM OF ASSOCIATION

1 The company's name is 'Gwestai Glyndwr, cwmni cyfyngedig cyhoeddus'.

2 The company is to be a public company.

3 The company's registered office is to be situated in Wales.

4 The company's objects are facilitating travelling in Wales by providing hotels and conveyances by sea and by land for the accommodation of travellers and the doing of all such other things as are incidental or conducive to the attainment of those objects.

5 The liability of the members is limited.

6 Every member of the company undertakes to contribute such amount as may be required (not exceeding £100) to the company's assets if it should be wound up while he is a member or within one year after he ceases to be a member, for payment of the company's debts and liabilities contracted before he ceases to be a member, and of the costs, charges and expenses of winding up, and for the adjustment of the rights of the contibutories among themselves.

7 The Company's share capital is £50,000 divided into 50,000 shares of £1 each.

We, the subscribers to this memorandum of association, wish to be formed into a company pursuant to this memorandum; and we agree to take the number of shares shown opposite our respective names.

| Names and addresses of subscribers | Number of shares taken by each subscriber |
|---|---|
| Thomas Jones, 13 Mountfield Street, Tredegar | 1 |
| Andrew Smith, 19 Merthyr Road, Aberystwyth | 1 |
| **TOTAL SHARES TAKEN** | **2** |
| Dated ...............19..... | |
| Witness to the above signatures, Anne Brown 'Woodlands', Fieldside Road, Bryn Mawr | |

## PART II - A PRIVATE COMPANY LIMITED BY GUARANTEE AND HAVING A SHARE CAPITAL

### MEMORANDUM OF ASSOCIATION

1 The company's name is 'The Highland Hotel Company Limited'.

2 The company's registered office is to be situated in Scotland.

3 The company's objects are facilitating travelling in the Highlands of Scotland by providing hotels and conveyances by sea and by land for the accommodation of travellers and the doing of all such other things as are incidental or conducive to the attainment of those objects.

4 The liability of the members is limited.

5 Every member of the company undertakes to contribute such amount as may be required (not exceeding £100) to the company's assets if it should be wound up while he is a member or within one year after he ceases to be a member, for payment of the company's debts and liabilities contracted before be ceases to be a member, and of the costs, charges and expenses of winding up, and for the adjustment of the rights of the contributories among themselves.

6 The company's share capital is £50,000 divided into 50,000 shares of £1 each.

We, the subscribers to this memorandum of association, wish to be formed into a company pursuant to this memorandum, and we agree to take the number of shares shown opposite our respective names.

| Names and addresses of subscribers | Number of shares taken by each subscriber |
|---|---|
| Kenneth Brodie, 14 Bute Street, Dundee | 1 |
| Ian Davis, 2 Burns Avenue, Dundee | 1 |
| **TOTAL SHARES TAKEN** | **2** |
| Dated ...............19..... | |
| Witness to the above signatures, Anne Brown 149 Princes Street, Edinburgh | |

# PART III - A COMPANY (PUBLIC OR PRIVATE) LIMITED BY GUARANTEE AND HAVING A SHARE CAPITAL

## ARTICLES OF ASSOCIATION

The regulations of Table shall constitute the articles of association of the Company.

## TABLE E - AN UNLIMITED COMPANY HAVING A SHARE CAPITAL

## MEMORANDUM OF ASSOCIATION

1   The company's name is 'The Woodford Engineering Company'.

2   The company's registered office is to be situated in England and Wales.

3   The company's objects are the working of certain patented inventions relating to the application of microchip technology to the improvement of food processing and the doing of all such other things as are incidental or conducive to the attainment of that object.

We, the subscribers to this memorandum of association, wish to be formed into a company pursuant to this memorandum, and we agree to take the number of shares shown opposite our respective names.

| Names and addresses of subscribers | Number of shares taken by each subscriber |
|---|---|
| Brian Smith, 24 Nibley Road, Wotton-under-Edge, Gloucester | 3 |
| William Green, 278 High Street, Chipping Sodbury, Avon | 5 |
| **TOTAL SHARES TAKEN** | 8 |
| Dated ...............19..... | |
| Witness to the above signatures, Anne Brown 108 Park Way, Bristol 8 | |

## ARTICLES OF ASSOCIATION

1 Regulations 3, 32, 34 and 35 of Table A shall not apply to the company, but the articles hereinafter contained and, subject to the modification hereinafter expressed, the remaining regulations of Table A shall constitute the articles of association of the company.

2 The words 'at least seven clear days notice' shall be substituted for the words 'at least fourteen clear days' notice in regulation 38 of Table A.

3 The share capital of the company is £20,000 divided into 20,000 shares of £1 each.

4 The company may by special resolution:

(a) increase the share capital by such sum to be divided into shares of such amount as the resolution may prescribe;

(b) consolidate and divide all or any of its share capital into shares of a larger amount than its existing shares;

(c) subdivide its shares, or any of them , into shares of a smaller amount than its existing shares;

(d) cancel any shares which at the date of the passing of the resolution have not been taken or agreed to be taken by any person;

(e)  reduce its share capital and any share premium account in any way.

# TABLE F - A PUBLIC COMPANY LIMITED BY SHARES

## MEMORANDUM OF ASSOCIATION

1  The company's name is 'Western Electronics Public Limited Company'.

2  The company is to be a public company.

3  The company's registered office is to be situated in England and Wales.

4  The company's objects are the manufacture and development of such descriptions of electronic equipment, instruments and appliances as the company may from time to time determine, and the doing of all such other things as are incidental or conducive to the attainment of that object.

5  The liability of the members is limited.

6  The company's share capital is £5,000,000 divided into 5,000,000 shares of £1 each.

We, the subscribers to this memorandum of association, wish to be formed into a company pursuant to this memorandum, and we agree to take the number of shares shown opposite our respective names.

| Names and addresses of subscribers | Number of shares taken by each subscriber |
|---|---|
| James White, 12 Broadmead, Birmingham | 3 |
| Patrick Smith, 145a Huntley House, London Wall, London EC2 | 5 |
| **TOTAL SHARES TAKEN** Dated ...............19..... | 8 |
| Witness to the above signatures, Anne Brown 13 Hute Street, London WC2 | |

## EXPLANATORY NOTE[1]

These regulations replace the Companies (Alteration of Table A etc.) Regulations 1984 which are revoked. They provide the regulations (Table A) and the forms of memorandum and articles of association (Tables B,C,D,E and F) for the purposes of sections 3 and 8 of the Companies Act 1985.

Certain amendments have been made to Table A and C. Table A has been amended as follows. The reference to 'the Companies Act 1948 to 1983' has been converted to 'the Companies Act 1985' and the references to 'the acts' to 'the act'. In regulation 33, the words 'subject to the provisions of the Act' have been inserted after the word 'including' in the words in parenthesis. In regulation 65, the words, 'resolution of ' have been inserted after 'approved by'. In regulation 87, 'directors, replaces 'company' as the second word of this regulation. In regulation 90, the words 'the continuing directors or director' are substituted for the word 'they'. In regulation 111, in the first sentence the words 'to or by

---

1    This note is not part of the Regulations.

any person' have been inserted after 'given' and the words 'except that a notice calling a meeting of the directors need not be in writing' after the word 'writing'. The remainder of the first sentence (with the deletion of the words 'and' and 'such') and the second sentence of regulation 111 are removed and become the first and second sentence of regulation 112. In regulation 116, the words 'by them' have been deleted.

The following amendments have been made to the Articles of Association in Table C. In regulation 1, the word 'inclusive' has been deleted in the third place where it appeared. In regulation 10, the words 'in both places where they occur' have been substituted for the words 'where they twice occur'. Regulation 12 has been amended to refer to regulation 112 of Table A.

The Regulations will come into operation simultaneously with the coming into force of the Companies Act 1985.

# CHAPTER 12

# PROMOTERS

## DEFINITION

When a company is set up there must be promoters. The promoters are those people who take preliminary steps to set the company up. They thus act for the company before it is properly formed.

There is no statutory definition of a promoter. A promoter is variously described. In *Twycross v Grant* (1877)[1], Cockburn CJ said that the promoter is 'one who undertakes to form a company with reference to a given project and to set it going, and who takes the necessary steps to accomplish that purpose'. In *Emma Silver Mining Company v Lewis* (1879)[2] Lord Lindley said that the word promoter had no very definite meaning.

## DUTIES

Promoters owe fiduciary duties although they are not trustees. Breach of promoters' duties may involve unpleasant consequences as was said by Sargant J in *Omnium Electric Palaces Ltd v Baines* (1914)[3]. A promoter must disclose any profit he is making from a transaction. This profit must be disclosed to an independent board or to all of the company's actual and potential members. The disclosure must be of all profits, direct or indirect.

## REMEDIES

If there is no appropriate disclosure of profits that have been made, then the company may rescind the transaction. The usual bars to rescission apply so there could be no rescission if there has been affirmation or if third party rights have intervened or if restitution is not possible.

---

1   (1877) 2 CPD 469 at p 541.
2   (1879) 4 CPD 396 at p 407.
3   [1914] 1 Ch 332.

An alternative remedy is for there to be recovery of the relevant profit. One instance where the remedy of disgorgement of profit is not available is where the property was acquired before promotion began. In such a situation, part of the profit should properly belong to the promoter and the courts will not interfere to decide what proportion of the profit relates to the pre-promotion period and what proportion of the profit relates to the post-promotion period (see *Re Cape Breton Co* (1885)).

## PRE-INCORPORATION CONTRACTS

### Introduction

Before the company has come into existence, contracts may well be concluded on behalf of the unformed company. These contracts cannot involve agency. There can be no agency where there is no principal in existence at the time the contract was concluded. Before the United Kingdom's entry into the European Community in 1972, the position was confused and depended upon the particular form of words used by the promoter in concluding the contracts. Sometimes the promoter was personally liable on the contract, sometimes he was not. Section 9(2) of the European Communities Act 1972 regularised the position. The position is now set out in s 36(1)(c) of the Companies Act 1985. This provides 'a contract which purports to be made by or on behalf of a company at a time when the company has not been formed has effect, subject to any agreement to the contrary, as one made with the person purporting to act for the company or as agent for it, and he is personally liable on the contract accordingly'. This has been interpreted as involving personal liability of the promoter who is also able to enforce the contract unless there is an *express* agreement to the contrary. Statute has thus clarified the position.

## RAISING FINANCE

### Issues of shares to the public

Ever since the passage of the Financial Services Act 1986 as a consequence of the Gower Committee's recommendations, the Stock Exchange has become the competent authority to administer Part IV of the Financial Services Act 1986. Those companies with shares listed on the Listed Market must ensure that they comply with the Stock

Exchange Yellow Book or the Rules on Admission of Securities to Listing as the Yellow Book is sometimes termed. The second tier market, the Unlisted Securities Market, also offers the chance for listing for medium size companies. There are currently proposals to abolish the Unlisted Securities Market.

The general framework of the law regulating the admission of securities to the official list of the Stock Exchange is governed by Part IV of the Financial Services Act 1986. The Act delegates detailed responsibility for the administration of the regime in relation to the listing particulars to the Council of the Stock Exchange by s 142(6) of the Act. The Stock Exchange in turn has delegated the functions in relation to listing particulars to its Committee on Quotations under s 142(8). The Secretary of State for Trade and Industry has reserve power under s 192 of the Financial Services Act 1986 to direct the Stock Exchange to comply with any international obligations in relation to listing particulars.

Section 143 of the Act requires where an application is made for listing of shares that this should be made to the competent authority, ie the Stock Exchange, and that the Stock Exchange should not admit the securities to the official list unless it is satisfied that the relevant rules are complied with. In addition to complying with the detailed rules set out in the Yellow Book, there is an overriding requirement in s 146 that the listing particulars should contain such information as investors and their professional advisers would reasonably require, and reasonably expect to find there, in order to make an informed assessment of: the assets and liabilities of the company, its financial position, profits and losses and its prospects; and the rights that attach to those securities.

Additionally, there is a requirement to submit supplementary particulars to the Stock Exchange and, with the approval of the Stock Exchange, publish these matters if between publication of the listing particulars and dealings opening in the company's securities significant changes occur or significant new matters arise. There is only an obligation to disclose such changes if the issuer is aware of them[4].

Certain exemptions exist from the requirement of disclosure. These are set out in the Yellow Book and also in s 148 of the Financial Services Act 1986. Section 3 of the Yellow Book provides that if the information is of minor importance only and would not influence an investor, then there is no need for it to be disclosed. Section 148 of the Financial Services Act 1986 provides exemption from disclosure on the grounds that it would be contrary to the public interest or on the grounds that it would be detrimental to the company and that non-disclosure would

---

4    Financial Services Act 1986, s 147.

not be likely to mislead investors. Section 148 also provides exemption from disclosure if the securities are debt securities such as debentures on the grounds that disclosure is unnecessary given the persons likely to deal in those securities, ie this is likely to be the type of security dealt with by more experienced investors.

## Remedies for misleading listing particulars

Sections 150-152 of the Financial Services Act 1986 provides a statutory remedy in relation to misleading listing particulars. The sections are not limited to subscribers from the company and may also be used by purchasers on the open market. It may even be that an investor is unaware of the content of the listing particulars or even of their existence. The critical factor is that the investor has suffered as a result of the particulars. This would be the case if the market had been misled by the particulars so that the price of the shares had altered accordingly.

## Defences

Section 151 sets out six defences in relation to the statutory remedy. Section 151(1) provides that a defendant will not be liable to pay compensation if he can demonstrate to the court that he had reasonable grounds for believing the statement made was true and not misleading or that the omission was appropriate and he continued in that belief until after dealings in the securities had opened. He must additionally demonstrate either:

(a) that he continued to hold the belief until the securities in question were acquired; or

(b) that they were acquired before it was reasonably practicable for him to publish a correction to potential investors; or

(c) they were acquired after he had taken all reasonable steps to publish a correction to potential investors; or

(d) the securities were acquired after such a period of time that in all the circumstances he ought reasonably to be excused.

The second defence is set out in s 151(2). This provides a defence if the defendant can show that the statement was made by an expert whom he believed on reasonable grounds to be competent to make the statement and whom he reasonably believed had consented to the inclusion of the statement in the form and context in which it appeared. The defendant must hold such belief until dealings in the securities in question have opened. Additionally the defendant must demonstrate one of the following:

(a) that he continued to hold this belief until after the securities in question were acquired; or

(b) that the securities were acquired before it was reasonably practicable for the defendant to issue a statement concerning the expert's lack of competence or lack of consent; or

(c) before the securities were acquired, he had taken all reasonable steps to issue a statement relating to the lack of competence or lack of consent; or

(d) that the securities were acquired after such a period of time that the defendant ought reasonably to be excused.

The third defence is set out in s 151(3). The defence provides that a defendant will not be liable to pay compensation if he can demonstrate that he took all reasonable steps to bring a correction, notification of a lack of competence or a lack of consent on the part of an expert, to the attention of potential investors in the securities before the securities were acquired.

The fourth defence provides that if a defendant can demonstrate that the statement was an accurate copy of an official document, he will not be liable to pay compensation[5].

If the defendant can demonstrate that the plaintiff had knowledge that the defendant's statement was false or misleading or knew of an omission, then he will not be liable to pay compensation[6]. This is the fifth defence.

A sixth defence is that if the defendant can demonstrate that he reasonably believed that a change or new matter was unimportant and that supplementary listing particulars were not required, then he will not be liable to pay compensation[7].

The persons responsible for listing particulars and supplementary listing particulars are set out in s 152. This provides that the persons responsible are as follows:

(a) the issuer of the securities, ie the company;

(b) every person who is a director of the issuing company at the time that the listing particulars are submitted to the Stock Exchange for registration;

(c) persons who are named and who have authorised themselves to be named as agreeing to become directors either immediately or at some time in the future;

---

5  Ibid., s 151(4).
6  Ibid., s 151(5).
7  Ibid., s 151(6).

(d) every person who accepts responsibility for any part of the listing particulars (such persons will be potentially liable in relation to those parts);

(e) any other person who has authorised the contents of part or all of the listing particulars (such persons will be liable in relation to the relevant part).

Alternatively, a plaintiff who has been induced to purchase securities on the strength of a misrepresentation may have a remedy for the misrepresentation.

He may seek rescission of the contract if rescission is appropriate although the court has the discretion to refuse this under s 2(2) of the Misrepresentation Act 1967.

Damages may be awarded under s 2(1) of the Misrepresentation Act 1967 unless the misrepresentor can prove that he had reasonable grounds to believe, and did believe up to the time the contract was made, that the facts represented were true.

Alternatively damages may be claimed in the tort of deceit against the person who has the responsibility for the listing particulars or part of those particulars. Fraud is difficult to prove, however.

It may be easier to demonstrate that there has been a breach of a duty of care and that damages should therefore be payable in the tort of negligent misstatement under the principle in *Hedley Byrne & Co Ltd v Heller & Partners Ltd* (1964).

## Remedies for misleading prospectuses

Currently prospectuses are subject to Part III of the Companies Act 1985 (ie in relation to offers of securities by companies not quoted on the official list of the Stock Exchange). This is to be replaced by Part V of the Financial Services Act 1986.

The rules on disclosure are similar to the rules on disclosure for companies on the official list.

The remedies are also similar, except that the statutory remedy is somewhat different.

Section 67 of the Companies Act 1985 does not enable purchasers on the open market to obtain compensation under the statute.

However, when Part V of the Financial Services Act 1986 is brought into force, this will provide a parallel remedy to that contained in Part IV so that those who purchase securities on the open market may also have a remedy where the prospectus has been misleading.

## Criminal liability

Section 47 of the Financial Services Act 1986 provides that those carrying on an investment business who issue false listing particulars will be guilty of an offence in certain situations. If such a person makes a statement, promise or forecast which he knows to be misleading, false or deceptive, or dishonestly conceals any material facts or recklessly makes (dishonestly or otherwise) a statement, promise or forecast which is misleading, false or deceptive, if it is for the purpose of inducing another to enter into any investment agreement, is guilty of an offence. The section also makes it an offence to do any act or engage in conduct creating a false or misleading impression as to the market in or value of any investment if done to induce another to acquire, dispose of, subscribe for or underwrite those investments or to refrain from doing so or to exercise or refrain from exercising any rights conferred by those investments.

It is a defence if the person concerned can prove that he reasonably believed that his act or conduct would not create an impression that was false or misleading. The maximum penalty is seven years' imprisonment or a fine or both.

Section 70 of the Companies Act 1985 making it a criminal offence to issue an untrue prospectus remains in force. The maximum penalty for infringing this section is two years' imprisonment or a fine or both.

Under Part IV of the Financial Services Act 1986 it is an offence to publish listing particulars without a copy of them having been delivered to the registrar of companies. It is also an offence to publish an advertisement of securities without approval of the Stock Exchange.

Under Part V of the Act (which is not yet in force), if an advertisement of securities is issued without the prospectus being both approved by an approved exchange and registered with the registrar, this also will constitute an offence.

It is of course an offence for a private company to issue an advertisement offering its securities to the public (s 170 of the Financial Services Act 1986 which is not yet in force) (s 81 of the Companies Act 1985 making this an offence remains in force until Part V is brought into force).

In addition, s 19 of the Theft Act 1968 provides that where an officer of a company, or person purporting to act as such, with the intention of deceiving members or creditors of a company publishes a statement or account which he knows is, or may be misleading he is guilty of an offence. This carries a maximum sentence of seven years' imprisonment.

# CHAPTER 13

# DIRECTORS

The board of directors of a company manages the company. This management is subject to certain controls exercised by the shareholders. Directors have duties and responsibilities towards the company. Section 282(1) of the Companies Act 1985 provides that every public company registered on or after the 1 November 1929 should have at least two directors. Section 282(2) provides that every company registered before that date other than a private company should have at least one director. Section 282(3) provides that every private company should have at least one director. There is no upper limit in the Act placed on the number of directors. The company's articles may place an upper limit on the number of directors. Table A Art 64 does not specify a maximum number. It does specify a minimum of two.

A company's articles will usually set out the method of appointment and retirement of directors. Table A Arts 73-80 deal with appointment and retirement.

In general, matters are left to the company and the procedures are therefore set out in the company's articles. However, the Companies Act does make some provisions relating to the appointment of directors. Section 291 of the Companies Act 1985 provides that it is the duty of every director who is required to hold qualification shares by the company's articles to obtain the qualification shares within two months from his appointment or such shorter time as may be fixed by the articles. If he fails to do so, then the office of director is vacated. Failure to vacate the office results in the person concerned being liable to a fine and for continued contravention to a daily default fine.

Section 292 requires that the appointment of directors be voted on individually at the general meeting where it is being considered, unless a resolution that it should be considered in a composite resolution has first been agreed to by the meeting without any vote being given against it.

Section 293 relates to the age limit for directors in public companies or in a private company which is a subsidiary of a public company. In such an instance no person is capable of being appointed as a director if at the time of his appointment he has attained the age of 70. A director who becomes aged 70 should vacate his office at the conclusion of the next annual general meeting after attaining that age. However, it is open to companies to vote in such people as directors if special notice has been served and if the members agree to it by ordinary resolution[1]. Section 294 requires that a person appointed as a director of a company subject to s 293 shall disclose his age to the company when he has attained the retiring age.

There is an additional provision of importance in relation to the first directors of a company. Section 10(2) of the Companies Act 1985 provides that there should be delivered with the memorandum a statement containing the names and particulars of the person or persons who are to be the first directors of the company. This document (Form 10) (see p 302) is sent to the registrar at the time when the company is seeking registration.

As has been noted, the matter of appointment of directors is generally dealt with in the company's articles of association. It is usual that directors may be appointed by ordinary resolution, see for example, Table A Art 78. Sometimes the directors themselves can appoint a person to the board but it is usual that where this happens, the person appointed will only hold office until the next annual general meeting and shall then be subject to election in the normal way, see for example Table A Art 79. The company's articles will usually deal with the matter of retirement of directors. Table A Art 73 for example provides that at every annual general meeting, one third of the directors should retire by rotation or, if the number is not divisible by three, the number nearest to a third (if only one director, he should retire and be subject to re-election at each annual general meeting). Retirement by rotation should depend upon length of service but as between persons who have been appointed at the same time should be determined by lot (Table A Art 74). If the company at the meeting at which a director retires by rotation does not fill the vacancy, the retiring director if willing to act should be deemed to have been re-appointed unless it is resolved not to fill the vacancy (Table A Art 75). In order to be appointed at a general meeting, a person must be either a retiring director or be recommended by the directors or not less than 14 and not more than 35 clear days before the date of the meeting must be proposed by a member qualified to vote and the notice of this intention must be accompanied by particulars relating to that director and an indication of the person's willingness to act as a director (Table A Art 76). This notice should be passed on to members entitled to vote (Table A Art 77).

When a director is appointed, there are certain formalities to be fulfilled. The company must keep at its registered office a register of its directors and secretaries and that register should contain certain particulars. The company should also within 14 days of the appointment

---

1    Companies Act 1985, s 293(5).

of a director or secretary send to the registrar of companies a notification in the prescribed form together with the required particulars. The particulars that are required are set out in s 289 of the Companies Act 1985. These are:

In the case of an individual:

- his present Christian name and surname;
- any former Christian name or surname;
- his usual residential address;
- his nationality;
- his business occupation, if any;
- particulars of any other directorships held by him or which have been held by him within the previous five years;
- the date of his birth.

The director concerned should also sign the Form 288 (see p 360) which has to be submitted to the registrar of companies and which contains the above information.

In the case of a corporation the particulars should set out the company's corporate name and its registered or principal office.

There are certain other matters that need to be considered in relation to directors. Directors must disclose any interest in the shares and debentures of the company or any company in the group held by them or by spouses or infant children[2]. Also, s 317 provides that a director must declare any interest that he has, whether direct or indirect in a contract or proposed contract with the company. This obligation is also extended to connected persons (as set out in s 346). It is usual practice for a director who has shares in other companies to send this list of shareholdings to the company secretary for circulation with board papers so that this may be taken to be disclosure of any interests that he has if the company is to conclude contracts with these other companies under s 317 of the Companies Act 1985. When a director is appointed he should be supplied with certain information and corporate documents. These would include a copy of the company's memorandum and articles, recent sets of accounts, a copy of his service agreement if he is an executive director and a schedule of board meetings together with a list of other directors.

If the company is a listed company then it is also necessary to notify the Stock Exchange of the appointment. If the company shows all of the

---

2    Ibid., s 324.

directors names on company notepaper, then new notepaper must be prepared showing this director's name[3].

The company's solicitors and auditors should be notified of the new appointment as should the company's bankers and a new mandate should be prepared if the director is a signatory of the company's bank account.

The register of directors and secretaries must be open to inspection of members without charge and to any other person on payment of a small sum[4].

In addition, director's service contracts or written memoranda of their terms and also contracts or memoranda of directors of subsidiaries have to be open to inspection of any member of the company without charge[5].

Mention should perhaps be made of particular types of directors at this juncture.

## ALTERNATE DIRECTORS

The Act makes no specific provision authorising directors to appoint alternates to act on their behalf in their absence. Alternate directors may only be appointed if the company's articles contain such a provision. Table A Arts 65-69 relate to alternate directors. Art 65 provides that any director other than an alternate director may appoint another as an alternate; either any other director or any other person approved by resolution of the directors and willing to act and may remove from office an alternate director so appointed by him. Alternates are regarded as directors of the company for the purposes of the Act and are subject to all the statutory rules and responsibilities imposed on directors. Particulars of alternate directors should be entered in the register of directors and secretaries and should be filed with the registrar on the same Form 288 as for other directors.

## MANAGING DIRECTORS

The post of managing director is not a post recognised by statute. It is not necessary for a company to have a managing director. Where a person is appointed as managing director, it is his role to ensure that the

---

3   Ibid., s 305.
4   Ibid., s 288(3).
5   Ibid., s 318(7).

company's day to day business is carried out by those responsible for the running of the company. Table A Art 84 provides that the directors may appoint one or more of their number to the office of managing director on such terms as they determine and they may remunerate any such director for his services as they think fit.

# EXECUTIVE DIRECTORS

The term 'executive director' is applied to those directors who have a service agreement with the company and will generally be working for the company full time. By contrast non-executive directors are those who are not employed under a Schedule E contract with the company and who will only provide services at board meetings and at other specified times.

If a director is an executive director, he will generally have a formal contract. A copy of the contract should be kept at the company's registered office as required by s 318 of the Companies Act 1985 and be there available for inspection of any member of the company without charge during business hours. Service contracts of directors cannot last for a period exceeding five years without the consent of the shareholders[6].

# SHADOW DIRECTORS

Section 741(2) defines a shadow director as a person in accordance with whose directions or instructions the directors of the company are accustomed to act. A person is not deemed to be a shadow director by reason only that the directors act on advice given by him in a professional capacity. This qualification ensures that banks and others advising the company in a professional way do not automatically become shadow directors. In general, the obligations and regulations set out in the Companies Act apply to shadow directors in just the same way as they apply to directors.

---

6    Ibid., s 319.

# CHAPTER 14

# DIRECTORS' DUTIES, INSIDER DEALING

## DIRECTOR'S DUTIES AND PERSONAL LIABILITY

### The director's duties to the company

A preliminary question that needs to be considered is: to whom do directors owe their duties?

The traditional view is to the providers of capital-shareholders, (*Percival v Wright* (1902))[1].

The British approach should be compared to the approach in other jurisdictions particularly Commonwealth jurisdictions (*Coleman v Myers* (1977))[2] in New Zealand.

The approach was broadened in the Companies Act 1980, now s 309 of the Companies Act 1985, to include the interests of employees. This is not as radical as it might seem as s 309(2) provides that the duty is enforced in the same way as other director's duties ie by the shareholders.

Sometimes, cases indicate that a duty is owed to creditors (*Liquidator of West Mercia Safetywear Ltd v Dodd* (1988))[3]. There is no clear indication from the decided cases that this is so. The Insolvency Act 1986 clearly contains provisions that protect creditors.

### The duty of care and skill

The leading statement of the duty of care and skill is still that of Romer J in *Re City Equitable Fire and Insurance Co Ltd* (1925)[4]. Romer J set out three clear propositions:

1 That a director need not exhibit in the performance of his duties a greater degree of skill than may reasonably be expected from somebody in that position. This meant that in *Re Denham & Co*

---

1   [1902] 2 Ch 421.
2   [1977] 2 NZLR 225.
3   [1988] BCLC 250.
4   [1925] Ch 407.

(1883)[5] a director who recommended the payment of a dividend out of capital was held not liable where he was a country gentleman and not an accountant!

2   A director is not bound to give continuous attention to the affairs of his company but only to do such things as he undertakes to do. This meant in *Re Cardiff Savings Bank, the Marquis of Bute's case* (1892)[6] that where the Marquis of Bute had been elected a director at the age of six months and in the next 38 years had only attended one board meeting when massive frauds were carried out which he failed to detect, that he was not liable. He had not undertaken to do more.

3   A director is entitled to delegate functions to professionals. This seems unexceptional. An example of this is *Dovey & Metropolitan Bank of England & Wales Ltd v Cory* (1901)[7] where the director Cory delegated the task of drawing up accounts to the accountants.

It may well be that the law is undergoing something of a sea change. Section 214 of the Insolvency Act 1986 places a statutory obligation on directors to act where they ought to realise that the company is insolvent. This clearly introduces in at least this situation an objective standard. In *Norman v Theodore Goddard* (1991)[8], Hoffman J considered that the standard in s 214 applied generally to other situations.

## Fiduciary duties

While little may be expected of directors in terms of care and skill, a great deal is expected in terms of honesty and integrity. Directors must not place themselves in a position where their personal interests may conflict with their duty to the company. This proposition is borne out by decided cases and also by provisions in the Companies Act.

In *Regal (Hastings) v Gulliver* (1942)[9], the House of Lords applied this principle. In that case, the directors of the company had put money into the company to expand the capital to enable the company to buy fresh cinemas. The company could not afford to do so. The company prospered as a result as did the directors. When the company's shares were sold, the purchaser then complained that the directors had profited from their position as directors. He was successful and the directors were forced to disgorge their profit back to the company. This is the 'high watermark' of cases indicating that directors must not profit from

---

5   (1883) Ch D 752.
6   [1892] 2 Ch 100.
7   [1901] AC 477.
8   [1991] BCLC 1028.
9   [1942] 1 All ER 378.

their position of director. It seems very tough on these directors who were doing their best for their company and the decision merely resulted in a windfall profit to the purchaser where he had freely agreed to the purchase price in question.

Other cases bear out this same line of reasoning, however. In *IDC v Cooley* (1972)[10] where Cooley falsely represented that he was extremely ill in order to secure release from his position as a director to take a contract personally, he was obliged to disgorge this profit back to the company. In *Horcal Ltd v Gatland* (1984)[11], where Gatland fraudulently took a contract personally where the person concerned wished to deal with the company, he was forced to disgorge the profit back to the company.

Statutory provisions reinforce the common law and equitable principles. Section 317 of the Companies Act 1985 obliges directors to disclose to the company where they are entering into a contract with it, or indeed if they have an interest in a contract as would be the case if it were concluded with the director's spouse or infant child or with a company associated with the director or a trust of which he is a trustee or with a partner of the director or of a connected person of the director.

Section 320 of the Companies Act 1985 provides that a director must obtain prior sanction of the company in general meeting if he is to enter into a substantial property transaction with the company. This is where he is buying from or selling to the company a piece of property which has a value of £100,000 or more or a value of more than 10% of the company's asset value.

Directors may protect themselves by disclosing the nature of their interest in the company and getting the company's consent to the agreement provided that this consent is given freely, see *Regal (Hastings) Ltd v Gulliver*. It may be sufficient that the company has turned down the corporate opportunity (*Peso Silver Mines Ltd v Cropper* (1966)[12] (Canada)).

Interestingly, despite the very high standard of honesty expected of directors, the only British case on competition *London & Mashonaland Exploration Co Ltd v New Mashonaland Exploration Co Ltd* (1891))[13]; indicates that a director is free to compete with his company either on his own account or by being a director of a competing company. This seems surprising and would almost certainly involve a breach of director's duties in relation to a director profiting from his position at the expense of his company. Commonwealth authority is inconclusive on the matter but it would seem that the *Mashonaland* case is of doubtful validity.

---

10   [1972] 1 WLR 443.
11   [1984] BCLC 549.
12   [1966] SCR 673.
13   [1891] WN 165.

Sometimes issues relating to director's duties may arise in relation to the exercise of director's powers, such as the issue of shares. Strictly speaking, shares should only be issued to raise necessary capital for the company. However, on occasion, the directors may issue capital for some other collateral purpose eg to prevent a takeover bid or indeed to facilitate one. If this is done bona fide, in the best interests of the company and without any thought of personal gain for the directors, this may be validated by the company in general meeting, see *Hogg v Cramphorn* (1966)[14] and *Bamford v Bamford* (1970)[15]. However, if the issue of shares is effected merely to 'feather the nests' of the directors and to further their own personal interest, then the matter cannot be validated by the company in general meeting, see *Howard Smith Ltd v Ampol Petroleum Ltd* (1974)[16], a Privy Council case from Australia.

Similarly, in *Lee Panavision Ltd v Lee Lighting Ltd* (1992)[17], a decision was reached in relation to a management agreement where the directors exercised their powers to enter into a new management agreement to further their own personal interests rather than those of the company. The Court of Appeal upholding Harman J held that this was voidable as it was not done in the best interests of the company.

## Personal liability of directors

In addition to the liability to the company for breach of director's duties, directors may be personally liable in the following ways:

### *Contractual*

- Breach of warranty of authority:

  if directors indicate to outsiders that they have authority to conclude a contract but do not have such authority, they may be liable for breach of warranty of authority;

- Collateral guarantee:

  a director may be asked to guarantee a company's overdraft or indeed some other contract;

- Pre-incorporation contracts:

  under s 36C(1) of the Companies Act 1985, those acting on behalf of an unformed company may be liable on pre-incorporation contracts. Clearly this can include directors.

---

14 [1967] Ch 254.
15 [1970] Ch 212.
16 [1974] AC 821.
17 [1992] BCLC 22.

### Tortious

- A director may be liable in fraud in relation to a prospectus, see *Derry v Peek* (1889)[18].
- A director may be liable for negligent misstatement in relation to prospectuses, see *Hedley Byrne v Heller* (1964)[19].
- Personal skill and care:

  on occasion if a director has given a personal guarantee of his own ability or skill in a particular area, he may be personally liable, see for example *Fairline Shipping Corporation v Adamson* (1975)[20] where Mr Adamson warranted his own personal skill in saying that a refrigeration plant was effective and it proved not to be. The company itself had gone into liquidation.

### Under Statute

- Under the Financial Services Act 1986 s 150 a director may be liable for damages in relation to misleading listing particulars; and also under s 166 in relation to misleading prospectuses when this is brought into force[21].
- Directors may be personally liable for failure to repay subscription money where a minimum subscription has not been received under s 83(5) of the Companies Act 1985.
- Directors may be personally liable for irregular allotment of shares under s 85(2) of the Companies Act 1985.
- Directors may be liable for improper use of the company name under s 349(4) of the Companies Act 1985.

## Limiting the liability of directors

It is not possible to limit the liability of directors or other officers by the company's articles or by any contract[22]. Insurance is a possibility[23], a provision inserted by the Companies Act 1989.

It is possible for the court in any proceedings to grant relief to officers acting honestly and reasonably where they ought in all the circumstances to be excused[24].

---

18  (1889) 14 App Cas 33.
19  [1964] AC 465.
20  [1975] QB 180.
21  At present liability is under s 67 Companies Act 1985.
22  Companies Act 1985, s 310.
23  Ibid., s 310(3).
24  Ibid., s 727.

Where a director has acted in breach of his duties, it is open to the company to ratify what the director has done as long as he is acting honestly, see *Hogg v Cramphorn* and *Bamford v Bamford* discussed above (p 118).

# FRAUDULENT TRADING AND WRONGFUL TRADING UNDER THE INSOLVENCY ACT 1986

Section 213 of the Insolvency Act 1986 is a provision of some vintage. It provides that where any person continues to trade where he *knows* that the company is insolvent, then he is personally liable and may be called upon to contribute to the company's assets in liquidation. There is also a corresponding criminal provision, s 458 of the Companies Act 1985, making this a criminal offence.

The Cork Committee on Insolvency recommended that this be extended to cases where a director ought to know that the company is insolvent. In consequence, what is now s 214 of the Insolvency Act 1986, provides that where a director or shadow director ought to realise that the company is insolvent, he is personally liable in relation to matters that occur after he ought to have realised this, see *Re Produce Marketing Consortium* (1989)[25].

# REMOVAL OF DIRECTORS

First, directors may always be removed in accordance with what is set out in the company's constitution (the memorandum and articles). In addition directors may be removed under s 303 of the Companies Act 1985 by ordinary resolution. This is notwithstanding anything that is set out in the company's articles or memorandum to the contrary or to the contrary in any contract with the directors. This provision was first introduced in the Companies Act 1948 in response to the Cohen Committee's recommendations on company law.

A director has several ways of protecting himself, however:

- weighted voting provisions giving extra votes to certain shares; (*Bushell v Faith* (1970))[26];

- a special quorum provision, making the meeting inquorate in the absence of the director threatened with removal;

---

25   [1989] BCLC 520.
26   [1970] AC 1099.

- a service contract at high remuneration making it expensive to get rid of the director, (*Southern Foundries v Shirlaw* (1940))[27], but note s 319 which makes it difficult for a director's service contract to last for more than five years;

- in a private company it may be a breach of the understanding on which the company has been formed, giving rise to a petition for unfair prejudice, see s 459 of the Companies Act 1985 and a string of cases including *Re London School of Electronics* (1986)[28];

Although there is no detailed consideration in this textbook of the remedy for unfairly prejudicial conduct available to shareholders under ss 459-461 of the Companies Act 1985, this is an area of great importance. Members of a company now have a broad remedy available to them, a remedy which is often invoked successfully against those managing a company:

- in a private company, it may enable the director to petition to wind the company up on the just and equitable ground under s 122(1)(g) of the Insolvency Act 1986, see *Ebrahimi v Westbourne Galleries Ltd* (1973)[29]. However, it is unlikely that this would succeed in many cases where a petition on the basis of unfair prejudice may be presented[30]. Section 125(2) provides that a winding up order should not be made if the court is of the opinion that some other remedy is available to the petitioners and that they are acting unreasonably in seeking to have the company wound up instead of pursuing that other remedy;

- voting agreements where particular shareholders agree to vote in support of a director may block a director's removal, see for example *Stewart v Schwab* (1956)[31] from South Africa;

- procedural difficulties may make it a matter of some difficulty to dismiss a director, using s 303, see the provisions on special notice that are required and *Pedley v Inland Waterways Association Ltd* (1977)[32].

## DISQUALIFICATION OF DIRECTORS

Disqualification of directors is covered by the Company Directors Disqualification Act 1986.

---

27  [1940] AC 701.
28  [1986] Ch 211.
29  [1973] AC 360.
30  Insolvency Act 1986 s 125 and *Abbey Leisure v Virdi* (1992).
31  (1956) (4) SA 791.
32  [1977] 1 All ER 209.

Where a disqualification order is made, it prohibits the person concerned from being:

(a) a director of a company;

(b) a liquidator or administrator of a company;

(c) a receiver or a manager of a company's property;

(d) in any way directly or indirectly concerned or taking part in the promotion, formation or management of a company.

The period of disqualification may be for up to 15 years.

Application for a disqualification order may be made by the Secretary of State or the official receiver or the liquidator or any past or present member or creditor of the company in relation to which the person concerned has committed an offence or other default. Disqualification may occur in various situations:

- conviction of an indictable offence in connection with the promotion, formation, management or liquidation of a company;

- persistent breaches of companies legislation, proof of persistent breaches is by indicating three or more defaults in relation to delivering company documents, making returns etc;

- fraud etc in a winding up. If a director has been concerned in relation to fraudulent trading or some other fraud or breach of duty as officer, liquidator, receiver or manager, this may lead to disqualification;

- a director may be disqualified for unfitness. This may happen where a director has been a director or shadow director of a company which has become insolvent whether while he was a director or afterwards and his conduct as a director or shadow director of that company taken together with his conduct as a director of any other company makes him unfit to be concerned in the management of the company.

The provisions on disqualification were tightened after the recommendations of the Cork Committee on insolvency were incorporated into the Insolvency Act 1985 and subsequently consolidated in the Company Directors Disqualification Act 1986.

## LOANS TO DIRECTORS

Loans to directors used to be controlled by s 190 of the Companies Act 1948. However, there were many loopholes and the law was tightened by the Companies Act 1980, now consolidated into the Companies Act 1985 ss 330-344.

The provisions on loans etc control loans (which are straightforward), quasi loans where a company provides credit to a third party for the benefit of a director etc where the director reimburses the company - for example the director buys articles with a credit card and the company pays the bill where the director is to repay the company. The legislation also controls credit transactions where a company supplies goods or land under a hire purchase agreement or a conditional sale agreement or leases or hires lands or goods on periodic payments to a director on the understanding that the payment is deferred.

The legislation differentiates between relevant companies where a company is a public company or in a group with a public company and other companies.

In general, no company may make a loan to or enter into any guarantee or provide any security in connection with a loan made by any person to a director of the company or a director of its holding company.

Furthermore, a relevant company may not make a quasi loan to a director or to a director of its holding company nor make a loan or quasi loan to a person connected with such a director not enter into a guarantee or provide any security in connection with a loan or quasi loan made by anyone else to such a director or connected person.

Nor may a relevant company enter into a credit transaction as creditor for a director or a director of its holding company or a connected person of such a director or enter into a guarantee or provide security to anyone else for such a credit transaction. It may be seen, therefore, that in relation to credit transactions and quasi loans, the provisions are more lenient than in relation to loans where there is basically a blanket prohibition.

Further, there are certain permitted exceptions:

- loans of up to £5,000 for each director;
- loans from one member of a group to another;
- quasi loans by a relevant company to a director up to £5,000;
- credit transactions by relevant companies up to £10,000;
- loans etc to directors who are holding companies;
- payment of director's expenses up to £20,000 outstanding;
- loans by money lending companies up to £100,000 for any one director unless the company is a banking company;
- loans by a banking company - these may in general be made to directors provided that the loan is on normal credit terms;
- loans for house purchase or improvement made by money lending companies or banks up to £100,000 provided that the company ordinarily makes loans to its employees on terms that are no less favourable.

## Remedies for breach of s 330

Section 341 provides that where there is a contravention of s 330, the transaction is voidable at the instance of the company.

Section 342 of the Act provides that a director of a relevant company who authorises or permits the company to enter into a transaction or arrangement knowing or having reasonable cause to believe that it was contravening s 330 is guilty of an offence and a relevant company which enters into such a transaction and a person who procures a relevant company to enter into such a transaction are also liable at criminal law.

# INSIDER DEALING

The Criminal Justice Act 1993 Part V amends the law relating to insider dealing and became effective on 1 March 1994.

The new provisions implement the EC Directive on insider dealing[33]. Section 52 of the Act provides that it is an offence for an individual who possesses information as an insider to deal in securities in relation to that information. The dealing is only within the section if it takes place on a UK market or through a professional intermediary.

Generally, if an individual with inside information discloses it other than in the proper performance of his duties, this is also an offence. It is an offence, too, if an individual in possession of information as an insider encourages another to deal in securities affected by this information.

There are a number of defences set out in s 53 of the Act, eg if the individual dealing did not expect the transaction to result in a profit or the avoidance of a loss. There are also some particular defences set out in Sched 1 of the Act eg for market makers.

The scheme of the Criminal Justice Act 1993 just like its predecessor the Company Securities (Insider Dealing) Act 1985 is to render insider dealing a criminal offence. Section 61 of the Act provides that on summary conviction an individual may be sentenced to a maximum of six months' imprisonment and/or a fine not exceeding the statutory maximum. If an individual is convicted on indictment the maximum sentence is seven years' imprisonment and/or a fine. Prosecutions can only be commenced by the DPP or the Secretary of State for Trade and Industry.

---

33   89/592 OJ 1989 L334/30.

# CHAPTER 15

# COMPANY SECRETARY

The company secretary is the chief administrative officer of the company. Every company, whether it be public or private, must have a company secretary, s 283 of the Act so provides. Section 283(2) provides that a sole director shall not also be the company secretary. This is extended by s 283(4) which provides that no company shall have as secretary to the company a corporation the sole director of which is a sole director of the company or have as sole director of the company a corporation the sole director of which is secretary to the company.

The Companies Act 1980 introduced minimum qualifications for the company secretaries of public companies. It is the duty of the directors of a public company to take all reasonable steps to ensure that the secretary is a person who holds a qualification of one of the following:

- The Institute of Chartered Accountants in England and Wales;
- The Institute of Chartered Accountants in Scotland;
- The Chartered Association of Certified Accountants;
- The Institute of Chartered Accountants in Ireland;
- The Institute of Chartered Secretaries and Administrators;
- The Institute of Cost and Management Accountants;
- The Chartered Institute of Public Finance & Accountancy;

or is a solicitor, barrister or advocate, or a person who held the office of secretary or assistant or deputy secretary of the company on 22 December 1980 or a person who for at least three of the five years immediately preceding his appointment as secretary held the office of secretary of a company other than a private company. Alternatively the secretary may be a person who by virtue of his holding or having held any other position or his being a member of any other body appears to the directors to be capable of discharging the secretarial functions.

There is no required qualification for the company secretary of a private company.

A hundred years ago, a company secretary had few powers. In *Barnett Hoares & Co v South London Tramways Co* (1887)[1], the company secretary was described as a mere servant whose position was to do as

---

1    18 QBD 815.

he was told and that no person could assume that he had any authority to represent anything at all nor that any statements made by him were necessarily to be accepted as trustworthy without further enquiry (per Lord Esher MR). The position has changed significantly. In 1971 the Court of Appeal considered the role and importance of the company secretary in *Panorama Developments (Guildford) Ltd v Fidelis Furnishing Fabrics Ltd* (1971)[2]. Here Lord Denning MR said that times have changed and that a company secretary is a much more important person nowadays than he was in 1887. He is, said Lord Denning, an officer of the company with extensive duties and responsibilities.

The responsibilities of the company secretary are considerable. There is no definitive list of duties for a company secretary. A typical list of duties might include the following, however:

- the preparation and keeping of minutes of board and general meetings[3];
- dealing with share transfers and issuing share and debenture certificates;
- keeping and maintaining the register of members and debenture holders[4] (Note: in large public companies, a professional share registrar often maintains these registers as well as dealing with share transfers);
- keeping and maintaining the register of directors and secretary[5];
- the registration of charges and the maintaining of the company's register of charges[6];
- keeping and maintaining the register of directors' share interests[7],director's contracts[8], and the collation of director's interests that have to be disclosed[9];
- keeping and maintaining the register of material share interests[10];
- sending notices of meetings, copies of accounts etc;
- keeping the company's memorandum and articles up to date;
- submitting the annual return[11];

---

2    [1971] 2 QB 711.
3    Companies Act 1985, s 382.
4    Ibid., ss 352 and 190.
5    Ibid., s 288.
6    Ibid., ss 399 and 407.
7    Ibid., s 325.
8    Ibid., s 318.
9    Ibid., s 232 and Sched 6.
10   Ibid., s 211.
11   Ibid., ss 363-365.

- filing with the registrar of numerous returns and documents;
- preparation of the numerous returns required by government departments and official bodies;
- witnessing documents, that is, signing as witness (together with a director) against the company seal;
- payment of dividends and preparation of dividend warrants.

Depending on the size of the headquarters staff, the company secretary may also be chief accounting officer, have charge of staff employment and pensions matters, obtain legal advice from solicitors and confer with the auditors. If the company is quoted, he or she may deal with the Stock Exchange. It is entirely possible that still other responsibilities may be placed upon the secretary by the company's articles.

By virtue of s 744 of the Companies Act 1985, the company secretary is an officer of the company. The definition of officer in relation to a body corporate includes a director, manager or secretary. This leads to the company secretary's having certain duties imposed upon him by virtue of the office. Thus, in a winding up by the court under s 131 of the Insolvency Act 1986, the company secretary must verify the statement of the company's affairs submitted to the official receiver, as s 131(3) provides that all those who are or have been officers of the company must submit such a statement. In a similar way, the company secretary must verify the statement of affairs submitted to the receiver appointed by a debentureholder under s 47 of the Insolvency Act 1986 by virtue of s 47(3) of the Act. Either the company secretary or a director must sign the form on a limited company's application to change status and re-register as unlimited under s 49 and particularly s 49(4) of the Companies Act 1985. Similarly, if an unlimited company wishes to change status to become limited, then the application form must be signed by the company secretary or a director under s 51 and particularly s 51(4) of the Companies Act 1985.

## APPOINTMENT OF THE COMPANY SECRETARY

Where a person is appointed to the post of company secretary, certain information has to be forwarded to the company's registry set out in ss 288 and 289 of the Companies Act 1985. Section 288 in addition obliges every company to keep a register of directors and secretaries at its registered office. The register is open to inspection of any member without charge and for other people on payment of a small fee.

The information that should be kept on the register is set out in s 290. The particulars are the present Christian name and surname of the person appointed and any former Christian name or surname and his usual residential address, and in the case of a corporation or a Scottish firm being appointed its corporate or firm name and registered or principal office. Section 288(2) provides that the notification to the registrar should also contain the signature of the person appointed agreeing to the appointment.

In practical terms, the appointment of the company secretary is generally made by the board of directors, often from amongst their number. The powers and salary of the company secretary will usually be set out in a written contract. Table A Art 99 provides under the heading 'secretary', 'subject to the provisions of the Act, the secretary shall be appointed by the directors for such term, at such remuneration and upon such conditions as they may think fit; and any secretary so appointed may be removed by them'.

It has been noted in relation to directors that the appointment of the first secretary should be recorded on Form 10 (see p 302) which is submitted to the registrar notifying him of the first person appointed as secretary of the company.

# REMOVAL OF THE COMPANY SECRETARY

Unlike the removal of directors which has statutory backing in s 303 of the Companies Act 1985, there are no special provisions relating to the removal of the company secretary as such. It has been noted that the company secretary may also be a director in which case the provisions on the removal of that person as a director would come into play. In other instances, it is a matter of contract although certain matters affect the removal of the company secretary. These circumstances are the compulsory winding up of the company or a voluntary liquidation where the company is insolvent or the appointment of a receiver and manager of the company's affairs. In the case of a removal or a resignation of a company secretary, Form 288 (see p 360) must, of course, be filed. The company secretary is susceptible to prosecution for fraudulent trading under s 458 of the Companies Act 1985 and may incur civil liability for fraudulent trading under s 213 of the Insolvency Act 1986. The company secretary is not liable to civil consequences under s 214 for wrongful trading but may however be subject to disqualification under the Company Directors Disqualification Act 1986 (pp 121-122).

# CHAPTER 16

# CAPITAL

The term 'capital' is used in many senses in company law. It may be used to describe the excess of the company's assets over its liabilities. Often, however, it is used to describe what has been raised from shareholders and from debentureholders who provide respectively share capital and loan capital.

This section of the textbook, intends to look at raising share capital and the maintenance of share capital.

First it is helpful to look at various situations where the term capital arises.

## Nominal or authorised share capital

Every company with shares must state in its memorandum of association the amount of its authorised or nominal share capital. This is the amount that it may raise by issuing shares to shareholders. It is open to companies to increase the amount of their authorised share capital. This will be examined below.

## Issued share capital

This is the amount of capital that has been actually raised by the company by issuing shares.

## Paid up capital

When a company issues shares, they may be fully paid in which case the fully paid up capital and the issued capital will be the same. However, a company may issue shares partly paid eg £1 partly paid to 25p. In this case, the paid up share capital represents 25% of the amount of the value of the shares. The remaining amount constitutes uncalled capital.

## Uncalled capital

Uncalled capital is the difference between the amount paid up on the share and the price of the shares that have been issued.

## Reserve capital

The uncalled share capital represents a guarantee fund for creditors. It may be called up in the event of the company going into insolvent liquidation. It may be that the terms of issue specify that the unpaid share capital shall be payable at specified dates or payment of the unpaid portion may be left open. Section 120 of the Companies Act 1985 provides that a limited company may by special resolution determine that any portion of its share capital which has not been called up shall not be capable of being called up except in the event and for the purposes of the company being wound up.

# SHARE CAPITAL

There are strict rules that govern the raising of capital. These rules are largely for the protection of creditors.

Section 2(5)(a) of the Companies Act 1985 requires that a company limited by shares must state in its memorandum the amount of the share capital with which the company proposes to be registered and the division of the share capital into shares of a fixed amount. As has been noted (p 53), this will set out the maximum amount which the company may raise by issuing shares. It is possible to increase this amount by ordinary resolution under s 121 of the Companies Act 1985. In law there is no minimum capital requirement for a private company, although in practice, since a private company must have one member and a share must have a monetary value, the minimum amount would be 1p although this would not have to be paid up.

As has been noted, there is a minimum requirement for a public company of £50,000 paid up to at least 25% plus the whole of any premium if shares are issued at a premium[1] (the question of shares being issued at a premium will be considered below).

In relation to public companies, they may not trade or borrow until the minimum authorised capital has been raised and the registrar of companies has issued a trading certificate when satisfied of this under s 117 of the Companies Act 1985.

# ISSUE OF SHARES AT A DISCOUNT

There used to be a common law rule that prohibited companies from issuing shares at a discount ie if a share had a nominal value of £1, at

---

1   Companies Act 1985, s 118.

least a pound had to be raised. This was the decision in *Ooregum Gold Mining Co of India v Roper* (1892)[2]. This rule is now enshrined in statute[3].

These rules were first introduced by the Companies Act in 1980 in response to the second EC Directive on company law. They are now contained in the Companies Act 1985.

Section 100 provides that a company's shares shall not be allotted at a discount. This practice is objectionable as is misleads creditors into a belief that the company has more capital than it in fact has. It is also potentially unfair to some shareholders where some shareholders have paid the full price for their shares and others have purchased shares issued at a discount.

There are, however, three situations where shares may be issued at a discount:

- where shares are issued in a private company in exchange for property. There is no obligation in a private company to value the property. In a public company there is a need to have an independent valuation of the property[4]; the same principle would apply in relation to the issue of shares in exchange for services in a private company. This is illegal in a public company[5] but in a private company it is possible that a person's services may be overvalued;

- a company may issue shares in exchange for debentures. These debentures may be convertible into shares. It is thus possible by a 'back door route' to issue shares at a discount. However, debentures must not be immediately convertible into shares. This would offend against the rule in s 100, see *Mosely v Koffyfontein Mines Ltd* (1904)[6];

- shares may be issued to underwriters at a discount of up to 10%[7];

Section 100(2) of the Companies Act 1985 provides that if shares are allotted in contravention of the prohibition on issue at a discount, the allottee is liable to pay the company an amount equal to the amount of the discount together with interest at the appropriate rate.

## PAYMENT FOR SHARES

Section 99 of the Companies Act 1985 provides that shares allotted by a company and any premium on them may be paid up in money or

---

2   [1892] AC 125.
3   Companies Act 1985, s 100.
4   Ibid., s 103.
5   Ibid., s 99(2).
6   [1904] 2 Ch 108.
7   Ibid., s 97.

money's worth (including goodwill and know-how). In so far as a public company is concerned, it may not accept in payment for its shares or any premium on them an undertaking made by any person that he or another person would do work or perform services for the company or some other person. Therefore, in relation to a public company, shares must be paid for in cash or by means of non-cash assets. If a public company does accept an undertaking for payment for its shares or any premium on them, then the holder of the shares is liable to pay the company in respect of those shares an amount equal to the nominal value together with the whole of any premium, or such proportion as is represented by the undertaking, and to pay interest at the appropriate rate. Section 738(2) of the Act explains the situations where shares are paid up in cash or allotted in cash. It is stated that a share is allotted in cash or for cash if the consideration for the allotment is cash received by the company or a cheque received by it in good faith which the directors have no reason for suspecting will not be paid, or as a release of a liability of the company for a liquidated sum, or an undertaking to pay cash to the company at a future date. Section 739 defines the non cash asset as any property or interest in property other than cash (but that cash includes foreign currency).

Section 102 of the Companies Act 1985 provides that a public company may not allot shares if the consideration for the allotment is or includes an undertaking which is to be or may be performed more than five years from the date of the allotment. In such a situation, if shares are allotted in contravention of this provision, then the allottee is liable to pay the company at the end of the five year period an amount equal to the aggregate of the nominal value of the shares and the whole of any premium with interest at the appropriate rate.

Section 106 of the Companies Act 1985 provides that any shares taken by a subscriber to the memorandum of a public company shall be paid up in cash as well as the whole of any premium on those shares.

Section 104 of the Companies Act 1985 provides that a public company may not during the initial period enter into an agreement for the transfer of one or more non-cash assets to the company if the other party is a subscriber to the company's memorandum and the consideration for the transfer is equal in value at the time of the agreement to one tenth or more of the company's nominal share capital. The initial period is a two year period beginning with the date when the trading certificate is issued under s 117.

A valuation may need to be carried out where this section applies. The valuation will be carried out in a similar way to the valuation under s 108 (p 133). Section 105 provides that if there is contravention of s 104, then the company is entitled to recover from the other person the consideration given by it under the agreement and the agreement so far as not carried out is void[8]. In addition, if shares are allotted in return for a non-cash asset, then the allottee is liable to pay the company an amount equal to the aggregate of the nominal value of the shares and the whole of any premium represented by the non-cash consideration with interest at the appropriate rate[9].

It may be seen that private companies have more room for manoeuvre than do public. Private companies, for example, may allot shares in exchange for services which public companies cannot do. Private companies may also allot shares in exchange for non-cash assets without the need for an independent expert valuation of the non-cash asset. In the case of a public company, it is necessary to have such a valuation[10].

The independent expert valuation required by s 103 of the Companies Act 1985 must comply with certain conditions set out in s 108 of the Companies Act 1985.

Section 108(1) provides that an independent person should carry out the valuation, that is to say a person qualified at the time of the report to be appointed or continue to be an auditor of the company. Alternatively, under s 108(2), a person who appears to have the requisite knowledge and experience to value the consideration and who is not an officer or servant of the company or any other body corporate within the same group or a partner or employee of such an officer or servant may carry out the valuation.

The object of the valuation is to ensure that the value of the non-cash consideration is equivalent to that part of the nominal value of the shares and the premium that it is supposed to represent[11].

Section 111 of the Companies Act 1985 requires that the valuer's report is sent together with the return of allotments required under s 88 to the registrar of companies (discussed below).

There are, however, three situations where the consideration given in exchange for shares in a private company may be examined:

- where the consideration is past as this consideration is not good consideration, see *Hong Kong & China Gas Co Ltd v Glen* (1914)[12];
- where the contract is a fraud and there is evidence of this;

---

8   Ibid., s 105(2).
9   Ibid., s 105(3).
10  Ibid., s 103.
11  Ibid., s 108(4)(d).
12  [1914] 1 Ch 527.

- if the inadequacy of the consideration is apparent on the face of the contract, see *Re Wragg Ltd* (1897)[13].

When shares are issued; then within one month of the issue of shares a return of allotments should be made to the registrar of companies in the prescribed manner (Form 88(2)) (see p 325). The form should state the number of shares and the nominal amount of the shares and the names and addresses of the allottees together with the amount paid or due and payable on each share.

In relation to the payment of shares in a public company, a public company must also ensure that any shares that are issued are paid up to at least 25% plus the whole of any premium[14].

Together with the return of allotments should be sent any contract where the shares have been allotted otherwise than for cash. The contract should set out the title of the allottee to the allotment together with any contract of sale or for services or other consideration in respect of which those shares are allotted. There should also be set out the number and nominal amount of the shares represented by that consideration.

If there is no such contract in writing then Form 88(3) (see p 327) should be submitted to the registrar. This form should set out particulars of the contract where there has been a non-cash consideration.

# ALTERATION OF CAPITAL

Section 121 of the Companies Act 1985 sets out various courses of action that may be accomplished by a company limited by shares or limited by guarantee with a share capital if so authorised by its articles. It may alter the conditions of its memorandum in any of the following ways by ordinary resolution:

## Increase of issued share capital

A company may increase its share capital by new shares of such amount as it thinks expedient.

This is usually done where the company realises that it requires more capital than the amount set out in the company's memorandum, as its authorised capital is insufficient for this purpose. An extraordinary general meeting should be convened (or if convenient the matter may be

13 [1897] 1 Ch 796.
14 Companies Act 1985, s 101.

postponed to the next annual general meeting) and the resolution should be put to the members.

Within 15 days of the passing of the resolution, a copy should be signed by the chairman of the meeting and forwarded to the registrar for filing together with Form 123 (see p 337)[15] s 123(3) of the Companies Act 1985.

As has been noted, whenever the company's memorandum is altered, a new copy of the memorandum as altered should also be filed with the registrar[16].

There are various other capital changes that can be achieved under s 121, also by ordinary resolution. These are as follows:

## Consolidation of a company's shares

This involves the merging of existing shares into shares of a higher nominal value eg four shares of 25p may be consolidated into one share of £1.

## Conversion of shares

Shares may be converted into stock or vice versa. This has little practical effect now. Formerly shares had to be numbered which occasioned additional work where shares were being transferred. This is no longer the case where shares are fully paid and rank equally with each other for all purposes[17]. Stock is conceived as a whole though it would be subdivided into units whereas shares are seen as separate units.

## Subdivision of shares

This is the reverse process of consolidation. A company may subdivide its existing shares into shares of a smaller nominal value, for example a £1 share may be subdivided into four 25p shares.

## Cancellation of shares

A company is able to cancel unissued shares. This is the reverse process of an increase of a company's authorised share capital. This should not be confused with a reduction of issued share capital which will be considered subsequently (pp 137-139).

---

15   Ibid., s 123(1).
16   Ibid., s 18(2).
17   Ibid., s 182(2).

In each of these instances, the registrar should be notified of the alteration on Form 122 (see p 335) within one month of the passage of the resolution[18].

---

18   Ibid., s 122(1).

# CHAPTER 17

# MAINTENANCE OF CAPITAL

Many of the Companies Act's provisions govern the maintenance of capital.

## ISSUE OF SHARES AT A PREMIUM

Often companies issue shares at a higher price than their nominal value. The nominal value is treated as ordinary share capital; any excess above the nominal value is termed a premium. There are special provisions relating to treatment of the premium.

Section 130 of the Companies Act 1985 provides that the premium should be transferred to an account called the 'share premium account'. The share premium account cannot be applied to pay a dividend but may be applied to pay up unissued shares to be allotted to members as bonus shares or to write off the company's preliminary expenses or the expenses of or the commission paid or discount allowed on any issue of shares or debentures of the company. It may also be used to provide for the premium payable on redemption of debentures of the company. It may also be used to pay up the premium on redeemable shares where those shares are redeemed[1].

## REDUCTION OF CAPITAL

As has been mentioned, it is open to a company to cancel unissued shares by passing an ordinary resolution in general meeting. The procedure is more complex if the company wishes to reduce its issued share capital. This is governed by ss 135-141 of the Companies Act 1985.

There are three ways in which companies may wish to reduce capital:

- to extinguish or reduce the liability on any of the existing issued shares in respect of capital that has not been paid up;

---

1   Companies Act 1985, s 160(2).

- either with or without extinguishing or reducing liability on any of its shares to cancel any paid up share capital which is lost or unrepresented by available assets;
- either with or without extinguishing or reducing liability on any of its shares pay off any paid up share capital which is in excess of the company's needs.

In the second instance, it may be seen that no capital is actually being returned to the company's members. In the first instance, no capital is being returned but an existing liability is being extinguished and in the third instance, capital is actually being returned to members. Clearly the second type of capital reduction is not prejudicial to creditors as no capital is being returned, nor is any liability being extinguished.

The procedure to be followed to accomplish a reduction of share capital is as follows.

An extraordinary general meeting will be called to pass a special resolution to reduce the company's capital. If there is not authority to reduce the company's capital (Table A provides such authority), then the company's articles will need to be altered by means of s 9 by special resolution before the resolution may be put (if the matter is non urgent, it may be postponed to the next annual general meeting when the same procedure can be followed).

If the resolution is passed, the company will then make an application to the court seeking an order to confirm the special resolution under s 136(1) of the Companies Act 1985.

If the proposed reduction of share capital involves diminution or extinguishment of a liability in respect of unpaid shares or the payment to a shareholder of any paid up share capital (ie cases 1 and 3 above) and in any other case if the court so directs, then certain procedures must be followed. These procedures are as follows:

Every creditor of the company at the date fixed by the court who is entitled to any debt or claim which would be admissible in proof against the company if the company were going into liquidation is entitled to object to the reduction of share capital. The court will settle a list of creditors entitled to object and for that purpose shall ascertain as far as possible the names of those creditors and the nature and amount of their debts or claims and may publish notices fixing a day or days when such creditors not entered on the list are to claim to be so entered or alternatively to be excluded from the right of objecting to the reduction of capital. If there is a creditor entered on the list whose debt or claim is not discharged and who has not consented to the reduction, the court may, if it thinks fit dispense with the consent of that creditor on the company's securing payment of his debt or claim by appropriating the amount of the debt or such amount fixed by the court after enquiry and adjudication as if the company were being wound up by the court.

The court has the power to dispense with the requirements set out above where there is a diminution or extinguishment of liability or where capital is paid back to members if it considers this appropriate.

If the court is satisfied, an order confirming the reduction may be made under s 137(1). The order may be made on such terms and conditions as the court thinks fit. The court may also order that the company shall for a period of time specified in the order add to its name as the last words 'and reduced'. It may also order that the company publish the reasons for the reduction of capital or such other information as the court thinks expedient with a view to giving proper information to the public, concerning the causes which led to the reduction.

The registrar of companies on production of the court order confirming the reduction and the delivery to him of a copy of the order and a minute approved by the court showing with respect to the company's share capital as altered (a) the amount of the share capital; (b) the number of shares into which it is to be divided and the amount of each share; and (c) the amount (if any) at the date of the registration deemed to be paid up on each share, shall register the order and minute under s 138(1) of the Act. The reduction is effective from the date of registration[2]. The registrar shall certify the registration of the order and minute and the certificate which may be signed by the registrar or authenticated by his official seal is conclusive evidence that the requirements of the Act in relation to the reduction of share capital have been complied with and the company's share capital is as stated in the minute[3].

Where the court makes an order confirming a reduction of a public company's capital which has the effect of bringing the nominal value of its allotted share capital below the authorised minimum, then the registrar of companies should not register the order under s 138 unless the court otherwise directs or unless the company is first re-registered as a private company[4]. A Form 139 (see p 341) should be submitted in this case.

## ACQUISITION BY A COMPANY OF ITS OWN SHARES

There has been for some time a general rule enshrined in the decision in *Trevor v Whitworth* (1887)[5] to the effect that a company is not able to purchase its own shares. This rule was given statutory force in the

---

2    Ibid., s 138(2).
3    Ibid., s 138(4).
4    Ibid., s 139(2).
5    12 App Cas 409.

Companies Act 1980 and is now set out in s 143 of the Companies Act 1985. There are, however, exceptions to the general rule. Thus, it is possible for a company to redeem its shares under s 159 and indeed to purchase its own shares on fulfilling certain conditions under s 162. Provisions relating to a company's acquisition of its own shares are set out in ss 143-181 of the Companies Act 1985.

Section 143(2) provides that if a company purports to acquire its own shares whether by purchase, subscription or otherwise, then the company and every officer in default is liable to a fine and the purported acquisition is void. Section 143(3), however, provides certain exceptions to this general rule. The exceptions are as follows:

- a company may acquire its own fully paid shares other than for valuable consideration. For example, the shares may be left to the company by will;
- the redemption or purchase of shares in accordance with Part V Chapter VII of the Companies Act 1985;
- the acquisition of shares and a reduction of capital duly made (see s 135 above);
- the purchase of its own shares in pursuance of an order of the court under s 5 (relating to the alteration of objects clauses); s 54 (relating to objections to re-registration as a private company); or Part XVII (relating to the remedy for unfairly prejudicial conduct);
- the forfeiture of shares or the acceptance of shares surrendered in lieu in pursuance of a provision of the articles for failure to pay a sum due in respect of the shares.

The reason for the general prohibition on a company acquiring its own shares is that it is in effect a reduction of capital and is therefore likely to mislead creditors by giving a false impression of the value of the company's shares.

Section 144 provides that if shares are issued to a nominee of the company, then the shares are to be treated as held by the nominee on his own account and the company is not to be taken as having a beneficial interest in them. If a sum of money is owed on those shares and the nominee fails to pay the amount due, then if the shares were issued to him as a subscriber to the memorandum the other subscribers to the memorandum are jointly and severally liable with him to pay the amount, or alternatively if the shares were otherwise issued to him then the directors of the company at the time of the issue are liable jointly and severally with him for the amount owed. Section 144 does not apply if the nominee holds the shares for the company where the company is itself acting as trustee[6].

---

6    Companies Act 1985, s 145(2)(a).

The general prohibition, as has been noted, has been relaxed in certain instances. Many of these were introduced in the Companies Act 1981 and are now consolidated into the 1985 Act.

# REDEEMABLE SHARES

Section 159 of the Companies Act 1985 provides that a company limited by shares or limited by guarantee and having a share capital may, where there is authority in its articles, issue shares which are to be redeemed or liable to be redeemed at the option of the company or of the shareholder. The exercise of this power is subject to various conditions. Redeemable shares can only be issued if the company has some shares which are not redeemable. Redeemable shares can only be redeemed where they are fully paid and the terms of the redemption must provide for payment on redemption. The terms and conditions of redemption should be set out in the articles[7]. Table A provides in Art 3 that shares may be issued which are redeemable or are liable to be redeemed at the option of the company or of the shareholder on such terms and in such manner as may be provided by the company's articles. The actual issue of redeemable shares may be authorised by ordinary resolution.

When shares are redeemed, they must be redeemed out of distributable profits or out of the proceeds of a fresh issue of shares made for the purposes of the redemption and any premium payable on redemption must also be paid out of distributable profits of the company[8]. If the redeemable shares were issued at a premium, then any premium payable on the redemption may be paid out of the proceeds of a fresh issue made for the purposes of the redemption or the amount may be paid out of the company's share premium account (see above - p 137).

A private company may also redeem shares out of capital provided that it satisfies the conditions set out in ss 171-177 of the Companies Act 1985.

When the shares are redeemed, they must be cancelled and the amount of the company's issued share capital diminished by the nominal amount of the shares redeemed[9].

When shares are redeemed out of the company's profits, then the amount by which the company's issued share capital is diminished shall be transferred to a reserve termed the 'capital redemption reserve'[10].

---

7    Ibid., s 160(3).
8    Ibid., s 160(1).
9    Ibid., s 160(4).
10   Ibid., s 170(1).

The capital redemption reserve is treated as paid up share capital of the company except that the reserve may be used to pay up fully paid bonus shares to members of the company[11].

# THE PURCHASE BY A COMPANY OF ITS OWN SHARES

Another exception to the principle that a company cannot acquire its own shares is set out in s 162 of the Companies Act 1985. This provides that a company limited by shares or limited by guarantee with a share capital may, if authorised to do so by its articles, purchase its own shares including any redeemable shares on fulfilling certain conditions. The provisions relating to the acquisition of shares by purchase need not be set out in the articles but the same conditions that apply in relation to the redemption of shares also apply in relation to the acquisition of shares by purchase[12]. A company may not, however, purchase its shares if as a result of the purchase there would no longer be any member of the company other than a member holding redeemable shares[13].

The rules relating to the acquisition by a company of its shares by purchase differ according to whether it is a market or an off market purchase. The test for this is set out in s 163 of the Act. The purchase by a company of its own shares is an off market purchase if the shares are purchased otherwise than on a recognised investment exchange or are purchased on a recognised investment exchange but are not subject to a marketing arrangement on that investment exchange. A company is subject to a marketing arrangement if the shares are listed under Part IV of the Financial Services Act 1986 or if the company has been afforded facilities for dealing in those shares to take place on that investment exchange without prior permission for individual transactions from the authority governing that investment exchange and without limit as to the time during which the facilities are to be available. The procedure for an off market purchase is set out in s 164. The company must have power to purchase shares by means of an off market purchase, if necessary the company's articles can be changed by special resolution under s 9. A company may only make an off market purchase of its own shares if the contract is approved or where the contract is a contingent purchase contract under s 165. The terms of the proposed contract must be authorised by special resolution of the company.

In the case of a public company the authority conferred by the resolution must set out a date on which the authority is to expire and

11  Ibid., s 170(4).
12  Ibid., s 162(2).
13  Ibid., s 162(3).

that date must not be later than 18 months from the date of the resolution. A copy of the contract should be kept at the company's registered office for not less than 15 days after the date of the meeting when the resolution was passed and should be available at the meeting itself. (Note: it may also be a written memorandum of the terms of the contract where there is no written contract). This should include the names of any members holding shares to which the contract relates.

As noted, s 165 makes provision for contingent purchase contracts where a company does not contract to purchase the shares but under certain conditions may become entitled or obliged to purchase them. A company may only make a purchase of its own shares in pursuance of a contingent purchase contract if the contract is approved in advance by a special resolution of the company before it is entered into as set out under s 164.

If the purchase is made out of distributable profits, the purchase of the shares can proceed after the special resolution has been passed and the contract has been signed. Form 169 (see p 348) must be filed with the registrar after the shares have been purchased. This must be filed within 28 days of the purchase. It must set out the number of shares of each class purchased and their nominal value and the date on which they were delivered to the company. In the case of a public company, the return should also state the aggregate amount paid by the company for the shares and the maximum and minimum prices paid in relation to shares of each class purchased.

Where a company enters into a contract under s 164 or s 165 (an off market purchase contract or a contingent purchase contract) or under s 166 (a market purchase contract), the company must keep the contract or a memorandum of its terms at its registered office for a period of 10 years from the date on which the purchase of all the shares covered in the contract is completed. The copy of the contract is then available for inspection by any member of the company and in the case of a public company by any person.

## A MARKET PURCHASE

Section 163(3) defines a market purchase as a purchase by a company of its own shares on a recognised investment exchange, other than a purchase which is an off market purchase by virtue of the definition relating to off market purchases. The authority for a market purchase may be general or limited to the purchase of shares of a particular class or description and it may be unconditional or subject to conditions. The authority should set out the maximum number of shares authorised to be acquired, set out the maximum and minimum prices which may be paid for the shares and specify a date on which it is to expire. The date of expiry must be no later than 18 months from the date of the resolution (a resolution must be passed by special resolution as with off market and contingent purchase contracts).

# REDEMPTION OR PURCHASE BY A PRIVATE COMPANY OF ITS OWN SHARES OUT OF CAPITAL

Section 171 of the Companies Act 1985 provides that a private company limited by shares or limited by guarantee with a share capital may, if authorised by its articles, make a payment in respect of the redemption or purchase of its own shares out of capital. The payment out of capital must be approved by special resolution of the company[14]. The directors of the company should make a statutory declaration specifying the amount of the permissible capital payment and that having made full enquiry into the affairs and prospects of the company, they have formed the opinion that immediately following the date of the permissible capital payment, there will be no grounds on which the company could be found unable to pay its debts and that as regards the prospects for the year immediately following that date but having regard to their intentions with respect to the management of the business and the amount and character of the financial resources that will be available to the company, the company will be able to continue to carry on business as a growing concern throughout that year (the statutory declaration should be made on Form 173 (see p 350)). Section 173(5) provides that annexed to the report should be a report by the company's auditors addressed to the directors stating that they have enquired into the company's state of affairs and the amount set out as the permissible capital payment and that they are not aware of anything to indicate that the opinions expressed by the directors in the statutory declaration is unreasonable in all the circumstances. A director who makes a declaration without having reasonable grounds is liable to imprisonment or a fine or both, (s 173(6)).

The special resolution that needs to be passed must be passed within the week immediately following the date on which the directors make the statutory declaration and the payment out of capital must be made no earlier than five and no later than seven weeks after the date of the resolution (s 174).

---

14   Ibid., s 173(2).

Within a week of the special resolution being passed, the company must cause to be published in the Gazette a notice setting out that the company has approved a payment out of capital to acquire its own shares by redemption or purchase, the amount of the permissible capital payment, that the statutory declaration of the directors and the auditors' report are available for inspection at the company's registered office and stating that any creditor of the company may at any time within the five weeks following the resolution apply to the court under s 176 for an order prohibiting the payment. The statutory declaration and auditors' report should be available at the company's registered office throughout the period for objections and be available for inspection during business hours without charge to any member or creditor. If an inspection required under this section is refused, the company and every officer who is in default is liable to a fine and for continued contravention to a daily default fine.

When the purchase is completed, Form 169 (see p 348) must be filed with the registrar within 28 days.

# FINANCIAL ASSISTANCE GIVEN BY A COMPANY TOWARDS THE PURCHASE OF ITS OWN SHARES

Section 151(1) provides that where a person is acquiring or proposing to acquire shares in a company, it is not lawful for the company or any of its subsidiaries to give financial assistance directly or indirectly towards the acquisition before or at the same time as the acquisition takes place. This is supplemented by s 151(2) which provides that where a person has acquired shares and a liability has been incurred, then it is not lawful for the company or any of its subsidiaries to give financial assistance towards reducing or discharging that liability directly or indirectly. If a company acts in contravention of this section, it is liable to a fine and every officer in default is liable to imprisonment or to a fine or both. The purpose of the prohibition in s 151 is to supplement the rule prohibiting a company from acquiring its own shares by purchase in s 143 as without such a provision the general thrust of s 143 could be avoided.

Financial assistance is defined in s 152. It means as follows:

- financial assistance given by way of gift;
- financial assistance given by way of guarantee, security or indemnity, release or waiver;
- financial assistance given by way of loan or similar arrangement;
- any other financial assistance given whereby the net assets of the company are reduced to a material extent or which has no net assets.

There are certain exceptions to the basic prohibitions in relation to both private and public companies. These are set out in s 153. There is also a further relaxation which relates just to private companies set out in ss 155-158.

Section 153(1) provides that the basic prohibition does not prevent a company from giving financial assistance for the purpose of an acquisition of shares in it or in its holding company if the company's principal purpose in giving that assistance is not to give it for the purpose of the acquisition but as an incidental part of some larger purpose of the company and the assistance is also given in good faith in the interests of the company. Section 153(2) provides a parallel exemption where the assistance relates to the reduction or extinction of a liability. Section 153(3) provides that s 151 does not prohibit the following:

- a distribution by way of dividend lawfully made or a distribution in the course of a winding-up;
- the allotment of bonus shares;
- a reduction of capital confirmed by court order under s 137;
- a redemption or purchase of shares made in accordance with Part V of Chapter VII of the Act;
- anything done in pursuance of a court order under s 425 relating to compromises and arrangements with creditors and members;
- anything done under an arrangement made in pursuance of s 110 of the Insolvency Act 1986 relating to the acceptance of shares by a liquidator in winding up as consideration for the sale of property; or
- anything done under an arrangement made between the company and its creditors which is binding on the creditors by virtue of Part I of the Insolvency Act 1986.

Section 153(4) provides that where lending is part of the ordinary business of the company, then the lending of money by the company in the ordinary course of its business does not fall foul of the prohibition. In addition, if assistance is given in good faith in the interests of the company for the purposes of an employee share scheme, this does not offend against the prohibition. This is also true of assistance which is intended to enable or facilitate transactions in shares by bona fide employees or former employees of the company of another company in the group or wives, husbands, widows, widowers, children or step-children under 18 of such employees or former employees, nor does it prohibit the making by the company of loans to persons other than directors employed in good faith by the company with a view to enabling them to acquire shares in the company or of its holding company to be held by them by way of beneficial ownership. However, in relation to public companies, they may not provide financial assistance in pursuance of s 153(4) unless the company's net assets are not thereby reduced or to the extent that they are reduced that the assistance is provided out of distributable profits.

A private company is able to provide assistance in accordance with ss 155-158 or, if it is a subsidiary of another private company, in that company. Where these sections are utilised, the general prohibition in s 151 does not apply. The following conditions apply:

- financial assistance can only be made out of distributable profits;
- the section cannot be used by a subsidiary to provide assistance to a holding company if the company in question is also a subsidiary of a public company which is itself a subsidiary of that holding company;
- unless the company proposing to give the financial assistance is a wholly owned subsidiary, the giving of assistance must be approved by special resolution of the company in general meeting;
- if the financial assistance is to be given by the company in a case where the acquisition is an acquisition of shares in its holding company, that holding company and any intermediary holding company, except in any case a company which is a wholly owned subsidiary, shall also approve the provision by a special resolution;
- the directors of the company proposing to give the financial assistance and where appropriate the directors of the holding company and of any other company which is both the company's holding company and a subsidiary of that other holding company shall make a statutory declaration fulfilling the conditions set out in s 156. The statutory declaration should state that it is the directors' opinion that there will be no ground on which after giving the assistance the company could be found to be unable to pay its debts and either if it is intended to commence the winding up of the company within 12 months that the company will be able to pay its debts in full within 12 months of the commencement of the winding up, or that the company will be able to pay its debts as they fall due within the year immediately following the provision of financial assistance. An auditor's report should be annexed which should state that they have enquired into the state of affairs of the company and are not aware of anything to indicate that the opinion expressed by the directors is unreasonable in all of the circumstances. If a director makes a statutory declaration without reasonable grounds for the opinion expressed in it, he is liable to imprisonment or to a fine or to both. Form 155(6)(a) (see p 343) should set out the statutory declaration of the directors in relation to the assistance for the acquisition of shares in a private company, and Form 155(6)(b) should be used where the shares to be acquired are shares in the

holding company. This is the declaration by the directors of that holding company. The declaration should set out details of the assistance proposed in addition. The statutory declaration and auditors' report must be delivered to the registrar within 15 days of the making of the declaration. If a special resolution is required, this must also be filed[15].

- The financial assistance cannot be given before the expiry of four weeks from the passing of the resolution unless the resolution was passed unanimously[16]. During this time, there is the possibility of an application to the court to cancel the special resolution which has approved the financial assistance. This application may be made under s 157(2). It must be made by the holders of not less in aggregate of 10% in nominal value of the company's issued share capital or any class of it, or, if the company is not limited by shares, by not less than 10% of the company's members. The application may not be made by somebody who has voted in favour of the alteration. The application must be made within 28 days of the resolution. Once the application is made, the financial assistance is "put on hold" until the matter has been dealt with[17].

- The latest that the assistance can be given is on the expiry of eight weeks from the date on which the directors of the company proposing to give the assistance made their statutory declaration or where the company is the subsidiary and both its directors and the directors of any of its holding companies made such a declaration, the date on which the earliest of the declarations is made unless the court on an application under s 157 orders otherwise.

# SERIOUS LOSS OF CAPITAL

This provision was added by the Companies Act 1980 which relates to a public company experiencing a serious loss of capital. This is now set out in s 142 of the Companies Act 1985. It provides that if the net assets of a public company are half or less of its called up share capital, then the directors shall not later than 28 days from the day on which that fact is known convene an extraordinary general meeting of the company for a date not later than 56 days from that day to consider what if any steps should be taken to deal with this situation. Section 142(2) provides that if there is a failure to convene an extraordinary general meeting in

---

15   Ibid., s 380.
16   Ibid., s 158(2).
17   Ibid., s 158(3).

compliance with the section, then each of the directors of the company who knowingly and wilfully authorises or permits the failure or after the expiry of the period during which the meeting should have been convened knowingly or wilfully authorises or permits the failure to continue is liable to a fine.

# DIVIDENDS

It is proposed to consider the question of dividends at this juncture. Dividends may not be paid out of capital. It is therefore appropriate to look at the matter of dividends in relation to the maintenance of a company's capital.

The principle was formerly rooted in common law as laid down in *Re Exchange Banking Co, Flitcroft's Case* (1882)[18]. This decision is authority for the proposition that dividends could not be paid out of capital.

The present statutory rules were first introduced by the Companies Act 1980. They are now found in Part VIII of the Companies Act 1985, ss 263-281.

The statutory provisions lay down the rules regarding when the dividend may be paid. In addition to the rules in the Companies Act 1985, the company's memorandum and articles may make further provision. In addition, a company will clearly be constrained by financial prudence and by possible comment in the market place such as the financial press on the company's dividend record. If the company is a quoted company it will also need to comply with the rules of the Stock Exchange. Section 263(1) of the Act provides that a company may not make a distribution except out of profits available for that purpose. In this context, distribution means payment of a dividend. The rule applies to both public and private companies.

Section 263(3) provides that the profits available for distribution are the accumulated, realised profits so far as not previously utilised by distribution or capitalisation, less the accumulated, realised losses, so far as not previously written off in a reduction or reorganisation of capital duly made.

There is no definition of the concept 'realised' within the Companies Act. SSAP2 (Statement of Standard Accounting Practice No 2) provides in paragraph 14(d) that profits should be shown in the profit and loss account 'only when realised in the form either of cash or other assets the ultimate cash realisation of which can be assessed with reasonable certainty'. The Act does provide for certain particular situations:

---

18   21 Ch D 519.

- section 275(1) provides that a provision for depreciation of a fixed asset is to be regarded as a realised loss;
- in the situation where a fixed asset is revalued such that an unrealised profit is made and consequent upon that revaluation a sum is written off or retained for depreciation, then the amount by which that sum exceeds the sum which would have been written off or retained for depreciation there has been no revaluation, it is treated as a realised profit[19];
- where there is no record of the original cost of an asset or a record cannot be obtained without unreasonable expense or delay, then for the purpose of determining whether the company has made a profit or loss in respect of that asset its cost is taken to be the value ascribed to it in the earliest available record of its value made on or after its acquisition by the company[20];
- it is provided that a company shall not apply any unrealised profit to pay up debentures or any amount unpaid on its issued shares[21].

The significance of the term 'realised' is clearly that in order to finance a distribution, the company must actually have received cash or the equivalent of cash before a distribution can be contemplated.

The significance of the term 'accumulated' is that the company cannot look at one year in isolation. Losses from previous years must be rolled forward and made good before a company can make a distribution even if there is a profit in the trading year in question.

## The relevant accounts

In deciding whether a distribution is justified, reference must be made to the company's accounts. The relevant accounts are generally the last annual accounts[22]. There are two exceptions to this general principle. These two cases are:

- where the distribution would be found to contravene the relevant section if reference were made only to the company's last annual accounts; or
- where the distribution is proposed to be declared during the company's first accounting reference period or before any accounts are laid in respect of that period. The accounts in these two situations are called respectively 'the interim accounts' and 'the initial accounts'.

---

19  Companies Act 1985, s 275(2).
20  Ibid., s 275(3).
21  Ibid., s 263(4).
22  Ibid., s 270(1).

If the accounts that are being used are the last annual accounts, the auditors must have made their report upon the accounts under s 235 and either the auditor's report must be unqualified or, if it is qualified, the qualification must be accompanied by a statement from the auditors as to whether the matter in respect of which their report is qualified, is material in determining whether a distribution would contravene the Act.

In the case of private companies in the two situations discussed above (p 150) interim and initial accounts must be prepared but the obligation is no wider than this[23]. There are further requirements for public companies.

If interim accounts have been prepared for a proposed distribution by a public company, s 272 will apply. The accounts must have been properly prepared or have been so prepared subject only to matters which are not material in determining whether the proposed distribution would be lawful. The accounts should comply with s 226 and Sched 4 of the Act and any balance sheet comprised in the accounts must have been signed in accordance with s 233. The balance sheet and profit and loss account must give a true and fair view of the company's affairs and of the company's profit or loss for the period for which the accounts apply[24]. A copy of these accounts must have been delivered to the registrar of companies[25].

Where initial accounts have been prepared for a proposed distribution by a public company, s 273 of the Companies Act 1985 applies. The accounts must have been properly prepared or have been so prepared subject only to matters which are not material in determining whether a proposed distribution will contravene the Act. The company's auditors must have made a report stating whether in their opinion the accounts have been properly prepared.

In the event of the auditor's report being qualified, the auditors must also make a statement as to whether in their opinion the matter in respect of which their report is qualified is material for determining whether the distribution would contravene the provisions of the Act.

## Dividends in public companies

Public companies are subject to further restrictions in relation to the payment of dividends. Section 264 provides that a public company can only pay a dividend if at the time the amount of its net assets is not less

---

23  Ibid., s 270(4).
24  Ibid., ss 272(2) and 272(3).
25  Ibid., s 272(4).

than the aggregate of its called up share capital plus undistributable reserves and if; and to the extent that the distribution does not reduce the amount of those assets to less than that aggregate. It is therefore clear that a public company must retain profits to maintain its fixed capital where its fixed capital has fallen below the level of its share capital plus undistributable reserves.

As has been seen above, it is also necessary for public companies to prepare initial accounts and interim accounts and to have these audited where these are appropriate where it wishes to pay dividends. The requirements of auditing interim and initial accounts do not apply to private companies.

## The unlawful payment of dividends

Section 277 provides that where a distribution is made by a company in contravention of the Act and at the time of the distribution the member knows or has reasonable grounds for believing that it is unlawful he is liable to repay it to the company.

Section 277(1) which sets out this rule is without prejudice to any obligation that exists apart from this section on a member to repay a distribution unlawfully made to him. In addition to this provision, there is a common law rule that directors who authorise unlawful distributions are liable to repay the money to the company. This is the rule in *Re Exchange Banking, Flitcroft's Case* (1882)[26]. However, directors will not be liable in all circumstances and where they have reasonably delegated the function of drawing up the accounts to accountants and trusted them, they will not be liable, see *Dovey v Cory* (1901)[27]. In such circumstances the accountants may well be liable to the company for drawing up the accounts negligently and for failing to detect that a dividend is being paid out of capital.

## The payment and declaration of dividends

Section 281 of the Act provides that the provisions of the Act operate without prejudice to any other enactment or rule of law or any provision in the company's constitution restricting the sum out of which, or the cases in which a distribution may be made. Table A Arts 102-108 contain the rules relating to the payment of dividends where Table A applies. Art 102 provides that the company may by ordinary resolution declare

---

26   (1886) 21 Ch D 519.
27   [1901] AC 477.

dividends but that no dividend may exceed the amount recommended by the directors.

Article 103 provides that the directors may pay interim dividends if it appears to them that they are justified by the profits of the company and if the share capital is divided into different classes, the directors may pay interim dividends on shares which confer deferred or non-preferred rights with regard to dividends as well as on shares which confer preferential rights with regard to dividend but no dividend shall be paid on shares with deferred or non-preferred rights if at the time of payment any preferential dividend is in arrears. Article 104 provides that dividend shall be declared and paid according to the amounts paid up on the shares on which the dividend is paid. Article 105 provides that a general meeting declaring a dividend may on the recommendation of the directors direct that it shall be satisfied wholly or partly by the distribution of assets (dividends in specie). Article 106 provides that dividend or other monies payable in respect of a share may be paid by cheque sent by post to the registered address of the person entitled, or if two or more persons are the holders of the share or are jointly entitled to it by reason of the death or bankruptcy of the holder to the registered address of the person who is first named in the register. Every cheque should be made payable to the order of the person or persons entitled or to such other person as the person or persons entitled may in writing direct and the payment of the cheque shall be a good discharge to the company. Article 107 provides that no dividend shall attract interest unless otherwise provided by the rights attached to the share.

Article 108 provides that any dividend which has remained unclaimed for 12 years from the date when it became due for payment shall if the directors so resolve be forfeited and cease to remain owing by the company.

It is not uncommon for companies to ask members to agree to have dividends paid directly into their bank accounts. This is clearly expeditious and less expensive than sending out cheques to members.

# CHAPTER 18

# TRANSFER OF SHARES

Shares are classed as personal property. Therefore a person is able to transfer his shareholding by sale or gift to another person.

Shares are freely transferable subject to the relevant provisions of the Companies Act 1985, the company's articles of association and the Stock Transfer Act 1963.

Section 182(1)(b) of the Companies Act 1985 provides that shares registered in the company's register of members are transferable in the manner provided by the company's articles but subject to the Stock Transfer Act 1963.

Generally, public companies do not place any restrictions on the transferability of shares apart from partly paid shares.

Private companies generally do impose restrictions on transferability, usually allowing the directors a discretion to refuse to register and including a pre-emption provision.

Section 183 of the Companies Act 1985 states that the transfer must be in writing and that a proper instrument of transfer must be used if the transfer is to be lawful.

The Stock Transfer Act 1963 governs the forms to be used for transfer.

The company may in its articles specify a form to be used eg Table A Art 23 specifies the usual form or any other form which the directors may approve.

However, regardless of any provision in the articles, the standard form set out in the Stock Transfer Act 1963 may always be used - s 2(1) of the Stock Transfer Act 1963 (this is the form invariably used).

Section 1(1) and s 1(4)(a) of the Stock Transfer Act 1963 provides that fully paid company shares may be transferred by executing a document in one of the forms set out in Sched 1 to the Act.

The forms now set out in Sched 1 to the Act as amended are:

(a) Stock Transfer Form for non Stock Exchange transactions

(b) Sold Transfer Form (SI 1990 No 18) Stock Exchange transactions

(c) Bought Transfer Form (SI 1979 No 277) Stock Exchange transactions

The procedure for transferring shares listed on the Stock Exchange and that for non Stock Exchange transactions differ substantially.

# PROCEDURE FOR TRANSFERRING SHARES: A NON STOCK EXCHANGE TRANSACTION

There are various stages that have to be followed:

- the transferor fills in a stock transfer form which he hands to the transferee in exchange for the agreed consideration;
- the transferee will complete his details - name and address - on the form. He will pay the necessary stamp duty to the Inland Revenue. The rate has been one half per cent from 27 October 1986;
- the transferee then lodges the stamped transfer and share certificate (which will have been handed to the transferee by the transferor) with the company;
- the company will then cancel the old share certificate, produce a new one and place the transferee's name on the register of members provided it is approved by the directors[1].

If the transferor wishes to transfer part of his shareholding and to retain part himself or to transfer the other shares to somebody else the procedure is different. The transferor sends the signed transfer(s) to the company together with his share certificate. The company will then endorse the transfer(s) to indicate that the company has the share certificate with the words 'certificate lodged' and will return the transfers to the transferor who will then negotiate the transfers for the agreed consideration.

## Transferability

If the articles contain no restriction at all, then the motive of the transferor in disposing of his shares is immaterial. In *Re European Bank, Masters Case* (1872)[2],12 days before a banking company stopped business, a shareholder transferred shares to his son-in-law. The shares were partly paid shares. The court held that the transfer could not be set aside. The court would not inquire into the bona fides of the transferor. In *Re Smith, Knight & Co* (1868)[3], the court held that the directors of the company have no discretionary powers except those that are given to them by the company's constitution to refuse to register a transfer which has been made bona fide.

What happens where there is some restriction on transferability? The restriction may take one of many forms. Articles of association may give

---

1    Companies Act 1985, s 185.
2    (1872) 7 Ch App 292.
3    (1968) 4 Ch App 20.

the directors an absolute discretion to refuse to register a transfer of shares. This was the position in *Re Smith & Fawcett Ltd* (1942)[4] In this case the court held that the directors had a total discretion as to registering transfers. The only limitation on their discretion was that it should be exercised bona fide in the interest of the company. The Court of Appeal refused to draw an inference that it was being exercised mala fide. It is clear that where the directors have an absolute discretion to refuse to register a transfer, the courts are reluctant to interfere. It should be noted, however, that a refusal to register a transfer of shares may justify a petition under ss 459-461.

Sometimes the refusal to register may only be exercised on certain grounds. A familiar power is one that the directors can exercise if, in their opinion, it is contrary to the interests of the company that the proposed transferee should become a member.

In *Re Bede Shipping Co Ltd* (1917)[5] which concerned a Newcastle based steamship company, the court held that such a power only justifies a refusal to register on grounds that are personal to the proposed transferee. It does not, for example, justify a refusal to register transfer of single shares or shares in small numbers because the directors do not think it is desirable to increase the number of shareholders. The refusal to register was exercised on the ground that the directors did not want the shares to be held by many people. Lord Cozens-Hardy MR at p 134 cited Chitty J in *Re Bell Bros* (1895)[6] with approval: 'If the reasons assigned are legitimate, the court will not overrule the director's decision merely because the court itself could not have come to the same conclusion, but if they are not legitimate, as, for instance, if the directors state that they rejected the transfer because the transferor's object was to increase the voting power in respect of his shares by splitting them among his nominees, the court would hold the power had not been duly exercised'.

Occasionally the restriction on transfer may be one of pre-emption giving other shareholders the right to purchase the shares of the transferor at a fair value before they are offered elsewhere. This situation arose in *Curtis v JJ Curtis & Co Ltd* (1986)[7] in the New Zealand Court of Appeal. Here the company's articles of association provided that a shareholder who wished to transfer his shares to an outsider had first of all to offer them to existing shareholders. This was not done. Cooke J held that a perpetual injunction would be granted against the transferor

---

4    [1942] 1 All ER 542.
5    [1917] 1 Ch 123.
6    (1985) 65 LT 245, 246.
7    [1986] BCLC 86.

preventing him from transferring them other than in accordance with the articles.

A pre-emption clause was the restriction which was utilised in *Rayfield v Hands* (1960)[8] to preserve control in a few people in a small company. Similarly in *Greenhalgh v Mallard* (1943)[9], an article provided that if a member wished to transfer his shares to a non-member, they must first be offered to existing members. Another article provided that if a member wished to sell his shares, he must notify the fact to the directors. A member transferred his shares to other members. Greenhalgh, another member, sought to have the transfers declared invalid on the ground that the restriction on transfer of shares applied to sales to existing members as well as to non-members and in this case the shares had not been first offered to members as a whole.

This argument was rejected by the Court of Appeal because the articles were not sufficiently clear to restrict a transfer to existing members. The restriction was held to apply only to the case of sales of shares to non-members.

Lord Greene MR stated:

'Questions of constructions of this kind are always difficult, but in the case of the restriction of transfer of shares I think it is right for the court to remember that a share, being personal property, is prima facie transferable, although the conditions of the transfer are to be found in the terms laid down in the articles. If the right of transfer, which is inherent in property of this kind is to be taken away or cut down, it seems to me that it should be done by language of sufficient clarity to make it apparent that this was the intention'.

The issue of pre-emption also came up in *Tett v Phoenix Property Investment Co Ltd & Others* (1984)[10] where the articles of association of the company restricted the right of the shareholder to transfer his shares. On the facts of the case it was held that the directors had offered the shares to existing shareholders and the offer had not been taken up so that sale elsewhere was effective. Registration of the transfer was appropriate.

The courts will lean against an interpretation of any power in the directors which hampers the right to transfer shares.

On the other hand, the courts will not carry out a literal construction so far that it defeats the obvious purpose of the provision. Thus in *Lyle & Scott Ltd v Scotts Trustees* (1959)[11] where the articles provided for a right

8    [1960] Ch 1.
9    [1943] 2 All ER 234.
10   [1984] BCLC 599.
11   [1959] AC 763.

of pre-emption in the other shareholders where a shareholder was desirous of transferring his ordinary shares, and some shareholders sold their shares to a take-over bidder and received the purchase price and gave him irrevocable proxies to vote on his behalf, the House of Lords held that in the context 'transferring' meant assigning the beneficial interest and not the process of having a transfer registered. The shareholders had indicated their intention to sell their shares and could not continue with the sale without giving the other shareholders their right to exercise their pre-emption rights.

It is most important, if the company wishes to protect some shareholders from the effect of shares being held by others, to ensure that the power of refusal to register a transfer of shares also applies on transmission (cases where shares pass on death or bankruptcy).

In *Safeguard Industrial Developments Ltd v National Westminster Bank Ltd* (1982)[12], a shareholder held the balance of control between two rival brothers. He died leaving the shares to one of the brothers' children. The question arose as to whether pre-emption applied on transmission or simply where a shareholder wished to transfer his shares during his lifetime.

The court held that the provision could only apply in respect of transfer not transmission. Careful wording is therefore needed to protect companies and their shareholders in such a situation.

If, on the true construction of the company's articles, the directors are only entitled to reject on certain prescribed grounds, and if it is proved that they have rejected on others, the court will interfere as in *Re Bede Steam Shipping Co Ltd*. Interrogatories may be administered to determine on which of certain prescribed grounds the directors have acted but not as to their reasons for rejecting on those particular grounds, see *Sutherland (Jute) v British Dominions Land Settlement Corporation Ltd* (1926)[13].

However, if the directors do state their reasons, the court will investigate them to determine whether they have acted on those grounds. They will overrule their decision if they have acted on considerations which should not have influenced them.

Even where the right to refuse is a qualified one, in certain situations the directors may not be obliged to give their reasons. In a case concerning Tottenham Hotspur Football Club, it was established that even if the directors can only refuse to register a transfer on certain grounds, they cannot be obliged to give the reason if the articles provide

12   [1982] 1 WLR 589.
13   [1926] Ch 746.

they need not do so (*Berry & Stewart v Tottenham Hotspur Football & Athletic Co Ltd* (1935)[14]).

In relation to transfer generally, it should be noted that a refusal to register a transfer must be a positive act of the board. In *Re Hackney Pavilion Ltd* (1924)[15], the two directors of the company were divided on the question of whether the proposed transfer should proceed. The company secretary was asked to write to the executrix's solicitors and return the transfer documents indicating that the transfer could not go ahead. The High Court ordered that the transfer must go ahead.

Astbury J said at p 280:

'Now the right to decline must be actively exercised by the vote of the board ad hoc. At the actual board meeting there was a proper quorum but as the board was equally divided, it did not and could not exercise its rights to decline'.

In such situations, the transfer must therefore go ahead.

Another restriction on refusal of registration of a transfer is that the refusal must be exercised within a reasonable time. This rule has been given statutory force in s 183(3) of the Companies Act 1985 which provides that the refusal must be exercised within two months after the date the transfer is lodged with the company. During this two month period, however, the transferee cannot claim to be registered as a member even though there are no directors so that the company cannot exercise the right to refuse to register - see *Re Zinotty Properties Ltd* (1984)[16].

The Jenkins Committee recommended in 1962 that directors should also be obliged to give a reason for refusing to register a transfer and also the refusal must be notified within five weeks. These recommendations have never been implemented.

However, s 459 of the Companies Act 1985 probably enables members to apply for a remedy in cases where directors fail to register a transfer of shares and this failure constitutes unfair prejudice to the members concerned. This may now enable a member to obtain a remedy in cases such as *Re Smith & Fawcett Ltd*. Other transfer situations may involve this section. Section 459 was involved in *Re a Company (No 007623 of 1984)* (1986)[17] where a rights issue was made which the petitioning shareholder was unwilling to accept.

Hoffmann J held that the remedy was to offer to sell his shares to the other members under pre-emption provisions. The pre-emption

14 [1935] Ch 718.
15 [1924] 1 Ch 276.
16 [1984] 1 WLR 1249.
17 (1986) 2 BCC 99, 191.

provisions of this company contained a mechanism for determining a fair value of the shares by means of a valuation conducted by auditors. This procedure should have been employed without recourse to the courts. The inference of the decision is that a remedy would have been available under s 459 had there been no pre-emption provisions.

The area of law relating to share transfer, and particularly restrictions on transferability, is increasingly important as more and more people buy shares and as more and more set up their own businesses where they may wish to keep control and ownership within a tightly knit group.

## Priorities

Sometimes there may be two transferees with claims to the same shares. For example, the company may certify a transfer without ever obtaining the share certificate or it may mistakenly return the share certificate to the transferor so enabling him to negotiate another sale.

Before registration, each transferee has a beneficial interest in the shares, although the equitable principle is that the first in time prevails. However, when a transferee registers he obtains legal title to the shares if he has no notice of the equitable claim.

If the person who registers the transfer is the second transferee, then the first transferee may still have a remedy against the company under s 184 of the Companies Act 1985.

The register of members does not provide any evidence of *beneficial* ownership. Section 360 of the Companies Act 1985 provides 'No notice of any trust, expressed, implied or constructive shall be entered on the register, or be receivable by the registrar, in the case of companies registered in England and Wales'.

A beneficial owner may, however, protect his interest. He may serve a 'stop notice' on the company and the company must then notify the beneficial owner before dealing in any way with the shares.

## Defective title

The register of members and the share certificate do not amount to conclusive evidence of ownership. They provide merely prima facie evidence of this. Where a person seeks to transfer shares and he has imperfect title, he is also passing on the same imperfect title.

The true owner of the shares may enforce his rights to registration[18]. There may be circumstances where the true owner of the shares is

---

18  Companies Act 1985, s 359.

estopped from challenging another person's title. This is so if he invests another person with apparent authority to deal with the shares and that person acting as agent fills in the transferee's name for example.

# APPENDIX 1 TO CHAPTER 18

## SHARE CERTIFICATE

Certificate No ...............................Date...............Number of Shares..............

Shareholder ......................................................................................................

Certificate No ...............................Number of Shares...........

### Limited

THIS IS TO CERTIFY THAT ...................................................... of
................................................................................................................

is/are the Registered holder(s) of .................................................. shares of
        (insert par value)        each .............................................. paid in the

above-named Company, subject to the Memorandum and Articles of
Association of the Company.

* This document is hereby executed by the Company/
The Common Seal of the Company was hereto affixed in the presence
of:

...............................Directors

...............................

...............................Secretary

on .........................19..........

* Delete as appropriate

NO TRANSFER OF ANY OF THE ABOVE MENTIONED SHARES
CAN BE REGISTERED UNTIL THIS CERTIFICATE HAS BEEN
DEPOSITED AT THE REGISTERED OFFICE OF THE COMPANY

**STOCK TRANSFER FORM**

(Above this line for Registrars only)

|  | Certificate lodged with Registrar |
|---|---|
| | (For completion by the Registrar/ |
| Consideration Money £1000 | Stock Exchange) |

| Full Name of Undertaking | Aegean Holidays Limited |
|---|---|

| Full description of Security | Ordinary Shares of One Pound Each |
|---|---|

| Number or amount of Shares, Stock or other security and, in figures column only, number and denomination of units, if any | Words One Thousand | Figures 1000 ( units of £1) |
|---|---|---|

| Names(s) of registered holder(s) should be given in full, the address should be given where there is only one holder<br><br>If the transfer is not made by the registered holder(s) insert also the name(s) and capacity (e.g. Executor(s) of the person(s) making the transfer | In the name(s) of<br><br>Anita Jean Jones<br>6 Tolpuddle Street<br>Bridgend<br>Mid Glamorgan<br>BD3 2XY | Account Designation (if any) |
|---|---|---|

| I/We hereby transfer the above security out of the name(s) aforesaid to the person(s) named *or to the several persons named in Parts 2 of Brokers transfer Forms relating to the above security*<br>   Delete words in italics except for stock exchange transactions | Stamp of Selling Broker(s) or for transactions of Agent(s), if any, acting for the Transferor(s) |
|---|---|

Signature(s) of transferor(s)

1._____

2._____

3._____

4._____          Date _____
   Bodies corporate should execute under their
   common seal

| Full name(s) and full postal address(s) (including County or if applicable, Postal District number) of the person(s) to whom the security is transferred<br><br>Please state title, if any, or whether Mr, Mrs or Miss<br><br>Please complete in typewriting or in Block Capitals | Account Designation (if any)<br><br>John Rees<br>17 Roberts Street<br>Swansea<br>West Glamorgan<br>SA7 2ZA |
|---|---|

I/We request that such entries be made in the register as are necessary to give effect to this transfer

| Stamp of Buying Broker(s) (if any) | Stamp or name and address of person lodging this form (if other than the Buying Broker(s)) |
|---|---|

**FORM OF CERTIFICATE REQUIRED WHERE TRANSFER IS NOT LIABLE TO STAMP DUTY**
**Pursuant to the Stamp Duty (Exempt Instruments) Regulations 1987**

| | |
|---|---|
| (1) Delete as appropriate | (1) I/We hereby certify that this instrument falls within category(2)_____ in the schedule to the Stamp Duty (Exempt Instruments) Regulations 1987, set out below |
| (2) Insert 'A', 'B' or appropriate category | |
| * Signature(s) | * Description: 'Transferor','Solicitor', or state capacity of other person duly authorised to sign and giving the certificate from his known knowledge of the transaction |

_____     _____

_____     _____

_____     _____

Date _____ 19\_\_\_

*NOTE - The above certificate should be signed by (i) the transferor(s) or (ii) a solicitor or other person (e.g. bank acting as trustee or executor) having a full knowledge of the facts. Such other person must state the capacity in which he signs, that he is authorised so to sign and gives the certificate from his own knowledge of the transaction.

**SCHEDULE**

A. The vesting of property subject to a trust in the trustees of the trust on the appointment of a new trustee, or in the continuing trustees on the retirement of a trustee.

B. The conveyance or transfer of property the subject of a specific devise or legacy to the beneficiary named in the will (or his nominee).

C. The conveyance or transfer of property which forms part of an intestate's estate to the person entitled on intestacy (or his nominee).

D. The appropriation of property within section 84(4) of the Finance Act 1985 (death: appropriation in satisfaction of a general legacy of money) or section 84(5)of (7) of that Act (death: appropriation in satisfaction of any interest of surviving spouse and in Scotland also of any interest of issue).

E. The conveyance or transfer of property which forms part of the residuary estate of a testator to a beneficiary (or his nominee) entitled solely by virtue of his entitlement under the will.

F. The conveyance or transfer of property out of a settlement in or towards satisfaction of a beneficiary's interest,not being an interest acquired for money or money's worth, being a conveyance or transfer constituting a distribution of property in accordance with the provisions of the settlement.

G. The conveyance or transfer of property on and in consideration only of marriage to a party to the marriage (or his nominee) or to trustees to be held on the terms of a settlement made in consideration only of the marriage.

H. The conveyance or transfer of property within section 83(1) of the Finance Act 1985 (transfers in connection with divorce etc).

I. The conveyance or transfer by the liquidator of property which formed part of the assets of the company in liquidation to a shareholder of that company (or his nominee) in or towards satisfaction of the shareholder's rights on a winding-up.

J. The grant in fee simple of an easement in or over land for no consideration in money or money's worth.

K. The grant of a servitude for no consideration in money or money's worth.

L. The conveyance or transfer of property operating as a voluntary disposition *inter vivos* for no consideration in money or money's worth nor any consideration referred to in section 57 of the Stamp Act 1891 (conveyance in consideration of a debt etc).

M. The conveyance or transfer of property by an instrument within section 84(1) of the Finance Act 1985 (death: varying disposition).

**Instructional Notes**

1. In order to obtain exemption from Stamp Duty on transactions described in the above schedule the Certificate must be completed and may then be lodged for registration or otherwise acted upon. Adjudication by the Stamp Office is not required.
2. This form does not apply to transactions falling within categories (a) and (b) in the form of certificate required where the transfer is not liable to ad valorem stamp duty set out below. In these cases the form of certificate printed below should be used. Transactions within either of those categories require submission of the form to the Stamp Office and remain liable to 50p duty.

**FORM OF CERTIFICATE REQUIRED WHERE TRANSFER IS NOT LIABLE TO**
*AD VALOREM* **STAMP DUTY**

Instruments of transfer are liable to a fixed duty of 50p when the transaction falls within one of the following categories:

a. Transfer by way of security for a loan or re-transfer to the original transferor on repayment of a loan.
b. Transfer, not on sale and not arising under any contract of sale and where no beneficial interest in the property passes: (i) to a person who is a mere nominee of and is nominated only by, the transferor; (ii) from a mere nominee who has at all times, held the property on behalf of the transferee; (iii) from one nominee to another nominee of the same beneficial owner where the first nominee has at all times held the property on behalf of that beneficial owner. (NOTE: This category does not include a transfer made in any of the following circumstances; (i) by a holder of stock etc, following the grant of an option to purchase the stock, to the person entitled to the option or his nominee; (ii) to a nominee in contemplation of a contract for the sale of the stock etc, then about to be entered into; (iii) from the nominee of a vendor who has instructed the nominee orally or by some unstamped writing to hold stock etc, in trust for a purchaser, to such a purchaser).

(1) 'I' or    (1)    hereby certify that the transaction in respect of which
    'We'      this transfer is made is one which falls within the category(2) above

(2) Insert    (3) _____
  (a) or
  (b)      _____

(3) Here set    _____
  out
  concisely    _____
  the facts
  explaining    * Signature          * Description ('Transferor',
  the                             'Solicitor' etc)
  transaction.
  Adjudication    _____        _____
  may be
  required.    _____        _____

               _____        _____

        Date_____ 19___

NOTE: The above certificate should be signed by (1) the transferor(s) or (2) a member of a stock exchange or a solicitor or an accredited representative of a bank acting for the transferor(s); in cases falling within (a) where the bank or its official nominee is a party to the transfer, a certificate, instead of setting out the facts, may be to the effect that "the transfer is excepted from Section 74 of the Finance (1909-1910) Act 1910". A certificate in other cases should be signed by a solicitor or other person (e.g. a bank acting as trustee or executor) having a full knowledge of the facts.

# CHAPTER 19

# MEETINGS

There are essentially two types of shareholders' meetings:

- annual general meetings; and
- extraordinary general meetings.

In addition, class meetings occur where there are meetings of classes of shareholder.

## ANNUAL GENERAL MEETING

In principle, every company has to hold an annual general meeting in each calendar year and it has to be specified in the notice calling the meeting as an annual general meeting[1]. This rule is diluted somewhat in the case of the company's first annual general meeting which has to be held within 18 months of incorporation. After this, the company has to hold an annual general meeting in each calendar year with no more than 15 months between successive annual general meetings[2].

If there is default in holding an annual general meeting, the Secretary of State may on the application of any member of the company call an annual general meeting and may give directions in relation to the holding of the meeting including fixing the quorum at one.

Historically, the annual general meeting would consider matters termed 'ordinary business'. It was not necessary to set out in detail the items of ordinary business where these were set out in the articles as they were under Table A of the 1948 Act. Ordinary business constitutes the following: considering the company's accounts and their adoption; the election of directors; the appointment of the company's auditors and fixing their remuneration and the declaration of a dividend.

These matters now have to be specified in detail since ordinary business is not defined in Table A of the Companies Act 1985. It is possible for other business to be transacted at the annual general

---

1   Companies Act 1985, s 366(1).
2   Ibid., s 366(3).

meeting. Such business is termed 'special business' and must be set out in the notice.

Since the Companies Act 1985, it is now possible for a private company to dispense with the need to hold an annual general meeting by unanimous resolution. Such a resolution may be passed at a meeting or may be passed in writing. This provision is now contained in the Companies Act 1985 as s 366A. Section 366A(2) provides that where there has been an election to dispense with holding an annual general meeting, this has effect for the year in which the election is made and subsequent years. By virtue of s 379A, an elective resolution dispensing with the need for an annual general meeting requires 21 days notice in writing. At the meeting or in writing, every member has to agree to the proposal. Section 366A(3) provides that in any year where an annual general meeting should be held but for the passing of the elective resolution, any member can require the annual general meeting to be conducted within three months of the end of the year.

## EXTRAORDINARY GENERAL MEETINGS

Any meeting of the company's shareholders that is not an annual general meeting is termed an extraordinary general meeting. Such meetings are 'extraordinary' in the sense that there is no obligation in the normal run of events for such meetings to be held. However, there are various ways in which extraordinary general meetings may be convened. These are as follows:

- the company's articles may provide for the calling of an extraordinary general meeting by the directors of the company. Article 37 of Table A makes such provision;

- extraordinary general meetings may be called by the members of the company. Section 368 of the Act provides that directors must call a meeting when they are requisitioned to do so by members of the company holding one tenth of the paid up capital of the company with voting rights or in the case of a company without share capital, one tenth of the voting rights. It should be noted that the members are not calling the meeting directly but are requisitioning the directors to do so. The requisition from the members should set out the aim of the meeting and be signed by the requisitionists and should be left at the company's registered office. The directors have 21 days in which to convene the general meeting and the meeting must be held for a date not more than 28 days after the date of the notice convening the meeting. This latter point remedies a loophole in the Act where it was earlier possible under the terms of the

Companies Act to send out a notice convening the meeting within 21 days for a date well into the distant future[3].

- If the articles do not make contrary provision, the shareholders may call a meeting directly under s 370 of the Companies Act 1985. This provides that in the case of companies with a share capital, two or more members holding 10% of the share capital or in the case of a company without share capital 5% of the members may call a meeting. It is usual for the section to be disapplied. Table A makes contrary provision and this is the usual position.

- The court has a residual power to order the calling of a meeting under s 371 of the Companies Act 1985. The section provides that if for any reason it is impracticable to call a meeting or to conduct the meeting in the manner prescribed by the articles or by the Act, then the court may order a meeting to be called and conducted in such manner as the court thinks fit. The provision is often used where there is a deadlock and it is impossible to hold a valid meeting because a member or members are refusing to attend, for example *Re Sticky Fingers Restaurant Ltd* (1992)[4].

- Section 392A provides that where an auditor resigns from office, he may deposit with his notice of resignation a requisition calling on the directors to convene an extraordinary general meeting of the company to receive and consider the explanation of his resignation.

- In circumstances where a public company has suffered a serious loss of capital, s 142 of the Act provides that an extraordinary general meeting must be held. A serious loss of capital occurs where a public company's assets are worth half or less of its share capital. The directors must within 28 days of this fact becoming known convene an extraordinary general meeting for a date not later than 56 days from that date to consider what step if any should be taken in relation to this situation (p 148).

---

3   *Re McGuinness & Another* (1988) 4 BCC 161 and the Companies Act 1989 s 145 and Sched 19 para 9.
4   [1992] BCLC 84.

# ANGLO HELLENIC TRAVEL PLC

**<u>REGISTERED OFFICE</u>**
4 Cathedral Walk
Maidstone
Kent

---

NOTICE IS HEREBY GIVEN THAT THE ANNUAL GENERAL MEETING of the Company will be held at THE WESTERN HOTEL, PROMENADE, DEAL, KENT on 30 July 1993 at 12.00 noon for the following purposes:

1 To approve Directors' remuneration in respect of the period ended 31 March 1993.

2 To receive the Financial Statements for the period ended 31 March 1993 together with the Directors' and Auditor's Reports thereon.

3 To re-appoint MESSRS TICKIT AND FILE, Chartered Accountants, as the Company's Auditor and to authorise the Directors to agree their remuneration.

BY ORDER OF THE BOARD

W W JACOBS
SECRETARY

Dated 14.6.93

A member entitled to attend and vote at the meeting may appoint a proxy to attend and vote in his/her stead. Such proxy need not be a Member of the Company.

# NOTICE OF THE MEETING

In order for a valid meeting to be held, a proper notice must be served on members. Certain rules are set out in the Act. In the case of the annual general meeting, 21 days notice is required. In the case of other meetings, seven days notice is required if the company is unlimited and 14 days if it is limited. If a special resolution is to be proposed, then 21 days notice is required. Therefore, if an extraordinary resolution is to be proposed, 14 days notice is required if the company is limited and seven days notice if it is unlimited. Table A also makes certain provisions. If a director is to be appointed, then 21 days notice is needed. Table A provides that notice can be served personally or by post (Art 112) and that it is deemed to be received 48 hours after posting (Art 115). Days notice means clear days, that is, exclusive of the day of service and of the day of the meeting.

Meetings may be called on short notice under s 369(3) of the Companies Act 1985. In the case of the annual general meeting, the short notice has to be agreed to by all of the members and in the case of other meetings by 95% (in value of share capital) or if the company has no share capital, 95% in voting rights. This percentage may be reduced in the case of private companies if all of the members agree to this by elective resolution. It may be reduced to 90%. It should be noted that waiving short notice can only be done deliberately and cannot be done simply by all of the members attending the meeting, see *Re Pearce Duff* (1960)[5].

# THE CONTENTS OF THE NOTICE

The notice obviously has to set out certain matters. As has been stated, if the meeting is an annual general meeting, the notice must clearly state so. The notice should set out the date, time and place of the meeting and the nature of the business that is to be transacted. In the case of companies with a share capital, it is also mandatory that the notice should set out the member's right to appoint a proxy and that that proxy need not be a member.

It has already been noted that under Table A of the Companies Act 1948, certain matters of ordinary business did not have to be set out in detail. Under the Companies Act 1985 Table A, there is no equivalent definition of ordinary business so that it has to be spelled out in detail for those companies which adopt Table A under the 1985 regulations.

---

5    [1960] 3 All ER 222.

The notice should be fair and reasonable and should not be deceptive or 'tricky' as it is called in the cases *Baillie v Oriental Telephone & Electric Company* (1915)[6].

If the meeting is to consider a special or extraordinary resolution, the resolution should be spelled out verbatim and this is also true if an ordinary resolution is proposed but where special notice is required (p 177).

# THE SERVICE OF THE NOTICE

Section 370(2) of the Act provides that if a company's articles do not make other provision, the notice should be served on every member of it in the manner required by Table A. Table A Art 112 provides that it is not necessary to serve a notice on a member outside of the United Kingdom, see *Re Warden & Hotchkiss Ltd* (1945)[7]. Art 112 does, however, provide that a member whose registered address is not within the United Kingdom may give the company an address within the United Kingdom at which notices may be given to him and shall be entitled to have notices given to him at that address.

Article 39 of the current Table A provides that the accidental omission to give notice does not invalidate the meeting. At common law, notice has to go to everybody. The provision in Table A is therefore important. If the notice is not given by an oversight, then the meeting is valid, see *Re West Canadian Collieries Ltd* (1962)[8] However, if the error arose innocently, but it is a quite deliberate act not to send notices to given individuals, then Art 39 will not validate the meeting, see *Musselwhite v Musselwhite & Son Ltd* (1962)[9].

The notice should be served where Table A Art 38 applies on members, directors and the company's auditors. It should also be served even if the person concerned could not have attended the meeting, see *Young v Ladies Imperial Club* (1920)[10] Table A Art 116 provides that a notice may be given by the company to the persons entitled to a share, in consequence of the death or bankruptcy of a member by sending or delivering it in any manner authorised by the articles for the giving of notice to a member, addressed to them by name, or by the title of representatives of the deceased, or trustee of the bankrupt, or by any like

---

6   [1915] 1 Ch 503.
7   [1945] 1 Ch 270.
8   [1962] Ch 370.
9   [1962] Ch 564.
10  [1920] 2 KB 523.

description at the address, if any, within the United Kingdom supplied for that purpose by the persons claiming to be so entitled. Until such an address has been supplied, a notice may be given in any manner in which it might have been given if the death or bankruptcy had not occurred.

If a member attends a meeting either in person or by proxy, he is deemed to have received notice[11]. If a transferee derives title from somebody else whose name is currently on the register of members and notice is served on that person, that is effective notice to the transferee[12].

# THE CHAIRMAN

Section 370(5) of the Companies Act 1985 provides that where the articles make no contrary provision, the members at the meeting may elect one of their number to act as chairman. It is usual for the company's articles to make provision in relation to the chairman. Table A Art 42 provides that the chairman of the board of directors; or in his absence some other director nominated by the board; shall preside at meetings. If the chairman or some other nominated director is not present within 15 minutes from the time appointed for the start of the meeting, the directors present shall elect one of their number to be chairman. If there is no director willing to act or no director is present within 15 minutes, then the members present who are entitled to vote may elect one of their number to be chairman.

It is the chairman's functions to take the meeting through the agenda, to put matters to the vote and to keep order. If appropriate, the chairman should adjourn the meeting[13]. When a chairman puts a matter to the vote, he will first put a matter to a vote on a show of hands[14]. If a poll is properly demanded, the chairman will put the matter to a poll. In the event of an equality of votes, he will have a casting vote[15]. Obviously a vote on a poll overrides a vote on a show of hands.

It would seem that the chairman has an inherent common law power to adjourn a meeting to preserve order, see *John v Rees* (1969)[16] or where the accommodation for the meeting is clearly inadequate, see *Byng v London Life Association Ltd* (1990)[17].

---

11   Table A Art 113.
12   Table A Art 114.
13   Table A Art 45.
14   Table A Art 46.
15   Table A Arts 49 and 50.
16   [1969] 2 WLR 1294.
17   [1990] Ch 170.

# QUORUM

Section 370(4) provides that unless the company's articles make contrary provision, the quorum for a meeting shall be two members personally present. This is subject, of course, to the 12th EC Directive where a private company has only one member, then the quorum for the meeting shall be one[18]. Table A Art 40 provides that two persons entitled to vote on the business at the general meeting, either as member or proxy for a member or as a duly authorised corporate representative, shall constitute a quorum. Art 41 provides that if a quorum is not present within half an hour from the time scheduled for the start of the meeting or if during a meeting, the quorum ceases to be present, the meeting shall stand adjourned for the same day in the next following week at the same time and place or at such other time and place as the directors may determine.

Problems sometimes arise over quorums. This is sometimes because as a matter of practicality, only one person can attend.

At common law, a meeting must be made up of more than one person. In *Sharpe v Dawes* (1876)[19], a meeting of a company where only one member turned up at the meeting together with the company secretary who was not a member was held to be invalid. The same principle applied where one member present held proxies for the other members, see *Re Sanitary Carbon Co* (1877)[20].

This general principle at common law gives way to certain exceptions.

In relation to class meetings, it may be that there is only one shareholder of the class. In such circumstances, clearly the quorum cannot be higher than one, see *East v Bennett Brothers* (1911)[21].

This also applies in relation to private companies with only one member.

The Companies Act recognises two situations where the quorum may be set at one. Under s 367 of the Companies Act 1985, the Secretary of State for Trade and Industry may direct an annual general meeting to be held and may fix the quorum at one. Similarly, under s 371 of the Companies Act 1985, the court may order an extraordinary general meeting to be held and may fix the quorum at one. This is likely to happen where there is some problem with obtaining the attendance of

---

18  Companies Act 1985, s 370A.
19  2 QBD 26.
20  [1877] WN 223.
21  [1911] 1 Ch 163.

certain members. Members may wish to absent themselves and render a meeting inquorate, for example, because they fear removal as directors.

Another problem associated with quorums is in relation to the question of whether a meeting can be held where members are not in each other's physical presence. In *Re Associated Color Laboratories* (1970)[22], a Canadian court held that it was not possible to hold a meeting by telephone link. This was reversed by the Canada Business Corporations Act s 109(9). In Britain, *Byng v London Life Association Ltd* (1990)[23] considered that an audio-visual link was a valid way of holding a meeting.

## SPECIAL NOTICE

Special notice has been mentioned above (p 174). It is defined under s 379 of the Companies Act 1985. This provides that special notice (that is, 28 days notice of the resolution) has to be given to the company by the person who proposes the resolution. The notice is given by depositing a copy of the proposed resolution at the company's registered office.

Special notice is required in three situations. These are:

- to elect or re-elect a director aged 70 or above in a public company or a company which is a subsidiary of a public company[24];
- to remove a director[25];
- to remove the company's auditors[26].

Where the resolution concerns the removal of a director, this must be forwarded forthwith to the director in question. He may then make representations in writing which are then to be circulated to every member of the company, to whom notice is to be sent. If for some reason, this is not possible, then the representations must be read out at the meeting. An exception to this situation is where the representations contain defamatory matter. If this is the case, then application may be made to the court which would then decide if it so thought that circulation was inappropriate.

Notice of the resolution to remove the director should be included in the notice of the meeting that is to be called. The director who is

---

22 12 DLR 3d 388.
23 [1990] Ch 170.
24 Companies Act 1985, s 293.
25 Ibid., s 303.
26 Ibid., s 388.

threatened with removal would be allowed to speak in his own defence at the meeting. In all the three cases where special notice is appropriate (removal of directors; removal of auditors and the election or re-election of directors aged 70 or above in public companies or companies which are subsidiaries of a public company), the special notice is followed by the proposal of an ordinary resolution.

In general, if the requirements of special notice are not complied with, the meeting and the removal at the meeting and any consequent action will be void. This gives way to the principle that the court will not interfere with a decision that is reached at the meeting if it is clear that had the correct procedures been followed, the decision would have been the same, see *Bentley-Stevens v Jones* (1974)[27].

The mere serving of special notice by a member who wishes to propose a resolution will not of itself entitle the member to have resolution circulated. He must satisfy one of the other conditions for the holding of meetings as discussed above, see *Pedley v The Inland Waterways Association Ltd* (1977)[28].

Although the Companies Act has introduced a new regime whereby private companies may obviate the need to call meetings in general, the removal of directors and auditors are not covered by the new procedures. It will always, therefore, be the case that the proposed removal of an auditor or the proposed removal of a director under s 303 would involve the need for a meeting.

# RESOLUTIONS

## Extraordinary resolutions

An extraordinary resolution is one that is passed by a majority of least 75% or those voting at a general meeting of which notice specifying the intention to propose the resolution as an extraordinary resolution has been given[29]. As has been noted, such a resolution requires 14 days' notice in the case of a limited company and seven days' notice in the case of an unlimited company. These rules are subject to the provisions on short notice.

---

27  [1974] 1 WLR 638.
28  [1977] 1 All ER 209.
29  Companies Act 1985, s 378.

## Special resolutions

A resolution is a special resolution if it is passed by a majority of least 75% of those voting and passed at a general meeting of which notice has been given specifying the intention to propose the resolution as a special resolution. In the case of special resolutions, there must have been at least 21 days' notice whether the company is limited or unlimited, subject to the provisions on short notice.

## Ordinary resolutions

Ordinary resolutions are not actually defined in the Act. An ordinary resolution is one which is passed by a simple majority of those voting. It is used extensively under the Companies Act, for example increasing a company's authorised share capital under s 121 or removing a director under s 303 of the Act.

## Written resolutions

The Companies Act 1989 introduced a new procedure to allow private companies to act by unanimous written resolution. Where this method is employed, it is no longer necessary to convene a meeting. The members will agree to a course of action by signing a document. The date of the passing of the resolution is the date of the last signature[30]. This procedure cannot be used in certain situations, as has been noted, for example the removal of the company's auditors or the removal of directors. Where the method is employed, the company's auditors have currently certain rights in relation to written resolutions. These are set out in s 381B of the Act. If the resolution concerns the auditors as auditors, they may within seven days of receiving a copy of the notice of the written resolution require the company to convene a general meeting.

## Amendments to resolutions

Resolutions can be amended at the meeting provided that the amendment is within the general notice that has been sent out. This principle does not apply if the resolution has to be set out verbatim. In such a case, the amendment must also be set out verbatim in order to provide the necessary notice, see *Re Moorgate Mercantile Holdings Ltd* (1980)[31]. However, an amendment to resolve an ambiguity or to correct

---

30   Ibid., s 381A.
31   [1980] 1 All ER 40.

some grammatical error would be permitted without the prescribed notice.

Where amendments are properly proposed, the amendment is first put to the vote. If that amendment is passed, the amended resolution is then voted upon.

## Registration of resolutions

Certain resolutions have to be registered. These are set out in s 380 of the Companies Act 1985. They are as follows:

- special resolutions;
- extraordinary resolutions;
- resolutions or agreements of all the members of a company which would have been registrable had they been passed as special resolutions or extraordinary resolutions;
- resolutions or agreements of a class of members which bind all the members of the class although some have not agreed to it;
- a resolution for voluntary winding up;
- a resolution to give, vary, revoke, or renew authority to directors to issue securities;
- a resolution conferring, varying, revoking, or renewing authority to purchase a company's own shares on the market;
- an elective resolution or a resolution revoking such a resolution (these are discussed below).

In addition, certain other resolutions are registrable:

- under s 123(3) of the Companies Act 1985 a resolution increasing the authorised share capital of the company;
- resolutions approving certain acquisitions from the subscribers of the memorandum under s 111(2) of the Companies Act 1985;
- a resolution treating a meeting called by the Secretary of State as an annual general meeting under s 367(4) of the Companies Act 1985.

If such resolutions are not registered, they will result in criminal liability. The resolution itself is not invalid but the company may not be able to rely upon the resolution unless it has been officially notified[32] which provides that a company is not entitled to rely on the happening of certain events such as the making of a winding up order or the appointment of a liquidator, or the alteration of the company's constitution, or a change of directors or any change in the situation of the

---

32  Companies Act 1985, s 42.

company's registered office if the event has not been officially notified and was not known by the relevant person at the appropriate time. Official notification is where the registrar will announce the receipt of certain documents by himself in the *London Gazette*.

## Members' resolutions

Section 376 of the Companies Act 1985 provides for the circulation of members' resolutions. If requisitionists representing one twentieth of the voting rights of the company or not less than 100 members holding shares upon which there is paid up an average sum per member of not less than £100 require a resolution to be put on the agenda of the annual general meeting they may so require. They may also require the circulation of a statement either at the annual general meeting or any other meeting of not more than 1,000 words in relation to a matter that is referred to in any proposed resolution or the business to be dealt with at the meeting.

## Elective resolutions

The Companies Act 1989 introduced a new provision for private companies whereby they may pass an elective resolution dispensing with certain formalities. The elective regime is dealt with in s 379A of the Companies Act 1985. It covers the following matters:

- election as to the duration of authority to allot shares. This normally may only subsist for up to five years under s 80 of the Act. Now, by virtue of s 80A, a private company may dispense with the time limitation by unanimous resolution;
- election to dispense with the laying of accounts and reports before a general meeting each year. This election is provided for under s 252;
- election to dispense with the holding of an annual general meeting. This election is provided for under s 366A;
- election as to the majority required for authorising short notice of meetings, reducing this from 95% to 90% under s 369(4) or s 378(3);
- election to dispense with the annual appointment of auditors. This is provided for under s 386.

Where an elective resolution is to be passed, it must be agreed to at a meeting in person or by proxy by all of the members entitled to attend and vote at the meeting or by the written resolution procedure (p 179).

## VOTES

When matters are put to the vote at a meeting, a vote will be initially conducted on a show of hands. On a show of hands, each member has one vote. This may well be conclusive of the matter. This would be the case, for example, if all of the members are present and they all vote in the same way. Sometimes, a vote on a poll is necessary. Proxies are not allowed to vote on a show of hands and it may well be that a decision on a show of hands produces a different result from a decision on a poll. In such circumstances, a vote on a poll will override a vote on a show of hands. Section 370(6) of the Companies Act 1985 provides that unless the articles provide otherwise, every member has one vote in relation to each share or each £10 worth of stock held by him; and in any other case, every member has one vote. Table A Art 54 provides that subject to any rights or restrictions attached to any shares, on a show of hands every member who (being an individual) is present in person or (being a corporation) is present by a duly authorised representative, not being himself a member entitled to vote, shall have one vote and on a poll every member shall have one vote for every share of which he is the holder.

A poll may always be demanded on any matter other than the election of the chairman of the meeting or the adjournment of the meeting. These two matters may be excluded from this general provision by the company's articles[33].

A poll may be demanded by any five members present in person or by proxy or by a member or members representing not less than one tenth of voting rights at the meeting or by members holding shares in the company with voting rights on which an aggregate sum has been paid up equal to at least one tenth of the share capital. The company's articles may provide more generous rights than this; Table A Art 46 provides that a poll may be demanded:

- by the chairman; or
- by at least two members having the right to vote at the meeting; or
- by a member or members representing not less than one tenth of the total voting rights of all the members having the right to vote at the meeting; or
- by a member or members holding shares conferring a right to vote at the meeting, being shares on which an aggregate sum has been paid up equal to not less than one tenth of the total sum paid up on all of the shares conferring that right;

---

33   Ibid., s 373(1).

- a demand by a person as proxy for a member shall be the same as a demand by the member.

A vote on a poll may be taken after a vote by a show of hands or it may pre-empt such a vote[34]. Table A Art 51 also provides that a poll may be demanded on the election of a chairman or on the adjournment of the meeting.

Table A Art 50 provides that in the case of an equality of votes the chairman will have a casting vote.

The usual procedure for taking a poll is for votes to be recorded on poll cards. On the poll cards are spaces marked either for or against particular resolutions. The voter will mark the card to indicate which way he is voting and then sign the card. The scrutineers will collect the cards and count the votes and report the results to the chairman who announces the results.

# PROXIES

Section 372 of the Act provides that any member of a company who is entitled to attend and vote at a meeting may appoint a person as his proxy and that proxy need not be a member. It has already been noted that this right must be set out in the notice calling the meeting[35].

In the case of a private company, a proxy has a right to speak at the meeting in the same way as the member would have been able to speak.

In both public and private companies, a proxy cannot vote unless on a poll. The articles may provide otherwise[36]. The proxy may join in the demand for a poll[37].

Any provision in a company's articles requiring delivery of a proxy more than 48 hours before a meeting or adjourned meeting will be void[38]. A company's articles may be more generous; for example, a provision that a proxy may be delivered up to 24 hours before the meeting. The deposit of proxies as provided for in Table A Art 62 requires that a proxy instrument must be deposited not less than 48 hours before the holding of the meeting or adjourned meeting or in the case of a poll taken more than 48 hours after it is demanded should be deposited not less than 24 hours before the time appointed for the taking of the poll. Where the poll is not taken forthwith but is taken not more

---

34  Table A Art 46.
35  Companies Act 1985, s 372(3).
36  Ibid., s 372(2)(c).
37  Ibid., s 373(2).
38  Ibid., s 372(5).

than 48 hours after it is demanded it should be delivered at the meeting at which the poll is demanded to the chairman or to the secretary or to any director.

Where invitations are sent by a company to appoint a person as proxy, such invitations must be sent to all the members or the company's officers who have knowingly committed proxy invitations to be sent to selected members are liable to a fine[39].

Unless the articles provide otherwise, certain limitations apply[40]:

- the rules on proxies only apply to companies limited by shares;
- a member of a private company may only appoint one proxy to attend and vote on any one occasion[41];
- a proxy is not entitled to vote except on a poll ie he may not vote on a show of hands[42].

In the absence of a contract, a proxy is not obliged to attend and vote on behalf of a member. If he does attend, the proxy's authority is only to vote as directed by the member.

The company's articles generally require the appointment of a proxy to be in writing and require that the full extent of the proxy's powers should be set out. Table A Art 60 and Table A Art 61 set out instruments for appointing a proxy (*see below*). Table A Art 60 is an ordinary proxy and Table A Art 61 instructs the proxy to vote in particular ways on the various resolutions.

It is generally the case that proxy forms should be signed by the member who is appointing the proxy. This is the case in relation to both the proxy forms under Table A Arts 60 and 61.

Proxies may be revoked in various ways. They are determined by the death of the member appointing the proxy, by express revocation or by the member actually turning up at the meeting. This last point occurred in *Cousins v International Brick Co Ltd* (1931)[43]. Most companies' articles provide that where a proxy casts a vote, that vote shall be treated as valid notwithstanding the previous determination of the authority of the proxy unless notice that the determination was received by the company at its registered office or such other place at which the instrument of proxy was deposited has been received[44].

---

39   Ibid., s 372(6).
40   Ibid., s 372(2).
41   Ibid., s 372(2)(b).
42   Ibid., s 372(2)(c).
43   [1931] 2 Ch 90.
44   Table A Art 63.

Where companies hold shares in another company, they do not appoint proxies to attend meetings but corporate representatives. Such persons are entitled to exercise the same powers on behalf of the corporation as the corporation could exercise if it were an individual shareholder rather than a corporate one. Table A Art 63 in relation to the determination of proxy authority also applies in relation to the determination of the authority of a corporate representative.

# ORDINARY PROXY

An instrument appointing a proxy shall be in writing, executed by or on behalf of the appointor and shall be in the following form (or in a form as near thereto as circumstances allow or in any other form which is usual or which the directors may approve).

'..................PLC/Limited

I/We,..........................., of....................................., being a member/members of the above-named company, hereby appoint ............................................of ........................................, or failing him,........................of............................, as my/our proxy to vote in my/our name(s) and on my/our behalf at the annual/extraordinary general meeting of the company to be held on 19......., and at any adjournment thereof.

Signed on........................19..........'

# INSTRUCTION TO PROXY

Where it is desired to afford members an opportunity of instructing the proxy how he shall act the instrument appointing a proxy shall be in the following form (or in a form as near thereto as circumstances allow or in any other form which is usual or which the directors may approve)

'..................PLC/Limited

I/We,..........................., of....................................., being a member/members of the above-named company, hereby appoint ............................................of ........................................, or failing him,........................of............................, as my/our proxy to vote in my/our name(s) and on my/our behalf at the annual/extraordinary general meeting of the company to be held on 19......., and at any adjournment thereof.

Signed on........................19..........'

This form is to be used in respect of the resolutions mentioned below as follows:

Resolution No 1*for*against

Resolution No 2*for*against

* Strike out whichever is not desired.

Unless otherwise instructed the proxy may vote as he thinks fit or abstain from voting.

Signed this........................ day of................ 19..........'

# ANGLO HELLENIC TRAVEL PLC
# FORM OF PROXY FOR USE AT ANNUAL GENERAL MEETING

I, David Dickens of 16 Savoy Road, Windsor, Berkshire, a beneficial owner of shares of the above-named Company,

hereby appoint (see note 1).......................................

of (see note 2)................................................................

as my proxy to vote for me on my behalf, at the Annual General Meeting of the Company to be held on 30.7.93 and at any adjournment thereof.

Signature ...............................................

Name ..............................................

(In block capitals)

Dated ..................

Please indicate with an X in the spaces below how you wish your votes to be cast.

|  | FOR | AGAINST |
|---|---|---|
| **RESOLUTION 1**<br>To approve Directors' remuneration | | |
| **RESOLUTION 2**<br>To receive the report and accounts | | |
| **RESOLUTION 3**<br>To re-appoint the auditors | | |

NOTE 1: Please insert full name in block capitals

NOTE 2: Please insert full address in block capitals

To be valid this form should be returned to W W Jacobs, 4 Cathedral Walk, Maidstone, Kent not less than 48 hours before the time fixed for holding the meeting or adjourned meeting.

# ADJOURNMENT OF THE MEETING

Table A Art 45 provides that the chairman with the consent of the meeting may adjourn the meeting and shall adjourn the meeting if so directed by the meeting. The chairman may in certain circumstances be obliged to adjourn the meeting. This would be the case, for example, if there is disorder at the meeting, see *John v Rees* (1969)[45]. He may need to do so if the room allocated for the meeting is not large enough to accommodate all of those attending or if some audio-visual link between different rooms breaks down, as in *Byng v London Life Association Ltd* (1990)[46]. Table A Art 45 also provides that if the meeting is adjourned for 14 days or more, at least seven clear days notice shall be given specifying the time and place of the adjourned meeting and the general nature of the business to be transacted. Otherwise, it shall not be necessary to give any such notice.

Section 381 of the Companies Act 1985 provides that where a resolution is passed at an adjourned meeting of the company, the resolution is for all purposes to be treated as having been passed on the date on which it was in fact passed and is not to be deemed passed on any earlier date.

This might seem to be a statement of the obvious - indeed it is a statement of the obvious!

A member is entitled to attend an adjourned meeting even though he was not present at the original meeting, see *R v D'Oyly* (1840)[47].

A motion to adjourn a meeting is by ordinary resolution unless the articles provide otherwise.

# MINUTES

The minutes represent a permanent record of what happened at a meeting. Section 382 of the Act requires that every company shall keep minutes of all proceedings at general meetings as well as all proceedings of meetings of directors and where there are managers all proceedings of meetings of managers. Section 382(5) provides that if a company fails to comply with this provision, the company and every officer who is in default is liable to a fine and for continued contravention a daily default fine.

---

45 [1969] 1 All ER 274.
46 [1990] Ch 170.
47 (1840) 12 Ad & El 139.

Section 383 provides that the books containing the minutes of general meetings of a company shall be kept at the company's registered office and shall be open to the inspection of any member without charge.

Any member shall be entitled on payment of such fee as may be prescribed to be furnished within seven days after making a request with a copy of any such minutes as are referred to.

If an inspection is refused or a copy is refused, then the company and every officer in default is liable to a fine. The usual practice is for minutes to be taken in shorthand or to be taken down in rough form at the meeting and then to be written up subsequently. The minutes are then generally checked by the chairman of the meeting.

The minutes should be kept in a bound book or in some other permanent way, see s 722(1). It is important that the minutes are kept in such a way that there is no chance of falsification, see s 722(2). Section 723 provides that the company may record the matters otherwise than in a bound book and this includes the power to keep them in some form other than in a legible form so long as the recording is capable of being reproduced in a legible form. This permits the company to use computers to keep company records.

The minutes should be signed by the chairman of the meeting or the chairman of the next succeeding meeting[48]. The minutes are then evidence of the proceedings of that meeting. Evidence may be adduced to rebut the minutes or to add to them, as in *Re Fireproof Doors Ltd* (1916)[49]. If the minutes are stated in the articles to be conclusive of matters decided at the meeting, then it is not possible to challenge the minutes, see *Kerr v John Mottram Ltd* (1940)[50].

48   Companies Act 1985, s 382(2).
49   [1916] 2 Ch 142.
50   [1940] Ch 657.

# CHAPTER 20

# AUDITORS

## APPOINTMENT

Part XI Chapter V of the Companies Act 1985 deals with auditors. Section 384 of the Act provides that every company shall appoint an auditor or auditors. This is subject to the exception set out in s 388A that a dormant company is exempt from the obligation to appoint auditors. Section 384(4) provides that this obligation is subject to s 386 by which a private company may elect to dispense with the obligation to appoint auditors annually.

Section 385 provides that a company shall at each general meeting at which accounts are laid appoint an auditor or auditors to hold office from the conclusion of that meeting until the conclusion of the next general meeting at which accounts are laid[1]. The first auditors of the company may be appointed by the directors at any time before the first general meeting of the company at which accounts are laid and may hold office until the conclusion of that meeting[2].

### Appointment of auditors in private companies - election to dispense with laying of accounts

Where a private company has elected to dispense with the laying of accounts before the company in general meeting, s 385A applies unless the company has also elected to dispense with the annual appointment of auditors. Auditors shall be appointed by the company in general meeting before the end of the period of 28 days beginning with the day on which copies of the company's annual accounts for the previous financial year are sent to members under s 238 of the Act or, if notice is given under s 253(2) requiring the laying of the accounts before the company in general meeting, the conclusion of that meeting. The auditors so appointed shall hold office from the end of that period or the conclusion of the meeting until the end of the time for appointing

---

1    Companies Act 1985, s 385(2).
2    Ibid., s 385(3).

auditors for the next financial year[3]. It is usual for companies which elect not to lay accounts also not to appoint auditors annually.

The first auditors of the company may be appointed by the directors before the end of the 28 day period following the company's first annual accounts being sent to members or at the beginning of the meeting where notice is being given under s 253(2) requiring the laying of the accounts before the company in general meeting.

Auditors holding office when an election is made shall, unless the company in general meeting determines otherwise, continue to hold office until the end of the time for appointing auditors for the next financial year, Where an election ceases to have effect, auditors holding office shall continue to hold office until the conclusion of the next general meeting of the company at which accounts are laid[4].

## Election to dispense with annual appointment of auditors

Members of a private company may elect by unanimous elective resolution to dispense with the annual appointment of auditors[5]. Where such an election is made the auditors who held office continue to hold office.

## Eligibility for appointment as company auditor

Section 24 of the Companies Act 1989 provides that the main purposes of this part of the Act are to secure that only persons who are properly supervised and appropriately qualified are appointed company auditors and that audits by persons so appointed are carried out properly and with integrity and with a proper degree of independence.

Section 25 deals with the question of eligibility for appointment. A person is eligible for appointment as a company auditor only if:

- he is a member of a recognised supervisory body; and
- he is eligible for appointment under the rules of that body.

Unlike the former position, s 25(2) provides that a firm may be appointed as company auditor. The definition of 'firm' in s 53 is given as 'a body corporate or a partnership'. Formally, corporate bodies could not act as auditors.

---

3   Ibid., s 385A(2).
4   Ibid., s 385A(5).
5   Ibid., s 386.

Where a partnership is appointed as auditor, the appointment unless there is a contrary intention, is of the partnership and not of the partners. Where the partnership ceases, the appointment shall be treated as extending to any successor partnership that is eligible for appointment and to any person who succeeds to the practice, having previously carried it on in partnership if he is eligible for appointment. A partnership is to be regarded as succeeding to the practice of another firm only if the members of the successor partnership are substantially the same as those of the former partnership and a partnership or other person shall be regarded as succeeding to the practice of a firm only if it or he succeeds to the whole or substantially the whole of the business of the former partnership. If there is no succession within s 26(3) (above) where there is a successor partnership or successor individual, the appointment may with the consent of the company be treated as extending to a partnership or to some other person who is eligible for appointment who succeeds to the business of the former firm or some part of it.

Where the auditors are a body corporate or a partnership, the signature should be in the name of the body corporate or partnership by a person authorised to sign on behalf of the corporate body or firm and not in the name of an individual auditor[6].

There are certain grounds of ineligibility to act as auditors. Section 27 provides for ineligibility on the ground of lack of independence. A person is ineligible if he is an officer or employee of the company or a partner or employee of such a person or a partnership of which such a person is a partner or if he is ineligible for appointment as a company auditor of any associated undertaking of the company (this means a company within the same group). More generally, s 27(2) provides that a person is also ineligible for appointment as company auditor if there exists between him or any associate of his and the company or any associated undertaking a connection of any such description as may be specified by regulations made by the Secretary of State.

Where an auditor becomes ineligible during the course of his term of office, he should immediately vacate office and give notice in writing to the company that he has vacated it by reason of ineligibility[7]. It is an offence for a person to continue as auditor in contravention of this section and a person who does so is liable on conviction on indictment to a fine and on summary conviction to a fine not exceeding the statutory maximum. In the case of continued contravention, he is liable on a second or subsequent summary conviction to a fine not exceeding one

---

6  Ibid., s 236(5).
7  Companies Act 1989, s 28(2).

tenth of the statutory maximum in respect of each day on which the contravention is continued. It is a defence in proceedings for a person to show that he did not know and had no reason to believe that he was or had become ineligible for appointment. Section 29 provides that the Secretary of State may require a second audit where a person becomes ineligible to act as auditor during his period of office. The cost of such a second audit may be recovered against the ineligible auditor[8].

## Qualifications

A person must be a member of a supervisory body in order to act as an auditor. Section 30(1) of the Act provides that a supervisory body is a body which maintains and enforces rules as to the eligibility of persons seeking appointment as company auditors and the conduct of company audit work, such rules being binding on persons seeking appointment or acting as company auditors because they are members of that body or otherwise subject to its control. Sched 11 of the Act deals with the question of grant and revocation of recognition of supervisory bodies. Sched 11 Part II provides the requirements for recognition. The body must have rules providing that a person is not eligible for appointment unless he holds an appropriate qualification in the case of an individual, or in the case of a firm, the individuals responsible for company audit work on behalf of the firm each hold an appropriate qualification and the firm is controlled by qualified persons. There are more detailed rules on how one determines control. The body should also have adequate rules and practices designed to ensure company audit work is conducted properly and with integrity and that persons are not appointed company auditor in circumstances where they have an interest likely to conflict with the proper conduct of the audit. Rules and practices of the body relating to the admission and expulsion of members, the grant and withdrawal of eligibility for appointment as a company auditor and the discipline it exercises over its members must be fair and reasonable and include adequate provision for appeals. Section 31 of the Act deals with the issue of an appropriate qualification. The person holds an appropriate qualification for the purposes of this part of the Act if he was by virtue of membership of a body recognised under the Companies Act 1985 qualified for appointment as an auditor before 1 January 1990 and immediately before the commencement of s 25 of the Act. The bodies then recognised were:

- The Institute of Chartered Accountants in England and Wales;
- The Institute of Chartered Accountants of Scotland;

---

8    Ibid., s 29(7).

- The Chartered Association of Certified Accountants;
- The Institute of Chartered Accountants in Ireland;
- The Association of Authorised Public Accountants.

A person is also qualified if he holds an approved overseas qualification and satisfies any additional educational requirements which may be directed as necessary by the Secretary of State under s 33(4) of the Act. Section 31(2) of the Act provides that somebody who was previously qualified to act as auditor under the old law other than by being a member of a recognised body must notify the Secretary of State in writing if he wishes to retain the qualification to act as auditor within 12 months of the coming into force of s 25 of the Act. He is then treated as holding the necessary qualification. Section 31(4) provides that a person who began a course of study or training leading to a professional qualification in accountancy offered by a body established in the United Kingdom before 1 January 1990 and who obtains that qualification before the 1 January 1996 shall be treated as holding an appropriate qualification if approved by the Secretary of State for the purposes of this sub-section. Section 32 provides that a qualifying body is a body established in the United Kingdom which offers a professional qualification in accountancy. The rules detailing how a professional qualification may be recognised are set out in Sched 12 of the Act. The qualification must only be open to persons who have attained university entrance level or who have a sufficient period of professional experience. The qualification must be restricted to persons who have passed an examination at least part of which is in writing testing theoretical knowledge of the subjects prescribed in regulations made by the Secretary of State and an ability to apply that knowledge in practice and requiring a standard of attainment at least equivalent to that required to attain a degree from a university or similar establishment in the United Kingdom. There should be a course of theoretical instruction. Where a person is seeking entry to the qualifications on the basis of professional experience, this should be no less than seven years' experience in a professional capacity in the fields of finance, law and accountancy.

## Overseas qualifications

Section 33 of the Companies Act 1989 provides for the approval of overseas qualifications. The Secretary of State may declare that persons who are qualified to audit accounts under the law of some other country and who hold a professional qualification there which is recognised in that country shall be regarded as holding an approved overseas qualification. The qualification should be one equivalent to that afforded by a recognised professional qualification in this country and in exercising his power, the Secretary of State may have regard to reciprocity in recognition in that other country of professional qualifications for eligibility in this country. The Secretary of State may direct that a person holding an approved overseas qualification shall not be treated as holding an appropriate qualification unless he also holds an additional educational qualification which may be specified by the Secretary of State.

## Authorisations under the 1967 act

Section 34 of the Act provides that those people with authorisations granted by the Board of Trade or the Secretary or State under the old s 13(1) of the Companies Act 1967 may be eligible for appointment as an auditor of an unquoted company.

## Appointment of auditors by the secretary of state

Section 387 of the Companies Act 1985 provides that where no auditors are appointed or re-appointed or deemed to be re-appointed, the Secretary of State may appoint a person to fill the vacancy. In such an instance, the company must within a week of the end of the time for appointing auditors give notice to the Secretary of State of his power having become exercisable. Failure to do so results in the company and every officer in default being guilty of an offence and liable to a fine and for continued contravention to a daily default fine.

## Casual vacancies

Where a casual vacancy, exists the directors or the company in general meeting may fill a casual vacancy. While such a vacancy continues, any surviving or continuing auditor or auditors may continue to act. Special notice is required for a resolution at a general meeting where it is proposed to fill a casual vacancy in the office of auditor or to re-appoint as auditor a retiring auditor who was appointed by the directors to fill a casual vacancy.

# REMOVAL

Section 391 of the Companies Act 1985 provides that a company may by ordinary resolution remove an auditor from office notwithstanding anything in any agreement between the auditor and the company. Where a resolution removing an auditor is passed, the company must within 14 days give notice of that fact to the registrar. The auditor retains his right to compensation or damages for any breach of an agreement with him. Furthermore, the auditor of the company who has been removed has the right to attend the general meeting at which his term of office would otherwise have expired or at which it is proposed to fill the vacancy caused by his removal and is entitled to all notices etc in relation to such meetings. Section 391A provides that special notice is required of a resolution to remove an auditor or to appoint somebody other than a retiring auditor. Such a notice should be sent to the person whom it is proposed to remove or to the person whom it is proposed to replace and to the person whom it is proposed should replace him. The auditor who is proposed to be removed or who is proposed to be retired may make representations in writing to the company not exceeding a reasonable length and request their notification to members of the company. If the representations are not notified to members, the auditor can request that they be read out at the meeting. In addition, the auditor may be heard at the meeting itself. However, the company may argue before the court that the rights conferred by the section are being abused to secure needless publicity for defamatory matter and the court may order that the matter should not be circulated and that the costs should be awarded against the auditor.

*Note*: The written resolution procedure may not be used to remove the auditor of a private company.

## RESIGNATION

An auditor may resign from office by depositing a notice in writing to that effect at the company's registered office[9]. A copy of this notice should be sent within 14 days to the registrar of companies. Section 392A deals with certain rights of resigning auditors. Where the auditor's notice of resignation is accompanied by a statement of circumstances which he considers should be brought to the attention of members or creditors of the company, then the section applies. He may deposit with the notice a signed requisition calling on the directors of the company to convene an extraordinary general meeting for the purpose of receiving and considering such explanation of the circumstances concerned with his resignation. He may request the company to circulate to its members a statement in writing of the circumstances connected with his resignation before the meeting convened on his requisition or before any meeting at which his term of office would otherwise have expired. The company unless the statement is received too late shall in any notice of

---

9   Companies Act 1985, s 392.

the meeting given to members state the fact of the statement and send a copy of it to every member of the company to whom notice of the meeting has been sent. If a copy of the statement is not sent out as required, the auditor may without prejudice to his right to be heard at the meeting require that the statement be read out at the meeting. Copies of the notice need not be sent on application of the company or any other aggrieved person if the court considers that the rights conferred by s 392A are being abused to secure needless publicity for defamatory matter and the court may order the costs against the resigning auditors.

# CEASING TO HOLD OFFICE

Section 394 provides that where an auditor ceases for any reason to hold office, he should deposit at the company's registered office a statement of any circumstances connected with his ceasing to hold office which he considers should be brought to the attention of the members or creditors of the company or if he considers that there are no such circumstances a statement that there are none. In the case of resignation, the statement should be deposited along with the notice of resignation. In the case of failure to seek re-appointment, the statement should be deposited not less than 14 days before the end of the time allowed for next appointing auditors. In any other case, the statement should be deposited not later than the end of 14 days beginning with the date on which he ceases to hold office. If there is a statement of circumstances which the auditor considers should be brought to the attention of the members or the creditors of the company, the company shall within 14 days of deposit send a copy to every person who is entitled to be sent a copy of the accounts or apply to the court. The application to the court would be on the basis that the statement is being made to secure needless publicity for defamatory matter.

# AUDITORS' DUTIES

It is the auditors' duty to make a report to the company's members on all annual accounts of the company of which copies are to be laid before the company in general meeting during their tenure of office[10]. Their report should state whether in their opinion the accounts have been properly prepared in accordance with the Act and in particular whether a true and fair view is given:

---

10   Ibid., s 235(1).

- in the case of an individual balance sheet, of the state of affairs of the company at the end of the financial year;
- in the case of an individual profit and loss account, of the profit or loss of the company for the financial year;
- in the case of group accounts, of the state of affairs as at the end of the financial year and the profit or loss for the financial year of the undertakings included in the consolidation as a whole so far as concerns members of the company.

The auditors are also required to consider whether the information given in the directors' report for the financial year for which the annual accounts are prepared is consistent with those accounts and if they are of the opinion that it is not, they shall state that fact in their report. Section 236 of the Act requires the auditors' report to have the names of the auditors stated and for the accounts to be signed by the auditors.

## CONDUCT OF THE AUDIT

The auditors should audit the company's accounts[11].

In conducting the audit an auditor is now obliged to take a much stricter approach to his client, physically checking the stock, advising of unsatisfactory practices, and scrupulously following up any suspicious circumstances.

His best protection is professional insurance. A clear unequivocal letter of appointment from his client is also desirable. It will remind him of what he has agreed to do. He should beware of giving ad hoc advice and if he does so should stress it is provisional and not to be relied upon. Even here the extent to which he can now disclaim liability is limited by the Unfair Contract Terms Act 1977. The Institute's revised Statement on Unlawful Acts or Defaults by Clients of Members provides that 'A member who acquires knowledge indicating that a client may have been guilty of some default or unlawful act should normally raise the matter with the management of the client at an appropriate level. If his concerns are not satisfactorily resolved, he should consider reporting the matter to non-executive directors or to the client's audit committee where these exist. Where this is not possible or he fails to resolve the matter a member may wish to consider making a report to a third party.'

This is, of course, in addition to any statutory or common law obligations placed upon an auditor.

---

11   Ibid., s 236.

An auditor's statutory duties cannot be restricted by the company's articles or by any contract between him and the company[12]. He may, however, be relieved by the court under s 727 of the Act.

An auditor's basic duties have been lucidly and uncontroversially outlined by Lord Denning:

First, the auditor should verify the arithmetical accuracy of the accounts and the proper vouching of entries in the books.

Secondly, the auditor should make checks to test whether the accounts mask errors or even dishonesty.

Thirdly the auditor should report on whether the accounts give to the shareholders reliable information respecting the true financial position of the company. An auditor must approach his work 'with an inquiring mind - not suspicious of dishonesty ... but suspecting that someone may have made a mistake somewhere and that a check must be made to ensure that there has been none'. *Fomento (Sterling Area) Ltd v Selsdon Fountain Pen Co Ltd* (1958)[13], at p 23, *per* Lord Denning.

The main obligations of an auditor are to audit the accounts of the company and to report to the company on the accounts laid before the company in general meeting during his tenure of office[14].

These are the basic statements of what an accountant should ensure in auditing a company's balance sheet and profit and loss account but it is proposed to examine these duties in more detail.

Much of the case law is of decidedly Victorian flavour; too much is now at stake in terms of financial amount and prestige for many cases to get beyond the doors of the High Court and one can only speculate on the basis of out of court settlements.

## AUDITORS' LIABILITIES

The starting point of any survey of auditor's liability is the famous dictum of Lopes LJ in *Re Kingston Cotton Mill* (1896)[15] that 'an auditor is not bound to be a detective ... he is a watchdog but not a bloodhound'. The auditors in this case had taken on trust a management assessment of the amount of yarn in stock, failing to make a physical check themselves. The assessments were frauds which had been perpetrated by a manager

---

12  Ibid., s 310.
13  [1958] 1 All ER 11.
14  Companies Act 1985, s 235.
15  [1896] 2 Ch 279, 288.

to make the company appear to flourish by exaggerating the quantity and value of cotton and yarn in the company's mills.

The auditors took the entry of the stock-in-trade at the beginning of the year from the last preceding balance sheet, and they took the values of the stock-in-trade at the end of the year from the stock journal.

The book contained a series of accounts under various heads purporting to show the quantities and values of the company's stock-in-trade at the end of each year and a summary of the accounts which was adopted by the auditors.

The auditors always ensured that the summary corresponded with the accounts but they did not enquire into the accuracy of the accounts. The auditors were held not liable; the court concluded they were entitled to accept the certificate of a responsible official. This is a decision that would almost certainly be reversed today. The dictum of Lopes LJ, however, still finds approval and has fossilised into an immovable principle of law, though it is now generally accepted that an auditor is a watchdog which must bark loudly and relentlessly at any suspicious circumstance.

At the outset of the audit, an auditor must familiarise himself with the company's memorandum and articles of association, so that he can ensure that payments shown in the accounts have been properly incurred. It will be no defence to assert that he has not read these company documents.

In *Leeds Estate Building and Investment Co v Shepherd* (1887)[16] the terms of the articles had not been carried out, and it was held that it was no excuse that the auditor has not seen them. As a result of this neglect dividends, director's fees and bonuses were improperly paid and the auditor was therefore held liable for damages.

An auditor is required to investigate suspicious circumstances. In *Re Thomas Gerrard* (1967)[17], Pennycuick J noted that 'the standards of reasonable care and skill are, upon the expert evidence more exacting than those which prevailed in 1896' (*Re Kingston Cotton Mill*). Here, in addition to an overstatement of stock, there had been fraudulent practice in changing invoice dates to make it appear that clients owed money within the accounting period when in fact it was due outside of it and to make it appear that suppliers were not yet owed money for goods when such liability did exist.

In holding Kevans, the auditors, to be liable, Pennycuick J considered that the changed invoice dates should have aroused suspicion. 'I find the

---

16 (1887) 36 Ch D 787.

17 [1967] 2 All ER 525.

conclusion inescapable, alike on the expert evidence and as a matter of business common sense that at this stage (of discovering the altered invoice dates) he ought to have examined the suppliers' statements and where necessary have communicated with the suppliers.'

# CHAPTER 21

# ADMINISTRATION

## ADMINISTRATION ORDERS

The Insolvency Act 1985 (consolidated into the 1986 Act) introduced the new procedure of administration. This is a type of intensive care for companies which are in financial difficulties. It follows the recommendations of the Review Committee on Insolvency Law and Practice - the Cork Report[1]. There followed a government white paper, a revised framework for insolvency law which then brought in some of the recommendations of the Committee. The method of administration is to make possible the rescue of a company by placing its management in the hands of an administrator. The purposes of administration are:

- the survival of the company and the whole or part of its undertaking as a going concern;
- the approval of a voluntary arrangement with creditors under Part 1 of the Insolvency Act 1986;
- the sanctioning under s 425 of the Companies Act of a compromise or arrangement between the company and creditors or members;
- a more advantageous realisation of the company's assets than would be effected on a winding up;

Where an order is made, it will specify the purpose or purposes for which the order is made.

An order can only be made if the court is satisfied (a) that the company is or is likely to become unable to pay its debts within s 123 of the Insolvency Act 1986 and (b) that one or more of the purposes mentioned above is likely of achievement.

## Procedure

A petition for an administration order may be presented by the company or by its directors, by a creditor or by the clerk of a magistrate's court in relation to the enforcement of fines imposed on companies or by any combination of these[2].

---

1    Cmnd 8558 1982.
2    Insolvency Act 1986, s 9.

The petition should set out the purpose or purposes which the petitioners believe is likely of achievement, certain information about the company and certain details of the petitioner.

Once the petition is presented, notice of this should be given to any person who has appointed or is entitled to appoint an administrative receiver. The application should also contain the consent of the person named as administrator to act. There should also be an affidavit of service of the petition in support. The affidavit of service should also indicate that where there is an administrative receiver, the petition for an administration order has also been served upon him or somebody entitled to appoint an administrative receiver.

The petition and affidavit of service are filed with the court and copies are served on the company on any administrative receiver or somebody who may appoint an administrative receiver no later than five days before the date fixed for the hearing. Section 9(2)(b) provides that a petition can only be withdrawn with the leave of the court.

## Effect of application

Section 10 of the Insolvency Act 1986 provides that after the petition has been presented, the following are not possible:

- a resolution to wind the company up or any order to wind the company up;
- any steps to enforce any security over the company's property or to repossess goods in the company's possession under any hire purchase agreement, conditional sale or chattel leasing agreement or to enforce any retention of title clause without the consent of the court and subject to such terms as the court may impose;
- any proceedings and execution or other legal process and any distress against the company's property except with the leave of the court and subject to such terms as the court may set out.

Where an application is made, the court may not appoint an administrator where there is an administrative receiver unless it is satisfied that the person by whom or on whose behalf the receiver was appointed has consented to the making of the order, or that if an administration order were made, any security by virtue of which the receiver was appointed would be released or discharged or avoided or challengeable under the relevant provisions of the Act.

## Effect of an order

When an administration order is made, certain people must be notified. Where an administration order is made, the administrator should send a copy of the order to the company and publish it in *The London Gazette* and should within 28 days send notice of his appointment to all creditors of the company of whose address he is aware. He should also within 14 days notify the registrar of companies[3].

Where an administration order is made, any receiver of part of the company's assets may be required to vacate office by the administrator[4].

The following actions are prohibited during the currency of an administration order:

- a resolution or order to wind the company up;
- the appointment of an administrative receiver;
- any other steps taken to enforce any security over the company's property or to repossess goods in the company's possession under a hire purchase agreement, conditional sale or chattel leasing agreement or to enforce any retention of title clause except with the consent of the administrator or the leave of the court and subject to such terms as the court may impose[5].

Every invoice, order for goods or business letter should contain the administrator's name and a statement that the affairs, business and property of the company are being managed by an administrator.

The administrator should within three months of his appointment make a statement of his proposals for dealing with the administration and send a copy of his proposals to the registrar of companies and to all creditors of the company and should lay a statement before a meeting of the company's creditors summoned for that purpose on not less than 14 days' notice[6]. He should also supply copies of the proposals to members of the company[7].

The creditors' meeting called to consider the proposals has the ability to amend the proposals[8]. The administrator should report the result of the meeting to the court and give notice of that result to the registrar of companies[9].

Section 22 provides that the administrator should require a statement of affairs of the company to be submitted to him within 21 days of having given notice.

---

3   Ibid., s 21.
4   Ibid., s 11(2).
5   Ibid., s 11(3).
6   Ibid., s 23.
7   Ibid., s 23(2).
8   Ibid., s 24(1) and (2).
9   Ibid., s 24(4).

A creditors' committee may be formed[10]. This committee would be established by the creditors' meeting called under s 23. The committee, if established, may, on giving not less than seven days notice, require the administrator to attend before it at any reasonable time and furnish it with such information relating to the carrying out of the administrator's functions as it may reasonably require.

The administrator has powers given to him by s 14 of the Insolvency Act 1986 in relation to the carrying out of the administration. He may do all such things as may be necessary for the management of the affairs, business and property of the company and without prejudice to the generality of this, he has powers that are set out in Sched 1 of the Act. These powers include the power to take possession of, collect and get in the property of the company, the power to sell or dispose of property, the power to raise or borrow money, the power to appoint a solicitor or accountant, the power to bring or defend legal proceedings, the power to refer matters to arbitration, the power to use the company seal, the power to draw, accept, make and endorse any bill of exchange, the power to appoint agents, the power to make payments, the power to carry on the business of the company and the power to establish subsidiaries of the company.

## Discharge or variation of administration order

Section 18 provides that the administrator may at any time apply to the court for the order to be discharged or to be varied so as to specify an additional purpose. The administrator shall make an application if it appears that the purpose or each of the purposes specified has been achieved or is incapable of achievement, or if he is required to do so by a meeting of the company's creditors summoned for the purpose in accordance with the rules. If an administration order is discharged or varied, the administrator shall within 14 days of the making of the order effecting the discharge or variation send a copy of the order to the registrar of companies[11].

The administrator may at any time be removed from office by order of the court and may in certain circumstances resign his office by giving notice of his resignation to the court[12].

Insolvency Rules r 2.53(1)[13] provides that the administrator may resign on ground of ill health or because (a) he intends ceasing to be in

---

10  Ibid., s 26.
11  Ibid., s 18(4).
12  Ibid., s 19(1) and Insolvency Rules r 2.53.
13  SI 1986 No 1925.

practice as an insolvency practitioner, or (b) there is some conflict of interest, or change of personal circumstances, which precludes or makes impracticable the further discharge by him of the duties of administrator.

The administrator shall vacate office if he ceases to be qualified to act as an insolvency practitioner or if the administration order is discharged[14].

---

14  Insolvency Act 1986, s 19(2).

# CHAPTER 22

# DEBENTURES

## DEBENTURES AND THE LAW OF MORTGAGES

Companies issue shares to raise capital. This is, however, not the only way of raising finance. Companies may also borrow money. They will usually do this by the issue of debentures. Section 744 of the Companies Act 1985 defines debentures as including debenture stock, bonds and any other securities of the company whether constituting a charge on the assets of the company or not. In common parlance, however, a debenture is a secured borrowing.

Companies may have an express power to borrow money in their memorandum. However, insofar as trading companies are concerned, such a power is in any event inferred. Borrowed money is generally termed 'loan capital'. The terms of the loan are set out in a document. This document is also called a debenture.

## DEBENTURES COMPARED WITH SHARES

Debentures and shares do have certain similarities. They are both collectively called securities. Dealings in debentures on the Stock Exchange are carried out in the same sort of way as dealings in shares. Prospectus rules are applicable to both shares and debentures. The transfer procedure for debentures is much the same as for shares.

There are certain clear distinctions, however. The essential distinction is that a debentureholder is a creditor of the company whereas a shareholder is a member of the company.

The company is free to purchase its own debentures.

Debentures can be issued at a discount whereas shares cannot[1].

Dividends are only payable out of profits whereas interest on a debenture is a debt and can be paid out of capital.

---

1    Companies Act 1985, s 100.

# THE LAW OF MORTGAGES

In general the law of mortgages applies to debentures as it does to other mortgages. Certain equitable principles protect mortgagors against 'clogging' of the equity of redemption. These clogs sometimes include making the mortgage irredeemable or redeemable only after a long period of time or providing a commercial advantage to the lender of money. In relation to debentures, there is no rule prohibiting debentures from being irredeemable or redeemable only after a long period. Section 193 of the Companies Act 1985 provides that:

> 'a condition contained in debentures or in the deed for securing debentures is not invalid by reason only that the debentures are thereby made irredeemable or redeemable only on the happening of a contingency (however remote) or on the expiration of a period (however long), any rule of equity to the contrary notwithstanding.'

In *Knightsbridge Estates Trust Ltd v Byrne* (1940)[2], the company which had secured a loan by mortgaging its property to the lender of the money argued that the provision that the mortgage would last for 40 years was void as an unreasonable restriction on the mortgagor. The court held that the mortgage constituted a debenture and therefore it was not void.

## Charges

Although as has been noted s 744 of the Companies Act 1985 provides that any form of borrowing by a company constitutes a debenture, in practice as has been noted the term generally connotes a secured borrowing. There are different types of security that may be employed:

### A fixed charge

A fixed charge is similar to an ordinary mortgage. It is granted over a particular asset or assets identified when the charge is created. Typical examples may include land, buildings or plant or machinery. Fixed charges can only be created over fixed assets and not circulating assets.

It seems however that fixed charges may be created over a company's book debts provided that those book debts are paid into a separate bank account, see *Siebe Gorman & Co Ltd v Barclays Bank Ltd* (1979)[3], *Re Keenan Brothers Ltd* (1986)[4] and *Re New Bullas Trading Ltd*

---

2    [1940] AC 613.
3    [1979] 2 Ll Rep 142.
4    [1986] BCLC 242.

(1993). In the last named case, Knox J held that a charge over the company's book debts constituted a floating charge. This was reversed on appeal.

## A floating charge

A floating charge is an equitable charge over the assets of the company that are subject to change in the day to day operation of the company. It enables the company to raise finance by mortgaging its assets and undertaking back to the provider of finance and at the same time continue to trade. A floating charge does not attach to the property at the time of creation but only on *crystallisation*. Until this time, the company is free to carry on trading with the property subject to the charge, see *Re Yorkshire Woolcombers Association Ltd (Illingworth Holdsworth and Another)* (1904)[5].

Certain events cause the charge to crystallise:

- if the company goes into liquidation;
- if a receiver is appointed either by the court or under the express terms of the debenture;
- if there is a cessation of the company's business;
- if an event occurs which under the debenture causes the floating charge to crystallise.

In relation to the fourth mode of crystallisation, there are conflicting views. The Cork Committee argued against automatic crystallisation. Indeed, there is doubt as to whether the happening of an event causes automatic crystallisation or merely enables debenture holders to act to bring about crystallisation. In the New Zealand case; *Re Manurewa Transport Ltd* (1971)[6] the court held that crystallisation could occur automatically. This view was approved by Hoffmann J in *Re Brightlife Ltd* (1987)[7].

Under s 413 of the Companies Act 1985 the Secretary of State may make regulations requiring that notice should be given to the registrar of companies of events causing automatic crystallisation. The occurrence of such events will not be effective until the required information has been delivered.

---

5    [1904] AC 355.
6    [1971] NZLR 909.
7    [1987] 2 WLR 197.

## Registration of charges

Certain charges require registration as set out in s 396(1) of the Companies Act 1985. These are:

- a charge on land or an interest in land;
- a charge on goods or any interest in goods;
- a charge on intangible property which includes;
  - (a) goodwill;
  - (b) intellectual property;
  - (c) book debts;
  - (d) uncalled share capital or calls made but not paid;
- a charge for securing an issue of debentures;
- a floating charge on the whole or part of the company's property.

Each application to register is free. There is no charge for the certificate issued to the presenter. Copies of the certificate may be obtained for a fee.

## Prescribed particulars

The system of registration is now that prescribed particulars of the charge have to be sent to the registrar. These particulars must be sent within 21 days of the creation of the charge or the date of acquisition if property is acquired which is subject to an existing charge. The prescribed particulars include the date of the creation of the charge or acquisition of the property subject to the charge, the amount secured by the charge, short particulars of the property charged and the person who is entitled to the benefit of the charge. The obligation to register is placed upon the company and therefore if there is a failure to register, the company is guilty of an offence. The registrar on receiving the prescribed particulars files the details on the register and notes the date on which the details have been received.

Any person may require the registrar to provide a certificate stating the date on which the required particulars were delivered and such a certificate is conclusive that the particulars were delivered on or before the date stated.

## Failure to register within time

The company is liable to a fine for failure to register a charge within the prescribed time, s 398(3) of the Companies Act 1985. Furthermore, a charge may be declared void if it is not registered within the prescribed period. Section 399(1) provides that where a charge is created by a company and no prescribed particulars are delivered for registration within the 21 day period, then the charge is void against an administrator or liquidator of the company and any person who for value acquires an interest in or right over property which is subject to the charge. Voidness does not apply where the company has acquired property which is subject to a charge.

This is subject to the provision for late registration of charges under s 400. Where a charge is registered in such a way, the charge is not void against an administrator or liquidator or any person who for value acquires an interest in or right over the charged property unless the relevant event occurs within the specified time. It is no longer necessary to make application to the court by virtue of the changes made by the Companies Act 1989. Where prescribed particulars of a charge created by a company are delivered for registration more than 21 days after the charge's creation, the charge will be registered and the charge is effective from registration, except in two instances set out in s 400(2). These are where the company is at the date of delivery of the particulars unable to pay its debts or becomes unable to do so as a result of the transaction and secondly where insolvency proceedings begin before the end of the relevant period beginning with the date of the delivery. The relevant period is two years in the case of a floating charge in favour of a connected person, one year in the case of a floating charge in favour of an unconnected person and six months in any other case.

## Omissions and errors in registered particulars

Section 402(1) of the Companies Act 1985 provides that where particulars of a charge are incomplete or inaccurate the charge is void pro tanto and to the extent that rights are not disclosed by the registered particulars which would be disclosed if the particulars were complete and accurate. The instrument itself that creates the charge is no longer placed on file and therefore if there is not full disclosure the charge is void if the information on file is incomplete. However, s 402(4) provides that the court may order that the charge is effective against an administrator or liquidator if it is satisfied that the omission or error is not likely to have misled materially to his prejudice any unsecured creditor of the company or that no person became an unsecured creditor of the company at a time when the registered particulars of the charge were incomplete or inaccurate in a relevant respect. Section 402(5) provides that the court may order that a charge is effective against a person acquiring an interest in or right over property subject to the charge if it is satisfied that the person did not rely in connection with the acquisition on the registered particulars which were incomplete or inaccurate in the relevant respect.

The certificate issued by the registrar used to be conclusive evidence that all the requirements relating to registration had been complied with. It is now the obligation of the company or the chargee to check the particulars or to run the risk of the charge being declared void.

## Registration

Section 416(1) provides that a person taking a charge over a company's property is taken to have notice of any matter requiring registration and disclosed on the register at the time the charge is created. This is one of the situations where constructive notice is retained. Section 711A which generally abolishes the doctrine of constructive notice makes an exception in relation to s 416. Section 416(2) makes it clear that this constructive notice only applies to persons taking a charge on company property. A person can still be affected by constructive notice by s 711A(2) if he fails to make such enquiries as ought reasonably to be made.

## The company's responsibilities

The company must keep certain documents at its registered office by virtue of ss 411 and 412 of the Companies Act 1985. The company must keep at its registered office a copy of every instrument creating or evidencing a charge over the company's property as well as a register of all charges whether or not they are charges that have to be registered by the registrar[8]. There is a penalty in default. The register and copies of the instruments are open to inspection by any creditor or member without charge and to any other person on payment of a fee[9]. A copy of such an instrument or entry in the register should be sent within 10 days if requested by any persons[10].

## Memorandum of a charge ceasing to affect the company's property

Section 403(1) provides that where a charge of which particulars have been delivered ceases to hold sway over the company's property, a memorandum to that effect should be delivered to the registrar and be registered. A section is inserted into the Companies Act 1985 by the Companies Act 1989 and the memorandum should be signed by or on behalf of both the company and the chargee.

---

8   Companies Act 1985, s 411(1),(2) and (3).
9   Ibid., s 412(1).
10  Ibid., s 412(3).

## Priority of charges

It must be borne in mind that certain property which is not the company's property is entirely outside the scope of the provisions on priority. This would include property such as hire purchase property, leased property and property where there is an effective retention of title provision.

A floating charge is an equitable charge and does not attach to the property until there is crystallisation. A fixed charge by contrast is legal and attaches to the property from the moment of its creation. It is therefore the case that the fixed charge takes priority over the floating charge where both are properly registered. This is true even if the floating charge was created and registered before the fixed charge. The only exception to this is where a floating charge contains a provision that the company is prohibited from creating a later fixed charge that should rank ahead of it. Such a restriction is termed a negative pledge clause. Section 415(2)(a) of the Companies Act 1985 provides that a negative pledge clause may be included in the required particulars. If this were to be the case, then a subsequent chargeholder would have constructive notice of this provision because it would be a required particular. Until the particular is required, however, there must still be actual notice of the negative pledge before a subsequent chargeholder is bound.

It should be noted that in so far as a floating charge is concerned, preferential creditors are paid off ahead of a floating charge if there are insufficient assets elsewhere to pay off the preferential creditors. The categories of preferential debts are set out in Sched 6 of the Insolvency Act 1986. The categories rank equally and are as follows:

- Pay As You Earn contributions due in the previous 12 months;
- VAT which is due in the previous 6 months;
- car tax due in the previous 12 months;
- general betting duty, bingo duty and pool betting duty payable in the previous 12 months;
- NIC contributions owing during the previous 12 months;
- any sums owing to occupational and state pension schemes;
- wages due to employees for the previous four months up to £800 per employee;
- Any accrued holiday pay owed to employees.

Where there are two or more floating charges over the same assets, then the first in time would generally take priority over later charges. This is subject to an exception where a company creates a floating charge over all of its assets and then subsequently a floating charge over a specific class of assets where the earlier floating charge has left open the possibility of a later floating charge over specific assets taking priority. In this situation, the later floating charge can take priority, see *Re Automatic Bottlemakers* (1926)[11].

## Avoidance of floating charges

When an administration order is made or a company goes into liquidation, there are certain provisions in the Insolvency Act which may have the result of rendering void certain floating charges. Section 245 of the Insolvency Act 1986 deals with this situation.

Where the charge is created in favour of a connected person, then at any time within two years of its creation if insolvency ensues the charge is void unless created for good consideration. In the case of an unconnected person the 'cut-off point' is one year and additionally the company must be unable to pay its debts at the time it is created.

## Transactions at an undervalue

Where a company goes into liquidation or an administration order is made, certain transactions at an undervalue and certain preferences may be re-opened. A transaction is at an undervalue if it is a gift or if property etc is provided for significantly less consideration in value than it is worth[12].

## Preferences

The creation of a charge (fixed or floating) may be a preference if the result is a creditor is advanced in favour of others *not* as a result of commercial pressure. If the person is connected the 'cut-off point' is two years. If the person is unconnected it is six months. In both cases the company must be unable to pay its debts at the time of the creation of the preference[13].

---

11  [1926] Ch 412.

12  Insolvency Act 1986, s 238.

13  Ibid., s 239.

# CHAPTER 23

# RECEIVERSHIP

Where it is intended to enforce the terms of a debenture where there has been a default, the appropriate remedy would generally be to secure the appointment of a receiver. If it is desired to appoint a person under a floating charge, the person appointed would be an administrative receiver and must be a qualified insolvency practitioner[1]. If the person is appointed under a fixed charge, he will be a receiver. He will not need to be a qualified insolvency practitioner. Many of the rules that apply to receivers and administrative receivers are the same.

## ADMINISTRATIVE RECEIVER

The person appointed under a floating charge is termed an administrative receiver. His task is to take possession of the assets that are subject to the charge and to realise them for paying off the secured creditors. He must first secure payment of the preferential creditors.

## RECEIVER

A receiver is a person appointed under a fixed charge. There is no need for him to be qualified as an insolvency practitioner. He also takes control of the assets subject to the charge. He should pay off the chargeholder subject only to a prior claim of his own for the fees relating to the receivership.

Where a receiver is appointed, the business of the company does not necessarily end. The person appointed as a receiver may also act as manager in which case he will have additional powers in relation to the management of the company.

---

1    Insolvency Act 1986, s 388.

# APPOINTMENT

## Administrative receiver

A body corporate cannot be appointed as a receiver[2]. Certain people are disqualified from acting as administrative receivers. An undischarged bankrupt is disqualified from so acting[3]. A person disqualified under the Companies Directors Disqualification Act 1986 is also disqualified from acting as a receiver or administrative receiver.

When a person is appointed as administrative receiver, he must send notice of his appointment to the company and publish the notice in the prescribed form[4]. He must also send notice to all the creditors within 28 days unless the court directs otherwise[5].

Section 47 provides that an administrative receiver must require a statement of affairs in the prescribed form from the directors and others to be provided within 21 days of the request. The statement should set out the particulars of the company's assets, debts and liabilities, the names and addresses of creditors, securities held by them respectively, the dates on which the securities were effectively given and such further or other information as may be prescribed. Section 48(1) of the Act provides that an administrative receiver shall also send to the registrar of companies, to any trustees of secured creditors of the company and to all such creditors (in so far as he is aware of their addresses) a report within three months of his appointment relating to:

- the events leading up to his appointment so far as he is aware of them;

- the disposal or proposed disposal by him of any property of the company and the carrying or proposed carrying on by him of any business of the company;

- the amounts of principal and interest payable to the debentureholders by whom or on whose behalf he was appointed and the amount payable to preferential creditors; and

- the amount if any likely to be available for the payment of other creditors.

He should also within three months send a copy of the report to all unsecured creditors or publish a notice in the prescribed manner giving

---

2    Ibid., s 30.
3    Ibid., s 31.
4    Ibid., s 46(1)(a).
5    Ibid., s 46(1)(b).

the address where copies may be obtained free of charge. He will then lay a copy before a meeting of the unsecured creditors summoned for the purpose on not less than 14 days' notice[6].

## Company stationery etc

In a receivership it must be shown that the company is in receivership on company documents. Section 39(1) of the Insolvency Act provides that every invoice, order for goods or business letter issued by or on behalf of the company or the receiver or manager or the liquidator of the company being a document on or in which the company's name appears, shall contain a statement that a receiver or manager has been appointed.

A committee of creditors may be appointed where there is an administrative receivership. The committee of creditors may require the administrative receiver to attend and supply such information as they may reasonably require[7].

In the case of a simple receiver, s 38 of the Insolvency Act 1986 requires the receiver to deliver to the registrar the requisite accounts of his receipts and payments. These accounts must be delivered within one month after the expiration of 12 months from the date of his appointment and for every subsequent period of six months and also within one month after ceasing to act as a receiver or manager.

## EFFECTS OF RECEIVERSHIP

In every administrative receivership, the administrative receiver will have the powers specified in the debenture[8].

An administrative receiver may apply to the court for an order allowing him to dispose of property subject to a charge as if it were uncharged[9].

An administrative receiver also has the powers set out in Sched 1 of the Insolvency Act 1986.

The basic duty of each type of receiver is the same: it is to collect the assets in in order to realise them and to pay off the debentureholders. An administrative receiver must, of course, first pay preferential creditors out of the proceeds of the sale.

---

6    Ibid., s 48(2).
7    Ibid., s 49.
8    Ibid., s 42.
9    Ibid., s 43.

A receiver (other than an administrative receiver) appointed by a debentureholder is personally liable on contracts he enters into in the performance of his function, although he is entitled to an indemnity out of the company's assets[10].

An administrative receiver is in a similar position[11].

# VACATION OF OFFICE

## Receiver

If a receiver is appointed by the court, he may be discharged on his application or on the application of another person when his duties have been completed.

If appointed out of court, he should notify the registrar on the completion of his duties and give notice to the company and to the persons who appointed him.

The court can remove a receiver whether appointed by the court or not and replace him if he does not carry out his functions in a proper manner.

A receiver appointed out of court may also be removed from office in accordance with the provisions of the debenture under which he was appointed. He may of course resign at any time.

A receiver may also have to vacate office if he is subject to a disqualification order made under the Company Directors Disqualification Act 1986.

## Administrative receiver

Section 45 of the Insolvency Act 1986 provides for the vacation of office by an administrative receiver. Section 45(1) provides that he may be removed by the court at any time and may resign his office by giving notice of his resignation in the prescribed manner to such persons as may be prescribed. Prescribed notice is seven days notice to the company, to the person appointing him and to any liquidator.

Section 45(2) of the Insolvency Act 1986 provides that an administrative receiver must vacate office if he ceases to be qualified to act as an insolvency practitioner in relation to the company.

---

10  Ibid., s 37.
11  Ibid., s 44.

Section 45(4) provides that an administrative receiver who vacates office otherwise than by death shall within 14 days of the vacation of office send a notice to that effect to the registrar of companies.

Once again, if an administrative receiver is subject to a disqualification order under the Company Directors Disqualification Act 1986, he must cease to act as an administrative receiver.

# CHAPTER 24

# LIQUIDATION

The law governing company liquidation is largely contained in the Insolvency Act 1986.

The Insolvency Act 1986 consolidated the law on the subject in the Companies Act 1985 and the Insolvency Act 1985.

## TYPES OF LIQUIDATION

Liquidation or winding up may be broken down into two types:
- compulsory liquidation; and
- voluntary liquidation.

Voluntary liquidation (or winding up) may be further broken down into two types:
- members' voluntary winding up;
- creditors' voluntary winding up.

The procedures and requirements of the different types of liquidation differ in some respects although there are some rules common to all the types of liquidation.

## INSOLVENCY PRACTITIONERS

There is a requirement that only an authorised insolvency practitioner may act as a liquidator and the Insolvency Act has a system for authorising insolvency practitioners.

An insolvency practitioner by virtue of s 388 of the Insolvency Act 1986 is an individual acting as a liquidator, administrator, administrative receiver or as a supervisor of a voluntary arrangement. To be able to act in any of these roles he must be both qualified and authorised to do so.

Section 390(1) of the Insolvency Act 1986 provides that a person is not qualified to act as an insolvency practitioner at any time unless at that time:
- he is authorised so to act by virtue of membership of a professional body recognised under s 391, being permitted so to act by or under the rules of that body; or

- he holds an authorisation granted by a competent authority under s 393.

The intention is that only people who are specialists in insolvency work and demonstrate their fitness to the body of which they are a member may act as insolvency practitioners. Their independence is essential when examining the management of the company's affairs.

Section 391 of the Insolvency Act 1986 provides that the Secretary of State has the power to declare a body a recognised professional body if it satisfies certain requirements. These requirements are that it regulates the practice of a profession and maintains and enforces rules for securing that the persons permitted by its rules to act as insolvency practitioners:

- are fit and proper persons to act; and
- meet acceptable requirements as to education and practical training and experience.

The Insolvency Practitioners (Recognised Professional Bodies) Order 1986 provides that the bodies recognised are:

- The Chartered Association of Certified Accountants;
- The Insolvency Practitioners Association;
- The Law Society;
- The Law Society of Scotland;
- The Institute of Chartered Accountants in England and Wales;
- The Institute of Chartered Accountants in Scotland;
- The Institute of Chartered Accountants in Ireland.

Section 391(3) provides that people subject to the bodies' rules are treated as members even if not actually members.

Section 391(4) provides that the Secretary of State may revoke recognition of the body if it fails to satisfy the requirements.

As already mentioned s 390(2)(b) provides that the other method of becoming qualified to act as an insolvency practitioner is to gain authorisation from a competent authority under s 393.

The competent authority will be authorised by the Secretary of State or may be the Secretary of State himself.

The person wishing to act as an insolvency practitioner must make an application to the competent authority in the form that it prescribes accompanied by any information it requires and a fee[1].

Section 393(2) provides that the authority will grant the application if it appears to it:

---

1    Insolvency Act 1986, s 392.

- that the applicant is a fit and proper person to act as an insolvency practitioner; and

- that the applicant meets the prescribed requirements with respect to education and practical training and experience.

A further requirement to be satisfied before a person may act as an insolvency practitioner is that he must provide the requisite security for the proper performance of his functions. This is provided for in s 390(3) of the Insolvency Act 1986.

There are also provisions for the disqualification of a person to act as an insolvency practitioner. Section 390(4) of the Insolvency Act 1986 provides that a person is not qualified to act an insolvency practitioner at any time if at that time:

- he is an undischarged bankrupt, or sequestration of his estate has been awarded and he has not been discharged; or

- he is subject to a disqualification order made under the Companies Directors Disqualification Act 1986; or

- he is a patient within the meaning of Part VI of the Mental Health Act 1983.

## COMPULSORY LIQUIDATION

Compulsory liquidation is liquidation commenced by order of the court.

It is more expensive than voluntary liquidation but a useful last resort where the company refuses to wind up despite its insolvency and acts against the interests of a creditor or member.

There are seven grounds on which a petition for compulsory winding up may be based. There are specified in s 122(1) of the Insolvency Act 1986:

(a) a special resolution has been passed by the company to be wound up by the court;

(b) the company was formed as a public company and registered yet has not been issued with a certificate under s 117 (to trade) and a year has passed;

(c) it is an old company within the meaning of the Companies Consolidation (Consequential Provisions) Act 1985;

(d) the company does not commence its business within a year from its incorporation or suspends its business for a year;

(e) the number of its members is reduced below two (except a private company limited by share or guarantee);

(f) the company is unable to pay its debts;

(g) the court is of the opinion that it is just and equitable that the company should be wound up.

The most significant grounds are (f) and (g) inability to pay debts and the just and equitable ground.

## Company unable to pay its debts

The Act expands further on this in s 123 of the Insolvency Act 1986 giving a definition and the circumstances in which a company will be deemed unable to pay its debts.

According to s 123(1) a company is deemed unable to pay its debts if:

- a creditor whose debt from the company is worth more than £750 has served a written demand on the company at its registered office and in the next three weeks the company has neither paid the debt nor given security for its payment;

- in England and Wales a judgement has been obtained against the company for a debt and execution remains wholly or partly unsatisfied (the sum of in excess of £750 is not mentioned but this is probably the cut-off point);

- it is proved to the satisfaction of the court that the company is unable to pay its debts as they fall due (the same cut-off is again presumed to apply).

A company is also deemed unable to pay its debts if it is proved to the satisfaction of the court that the value of the company's assets is less than the amount of its liabilities, taking into account its contingent and prospective liabilities[2].

In practice the cut-off point is one of in excess of £750 in each case.

## Just and equitable ground (s 122(1)(g))

This ground allows the court wide discretion and is not restricted by or subject to the other grounds specified in s 122(1) of the Insolvency Act 1986.

The court has used this ground in a number of situations, for example, where:

- the substratum of the company has gone;

- there is a deadlock in the management of the company;

---

2    Ibid., s 123(2).

- there is a breakdown of mutual trust and confidence;
- there is lack of probity on the part of the management;
- there is exclusion from management in a quasi-partnership company.

# WHO MAY PETITION?

There are a number of people who may petition for compulsory winding up. However, their right to petition or grounds upon which they petition may differ.

Section 124 of the Insolvency Act 1986 specifies who may apply to the court for winding up. Section 124(1) provides for:

- the company;
- its directors;
- a creditor or creditors;
- a contributory or contributories.

| | |
|---|---|
| The company | may decide to petition by ordinary resolution. |
| The directors | normally a resolution of the board (most articles provide for a simple majority) |
| Creditors | a creditor will usually petition under s 123 bearing in mind the excess of £750 minimum. |
| Contributories | Section 124(2) provides that in order to be entitled to petition a contributory must have held shares for at least six months out of the 18 months before commencement of the winding up. This does not apply if the ground for winding up is that the number of members is reduced below two. |
| Secretary of State | Section 124(4) of the Insolvency Act 1986 provides that the Secretary of State for Trade and Industry may present a petition to wind the company up on grounds (b) and (c) of s 122(1) and also if following a report made or information received in relation to company investigations or information obtained under s 2 of the Criminal Justice Act 1987 in relation to fraud investigations or under s 83 of the the Companies Act 1989 in relation to assisting overseas regulatory authorities, he thinks that it is expedient in the public interest that a company should be wound up. |

Official receiver            Section 124(5) provides that where a company is being wound up voluntarily in England and Wales a winding up petition may be presented by the official receiver.

# PROCEDURE

The procedure commences when a person entitled to petition presents a petition to the court, supported by an affidavit verifying the grounds upon which he is relying.

Winding up petition:      *Form No 4.2*

Affidavit verifying it:      *Form No 4.3*

The petition will be made to the High Court which has jurisdiction to wind up any company in England and Wales under s 177(1) of the Insolvency Act 1986.

However, where the amount of a company's share capital paid up or credited as paid up does not exceed £120,000 then the County Court of the district in which the company's registered office is situated has concurrent jurisdiction with the High Court to wind the company up[3].

There is provision for the extension or reduction of the County Court jurisdiction under s 177(3) of the Insolvency Act 1986.

The procedure is governed by the Insolvency Rules 1986 as amended.

The procedure followed when a contributory presents a petition for a winding up order differs from that followed by other petitioners. There is no supporting affidavit and directions are required from the court. A contributory petitions on Form 4.14.

As already mentioned, any other petitioner uses *Form 4.2* as prescribed by the Insolvency Rules 1986[4].This petition is accompanied by an affidavit verifying the facts stated in the petition, *Form 4.3*[5].

There is also a requirement that a receipt for the deposit of security for the official receiver's fee issued by the court must also accompany the petition.

Also to be delivered to the court are:

- a copy of the petition for service on the company where it is not the petitioner;

---

3     Ibid., s 177(2).
4     Rules 4.7, 12.7, SCL 4.
5     Rule 4.7 Sched 4.

- a copy to be exhibited to the affidavit verifying service;
- a copy for service on a liquidator (if the company is already in voluntary liquidation), a copy for service on the administrator (if there is an administration order in force), on an administrative receiver (if appointed to realise security) or a supervisor (if there is a voluntary arrangement).

The petition must be served on the company at its registered office if possible or failing that at its last known registered office or principal place of business.

In the case of service at the registered office, it should be handed to a person acknowledging himself to be a director, officer, employee or person authorised to accept service to the best knowledge of the server. If none of these people is present, it may be left at the office in such a way that it is likely to come to the notice of a person attending the office.

Proof of service is by an affidavit in the prescribed form (*Form 4.4*) where served at the registered office (*Form 4.5* if it is not served at the registered office).

There is also a provision for the advertisement of the petition in order to give the creditors and interested parties sufficient time to be represented at the hearing.

The petition must be advertised in the London Gazette not less than seven business days after the service and not less than seven business days before the hearing unless the court directs otherwise. The contents of the advertisement are also regulated (*Form 4.6* advertisement of winding up petition).

The petitioner or his solicitor must file a certificate showing that the requirements of service and advertisement have been met at least five days before the hearing (*Form 4.7*). The petition is heard in open court.

On hearing the petition the court may dismiss it, adjourn it, make an interim order or any order it things fit or an order for compulsory winding up, but it may not refuse to make a winding up order on the ground only that the company's assets have been mortgaged for an amount equal to or more than the assets or that the company has no assets[6].

An order for winding up by the court is made on *Form 4.11*.

The commencement of the winding up of a company by the court is the time of the presentation of the petition for winding up[7].

---

6   Insolvency Act 1986, s 125.
7   Ibid., s 129(2).

If the company had already resolved to wind up the commencement is the time the voluntary liquidation commenced[8].

On the making of a winding up order, a copy of the order must forthwith be forwarded by the company (or otherwise as may be prescribed) to the registrar of companies who will enter it into his records relating to the company[9].

All actions against the company are stayed unless the court gives leave for them to continue or commence subject to any terms it imposes[10].

Any disposition of the company's property, any transfer of shares or alteration in the status of the members made after commencement of the winding up is void unless the court orders otherwise[11]. Also any seizure of the company's assets to satisfy a debt after commencement of the winding up is void[12].

Upon the making of the winding up order the official receiver becomes the provisional liquidator and will continue in office until another person is appointed as liquidator[13].

The official receiver may require a statement of affairs to be made[14]. The people he may require to make out the statement are specified in s 131(3) although it is usually a director or secretary that does so.

The statement of affairs will be made in the prescribed form (*Form 4.17*) verified by affidavit and it must show:

- particulars of the company's assets, debts and liabilities;
- the names and addresses of the company's creditors;
- the securities held by them respectively;
- the dates when the securities were respectively given;
- such further or other information as may be prescribed; or as the official receiver may require[15].

They have 21 days from the notice requiring the statement in which to submit it to the official receiver[16]. (*Note*: the prescribed notice to deponents requiring preparation and submission of a statement of affairs is made on *Form 4.16*).

---

8    Ibid., s 129(1).
9    Ibid., s 130(1).
10   Ibid., s 130(2).
11   Ibid., s 127.
12   Ibid., s 128.
13   Ibid., s 136(2).
14   Ibid., s 131(1).
15   Ibid., s 131.
16   Ibid., s 131(4).

The official receiver may summon separate meetings of the creditors and contributories in order to choose a liquidator to replace him[17].

He must decide if he is to do this within 12 weeks of the order. He must take into account any benefit to be gained from the meetings. It would be pointless to call meetings if he knows nobody will be nominated, for example, and he must consider the cost of the meetings.

However, he may be compelled to hold a meeting on the demand of one quarter in value of the creditors[18] (a request is made by the creditors on *Form 4.21*).

If these meetings are held, both the creditors and contributories may nominate a liquidator. If the people nominated are different, the creditors' nominee generally takes office. However, there is a right of objection. Within seven days any creditor or contributory may apply for an order either appointing the creditors' choice or some other person as liquidator[19].

The general function of the liquidator is to take control of the assets of the company, ensure they are got in, realised and distributed to the company's creditors, any surplus being given to those who are entitled to it[20].

The liquidator has certain powers some of which need the sanction of the court or a liquidation committee.

A liquidation committee may be established at the meetings held to nominate a liquidator or at a subsequent meeting summoned by the liquidator[21].

The committee will consist of three to five creditors if the company is being wound up on any ground. If is not on the ground of insolvency, the contributories may appoint up to three members.

A committee will be established even if one of the meetings think it unnecessary unless the court decides otherwise[22].

The committee will help supervise the winding up, the liquidator will maintain communication through the committee and keep it advised of his activities. He also requires the committee's sanction or the court's sanction before exercising certain powers, such as:

- bringing and defending actions on the company's behalf;
- paying any class of creditors in full;

---

17  Ibid., s 136(4).
18  Ibid., s 136(5)(c).
19  Ibid., s 139(4).
20  Ibid., s 143.
21  Ibid., s 141(1) and (2).
22  Ibid., s 141(3).

- making a compromise with creditors, contributories or debtors.

The liquidator has other powers which he may exercise without requiring authorisation in order to complete the winding up of the company. For example, he may:

- sell the company's assets;
- draw, accept and endorse bills of exchange in the company's name;
- do all such other things as necessary to wind up the company and distribute its assets.

The liquidator will use these powers to effect the winding up of the company and he may call meetings as necessary during the course of the liquidation.

He is under a duty to call a general meeting of the company's creditors when he is satisfied that the winding up is complete. This meeting will receive his report and decide if he should be released from office under s 174 of the Insolvency Act 1986[23].

He must also retain sufficient funds to cover the expense of the meeting[24].

The final step is to seek the dissolution of the company under s 205 of the Insolvency Act 1986.

The registrar of companies must be given notice of the final meeting having been held or a notice from the official receiver declaring that the winding up is complete[25].

The registrar will register the notice and at the end of a three month period from that date the company will be dissolved[26].

There is a way in which the dissolution may be deferred on the order of the Secretary of State[27].

There is also a procedure whereby on certain specified grounds the liquidator may apply for early dissolution of the company.

Section 202(1) of the Insolvency Act 1986 provides that if the official receiver is liquidator and it appears to him that the realisable assets of the company are insufficient to cover the expenses of the winding up and that the affairs of the company do not require any further investigation, he may at any time apply to the registrar of companies for the early dissolution of the company.

---

23  Ibid., s 146(1).
24  Ibid., s 146(3).
25  Ibid., s 205(1).
26  Ibid., s 205(2).
27  Ibid., s 205(3).

He must give not less than 28 days notice of his intention to make the application to the creditors, contributories and administrative receiver if there is one, before making the application[28].

Upon receiving this notice any creditor, contributory or receiver has a right to apply to the Secretary of State for directions that:

- the assets are sufficient to cover expenses;
- further investigation is needed;
- early dissolution is inappropriate for any other reason.

It is the duty of the registrar to register the application for early dissolution and at the end of the three months beginning with the day of registration the company shall be dissolved. It is during this period that any directions from the Secretary of State need to be sought[29].

# REMOVAL AND VACATION OF OFFICE OF LIQUIDATOR

## Resignation

A liquidator may in the prescribed circumstances resign office by giving notice of his resignation to the court[30].

He may only resign on the grounds of ill health, that he intends to cease practice as an insolvency practitioner, a conflict of interest or change of personal circumstances preventing his continuing to fulfil his duties as liquidator or making it impracticable for him to do so, or where he is one of two or more joint liquidators and it is no longer expedient that there should be the same number of joint liquidators.

He must go through the procedure of calling a creditors' meeting and gaining the necessary acceptance.

## Removal

A liquidator may be removed from office by order of the court or by a general meeting of the company's creditors summoned specially for that purpose in accordance with the rules[31].

---

28  Ibid., s 202(3).
29  Ibid., s 202(5).
30  Ibid., s 172(6).
31  Ibid., s 172(2).

A liquidator appointed by the Secretary of State may be removed by him[32].

Section 172(5) of the Insolvency Act 1986 provides that a liquidator, not being the official receiver, shall vacate office if he ceases to be a person qualified to act as an insolvency practitioner.

He will also vacate office following the giving of notice after the final meeting to complete winding up of the company[33].

## Release of liquidator

Section 174(6) provides that when the liquidator has his release under this section, he is, with effect from the time specified in the section, discharged from all liability both in respect of acts or omissions of his in the winding up and otherwise in relation to his conduct as liquidator.

However, he may still be liable for misfeasance under s 212 of the Insolvency Act 1986 despite his release.

# VOLUNTARY LIQUIDATION

There are two types of voluntary liquidation:

- members' voluntary winding up;
- creditors' voluntary winding up.

Section 84 of the Insolvency Act 1986 provides the circumstances in which a company may be voluntarily wound up:

- where the period fixed in the articles for the duration of the company expires or an event occurs on the occurrence of which the articles specify dissolution and the company passes a resolution in general meeting to wind up voluntarily;
- where the company resolves by special resolution to voluntarily wind up;
- where the company resolves by extraordinary resolution that it cannot continue business due to liabilities and it is advisable to wind up.

Therefore, each type of voluntary liquidation commences by passing a resolution in general meeting.

In accordance with s 380 of the Companies Act 1985 a copy of the resolution must be sent to the registrar within 15 days of being passed[34].

---

32 Ibid., s 172(4).
33 Ibid., s 172(8).
34 Ibid., s 84(3).

The next step is for notice of the resolution to be given by advertisement in the *Gazette* within 14 days of being passed[35].

The voluntary liquidation is deemed to have commenced on the passing of the resolution for voluntary winding up[36].

## Members' voluntary winding up

The essential difference between a members' voluntary liquidation and a creditors' voluntary liquidation is that in the former the company must be solvent.

The distinction between the two is that a statutory declaration under Section 89 is required in a members' voluntary winding up but not in a creditors' voluntary winding up[37].

A statutory declaration of solvency is one of the essential first steps in a members' voluntary liquidation.

The directors (or a majority of them in a company with more than two) must make a statutory declaration of solvency during the five weeks before the date of the resolution to wind up or on the date of the resolution but before the passing of the resolution.

It must contain the latest practicable statement of the company's assets and liabilities and state that in their opinion after full inquiry the company will be able to pay its debts within a stated period not exceeding 12 months from the commencement of the winding up[38].

(*Note*: the declaration of solvency embodying a statement of assets and liabilities is *Form 4.70*).

The declaration must then be delivered to the registrar of companies before the expiration of 15 days immediately following the date on which the resolution was passed for winding up[39].

A director commits a criminal offence if he makes a declaration without reasonable grounds[40].

A liquidator is appointed by the company in general meeting by ordinary resolution[41].

---

35   Ibid., s 85(1).
36   Ibid., s 86.
37   Ibid., s 90.
38   Ibid., s 89(1) and (2).
39   Ibid., s 89(3).
40   Ibid., s 89(4).
41   Ibid., s 91(1).

The creditors have no say in the appointment as the company is supposed to be able to pay all its debts in full.

The chairman of the meeting certifies the appointment and the liquidator keeps the certificate as part of his records.

Notice of the appointment must be published in the *Gazette* and delivered to the registrar of companies within 14 days[42]. All creditors must be notified within 28 days.

On the appointment of the liquidator the directors powers cease unless specified otherwise[43].

The general function of the liquidator in both types of voluntary liquidation is to wind up the company's affairs, make full payments to the creditors and distribute the surplus among the members according to their rights and interests in the company[44].

The liquidator may have to call meetings for several reasons in the course of the liquidation.

If the liquidation lasts for more than a year, he must summon a general meeting at the end of each year or at the first convenient date within three months from the end of the year or such longer period as the Secretary of State may allow[45].

The liquidator must make an account of the conduct of the liquidation and call a general meting to lay the account before it and explain it when the company's affairs are fully wound up[46] (the final meeting).

An advertisement in the *Gazette* at least one month before the meeting is the method of calling this final meeting[47].

Within one week after the meeting, the liquidator shall send to the registrar of companies a copy of the account and shall make a return to him of the holding of the meeting and of its date[48]. (Return of final meeting - *Form 4.71*)

There is a provision for the members' winding up to become a creditors' voluntary winding up where the liquidator is of the opinion that the company will be unable to pay its debts in full within the period stated in the directors' declaration[49].

---

42  Ibid., s 109.
43  Ibid., s 91(2).
44  Ibid., s 107.
45  Ibid., s 93(1).
46  Ibid., s 94(1).
47  Ibid., s 94(2).
48  Ibid., s 94(3).
49  Ibid., s 95(1).

The procedure for doing this and the duties of the liquidator are provided for in s 95(2) of the Insolvency Act 1986.

Section 95(2) provides that the liquidator shall:

- summon a meeting of the creditors for a day not later than the 28th day after the day on which he formed the opinion;
- send notice of the creditors' meeting to the creditors by post not less than seven days before the day on which that meeting is to be held;
- cause notice of the creditors' meeting to be advertised once in the *Gazette* and once at least in two newspapers circulating in the relevant locality;
- during the period before the day on which the creditors' meeting is to be held, furnish creditors free of charge with such information concerning the affairs of the company as they may reasonably require.

## Creditors' voluntary winding up

If the company resolves to wind up and no statutory declaration is made, this will be a creditors' voluntary winding up. A creditors' voluntary winding up occurs when the company is insolvent and the views of the creditors are important and regarded as preponderant.

The company will pass an extraordinary resolution to the effect that it cannot by reason of its liabilities continue business and that it is advisable to wind up[50].

At this point the liquidation commences and the company comes under certain duties towards the creditors.

A meeting of the creditors must be held within 14 days of the resolution. The creditors must be given seven days notice of the meeting. Notice must be published in the *Gazette* and in two local newspapers[51].

There are certain matters which must be included in the notice. These are specified in s 98(2) of the Insolvency Act 1986:

- the name and address of an insolvency practitioner from whom the creditors may obtain any information they require before the meeting; or
- the place where in the final two business days before the meeting the creditors may find a list of all the creditors for inspection free of charge.

---

50  Ibid., s 84(1)(c).
51  Ibid., s 98(1)(a)-(c).

The directors are under certain duties in relation to the creditors' meeting[52].

They must make out a statement of affairs in the prescribed form (*Form* 4.19) as to the affairs of the company which must be verified by affidavit[53].

The statement must be laid before the creditors meeting and the directors must appoint one of their members to preside over the meeting[54].

Section 99(2) of the Insolvency Act 1986 specifies the contents of the statement:

- particulars of the company's assets, debts and liabilities;
- names and addresses of the company's creditors;
- securities held by them respectively;
- dates when the securities were respectively given;
- such further information as may be prescribed.

Section 100 of the Insolvency Act 1986 provides for the appointment of the liquidator. Both the members and creditors may nominate individuals but the creditors' choice will prevail unless the court orders otherwise.

The liquidator must then within 14 days of his appointment publish notice in the *Gazette* and deliver a notice in the form prescribed (by the Secretary of State by statutory instrument) to the registrar for registration[55].

He must also within 28 days of the creditors' meeting send a summary of the statement of affairs and a report of the meeting to the company's creditors.

The members may have appointed a liquidator in the period before the creditors' meeting. He will have limited powers until replaced or confirmed by the creditors[56].

Provision is made for the appointment of a liquidation committee consisting of up to five creditors and the members may also appoint up to five of their number subject to any objections by the creditors[57].

---

52  Ibid., s 99.
53  Ibid., s 99(1)(a) Rule 4.34.
54  Ibid., s 99(1)(b) and (c).
55  Ibid., s 109.
56  Ibid., s 106.
57  Ibid., s 101.

Separate meetings of members and creditors must be called by the liquidator if the liquidation lasts for more than a year at which he will lay an account of his actions[58].

As soon as the company's affairs are fully wound up, the liquidator makes up an account of the winding up showing how it has been conducted and how the company's property has been disposed of and he calls a general meeting of the members and a meeting of the creditors to lay the account before them[59].

The meetings are called by advertisement in the Gazette specifying the time, place and object of the meeting and published at least one month before it[60].

Also the liquidator must within one week after the meetings send to the registrar a copy of the account and make a return to him of the holding of the meetings and of their dates[61].

# REMOVAL AND VACATION OF OFFICE OF LIQUIDATOR IN VOLUNTARY WINDING UP

## Resignation

A liquidator may in the prescribed circumstances resign office by giving notice of his resignation to the registrar of companies[62].

He may only resign on the grounds of ill health, that he intends to cease practice as an insolvency practitioner, a conflict of interest or change of personal circumstances preventing him continuing to fulfil his duties as liquidator or making it impracticable for him to do so or where two or more persons are acting as joint liquidators and one of them wishes to resign on the ground that it is no longer expedient that there should be so many joint liquidators.

He must go through the procedure of calling a meeting of members or creditors (as appropriate) and gaining the necessary acceptance.

---

58  Ibid., s 105.
59  Ibid., s 106(1).
60  Ibid., s 106(2).
61  Ibid., s 106(3).
62  Ibid., s 171(5).

## Removal

A liquidator may be removed from office by order of the court or by a general meeting of the company's members or creditors (as appropriate) summoned specially for that purpose[63].

A liquidator appointed by the court where there is no liquidator to act may only be replaced if the liquidator thinks fit or if the court so directs or by a meeting of members in a members' voluntary winding up or of creditors in a creditors' voluntary winding up[64].

A liquidator shall vacate office if he ceases to be a person qualified to act as an insolvency practitioner[65]. Section 171(6) of the Insolvency Act 1986 provides that he will also vacate office following giving notice after the final meeting of members or members and creditors to complete winding up of the company.

## Release of liquidator

Section 173(4) provides that when the liquidator has his release under this section, he is, with effect from the time specified in the section, discharged form all liability both in respect of acts or omissions of his in the winding up and otherwise in relation to his conduct as liquidator.

However, he may still be liable for misfeasance under s 212 of the Insolvency Act 1986 despite his release.

# PROVISIONS COMMON TO ALL TYPES OF LIQUIDATION

## Distribution of assets

The general function of the liquidator is to get in the assets, realise them and use this money to pay the company's debts and distribute any surplus to the shareholders.

The order of payment is as follows:

- the liquidation expenses are paid in the order specified in the Insolvency Rules 1986;

---

63  Ibid., s 171(2).
64  Ibid., s 171(3).
65  Ibid., s 171(4).

- a secured creditor with a fixed charge will have either realised the asset in part or full satisfaction of his debts, or if realised by the liquidator the proceeds will be used to satisfy the debt;
- preferential creditors are paid. They will be paid out of assets subject to a floating charge if other assets are insufficient. The categories of preferential debts are defined in Sched 6 of the Insolvency Act 1986;
- a floating charge that had not already crystallised before the liquidation will be paid out of the assets next;
- unsecured creditors who have proved their debts are paid next eg trade creditors and secured creditors whose security was insufficient;
- deferred debts will then be paid eg a sum owed to a member such as an unpaid dividend;
- if there are surplus funds remaining, these will be distributed to members according to their rights.

## Enforceable debts/proof of debts

The liquidator must ensure that he only pays legally enforceable debts.

There are procedures for creditors to prove their debts and for the liquidator to avoid some debts, reject claims and disclaim onerous property.

The court may fix a time or times within which creditors are to prove their debts or claims or be excluded from the benefit of any distribution made before those debts are proved[66].

The liquidator may be delegated the power to fix the time for proving debts[67].

A creditor may still prove his debt after this time if surplus funds are available and subject to any conditions the court may impose.

Proof of a debt or claim is usually made on the form 'Proof of Debt' (*Form 4.24*) and signed by or on behalf of the creditor.

The liquidator should send out forms of proof to every creditor known to him or identified in the company's statement of affairs. The court may dispense with the need to do this.

Creditors in a creditors voluntary winding up may use any form of proof.

---

66   Ibid., s 153.
67   Ibid., s 160.

## Invalidity of certain floating charges

A floating charge may be invalid in certain circumstances. Under s 245 of the Insolvency Act 1986, a floating charge which is created in favour of a connected person within the period two years before the onset of insolvency is invalid except to the extent that it is made for good consideration or within 12 months of the onset of insolvency if it is made in favour of an unconnected person. If it is made in favour of an unconnected person, it also needs to be demonstrated that at the time that the charge was created the company was unable to pay its debts. This condition does not apply where the charge was created in favour of a connected person.

## Voidable preferences

A preference is an act such as making a payment or giving some other benefit to a creditor which puts him in a better position than the other creditors when it is known that the company is going into insolvent liquidation.

There is a provision in s 239 of the Insolvency Act 1986 for an application to the court by the liquidator or administrator to restore the position to what it would have been if the company had not given that preference.

A number of conditions have to be satisfied.

Section 239(5) of the Insolvency Act 1986 provides that a court order avoiding the preference will not be made unless it is shown that the company was influenced by a desire to produce a preference.

The position is clearer if the preference is given to a person connected with the company. It is presumed unless the contrary is proven that it was influenced by such a desire[68].

A preference may only be avoided if created during time periods specified in s 240 of the Insolvency Act 1986:

- the time period if the person is connected with the company is the period of two years ending with the onset of insolvency;
- the time period is six months ending with the onset of insolvency if the person is not connected;
- the time between the presentation of a petition for the making of an administration order in relation to the company and the making of such an order on that petition.

---

68   Ibid., s 239(6).

(*Note*: connected persons include directors, shadow directors, associated companies etc.)

The court has power to make such order as it things just for restoring the position to what it would have been if the company had not given that preference[69].

## Transactions at an undervalue

Where the company goes into liquidation or an administration order has been made there is a provision for the liquidator or administrator to apply to the court for an order restoring the position if a company has entered into a transaction at an undervalue during the relevant time[70].

Section 238(4) of the Insolvency Act of 1986 provides that a transaction between the company and a person is at an undervalue if:

- the company makes a gift to that person or otherwise enters into a transaction with that person on terms that provide for the company to receive no consideration; or

- the company enters into a transaction with that person for a consideration the value of which in money or money's worth is significantly less than the value in money or money's worth of the consideration provided by the company.

However, s 238(5) of the Insolvency Act 1986 provides that the court will not set aside a transaction at an undervalue if it is satisfied:

- that the company which entered into the transaction did so in good faith and for the purpose of carrying on its business; and

- that at the time it did so there were reasonable grounds for believing that the transaction would benefit the company.

The transaction at an undervalue will only be set aside if it occurred within the period of two years ending with the commencement of liquidation or the petition for an administration order or six months if the other party is unconnected[71].

## Disclaimer of onerous property

The liquidator is given power under s 178 of the Insolvency Act 1986 to disclaim onerous property.

---

69   Ibid., s 239(3).

70   Ibid., s 238.

71   Ibid., s 240.

Section 178(2) of the Insolvency Act 1986 provides that the liquidator may by giving the prescribed notice (*Form 4.53*) disclaim any onerous property and he may do so notwithstanding that he has taken possession of it, endeavoured to sell it or otherwise exercised rights of ownership in relation to it. Onerous property is defined in s 178(3) of the Insolvency Act 1986 as:

- any unprofitable contract;
- any other property of the company which is unsaleable or not readily saleable or is such that it may give rise to a liability to pay money or perform any other onerous act.

There are circumstances in the Act where a liquidator will not be able to issue a notice to disclaim onerous property.

Section 178(5) of the Insolvency Act 1986 provides that a person interested in property which the liquidator has the opportunity to disclaim may apply to the liquidator requiring him to make a decision if he is to disclaim or not.

The person does this by delivering to the liquidator (*Form 4.54 - Notice to elect*).

The liquidator must then either give notice of disclaimer (*Form 4.53*) within 28 days or he loses his right to disclaim that property.

The effect of a disclaimer is stated in s 178(4) of the Insolvency Act 1986. The company loses all interests in the property and the person who suffers loss as a result becomes a creditor of the company for that loss.

## Restriction on re-use of company name

Section 216 of the Insolvency Act 1986 places a restriction on a director or shadow director of a company (in the year before liquidation) that has gone into liquidation becoming a director or otherwise concerned with a company with a similar name.

This prohibition lasts for five years although the person may apply for leave of the court.

The penalty for contravention is imprisonment of up to two years or a fine or both[72].

# MALPRACTICE

Another area of law of importance in a liquidation concerns the penalisation of directors and officers for malpractice. Section 212 of the

---

72   Ibid., s 216(4).

Insolvency Act 1986 provides a summary remedy in winding up where a person who has been an officer, liquidator, administrator or administrative receiver or concerned in the promotion, formation or management of the company has misapplied or retained or become accountable for the company's money or property or been guilty of any misfeasance or breach of any fiduciary or other duty in relation to the company. The court may order repayment of money or restoration of property or such contribution for breach of duty as the court thinks just. It would appear that s 727 of the Companies Act 1985 enabling the court to give relief to any officer does not cover liquidators, administrators or administrative receivers.

A provision of some importance enables the court on the application of the liquidator to declare that any persons knowingly party to the carrying on of the business of a company with intent to defraud creditors or for a fraudulent purpose be ordered to contribute to the company's assets. This is the so-called 'fraudulent trading' section[73]. The Cork Committee had recommended that whilst retaining the high standard of proof for criminal proceedings[74] a lower standard of proof founded on unreasonable behaviour should become the basis for civil liability. In the event a new provision - s 214 of the Insolvency Act -based on unreasonable behaviour - wrongful trading - supplements rather than replaces s 213 of the Act.

Under s 213 actual deceit on the part of the person carrying on the business must be shown. In *Re Gerald Cooper Chemicals Ltd* (1978)[75] it was said that where the company received forward payment for the supply of indigo knowing that it could not continue to trade because of insolvency and used this to pay off part of a loan, the company was carrying on business fraudulently. The person receiving the money was stated to be liable if he accepted money which he knew full well to have been obtained by the carrying on of a business with intent to defraud creditors.

When an order is made on the application of the liquidator the sum which the person is ordered to pay will generally contain a punitive side as well as a compensatory one, see *Re William C Leitch Bros Ltd* (1932)[76], *Re a Company (No 001418 of 1988)* (1991)[77].

Section 214 of the Insolvency Act 1986 extends liability for directors or shadow directors who should know or ought to have concluded that

---

73  Ibid., s 213.
74  Companies Act 1985 s 458.
75  [1978] 1 Ch 262.
76  [1932] Ch 71.
77  [1991] BCLC 187.

there was no reasonable prospect that the company would avoid going into insolvent liquidation. The section is therefore more limited in catchment than s 213 as s 213 applies to any person knowingly party to the carrying on of the business. Furthermore s 214 has no corresponding criminal sanction.

The section was considered in *Re Produce Marketing Consortium Ltd* (1989)[78]. The liquidator of the company sought an order under s 214 of the Insolvency Act 1986 against two directors. The auditors of the company which was in the business of importing fruit had warned the directors of the company's serious financial position. The judge found the directors liable to contribute £75,000. In determining how to decide whether directors ought to have known of the company's position, Knox J had this to say, 'The knowledge to be imputed in testing whether or not directors knew or ought to have concluded that there was no reasonable prospect of the company avoiding insolvent liquidation is not limited to the documentary material actually available at the given time. This appears from s 214(4) which includes a reference to facts which a director of a company not only should know but those which he ought to ascertain, a word which does not appear in s 214(2)(b). In my judgement this indicates that there is to be included by way of factual information not only what was actually there, but what given reasonable diligence and an appropriate level of general knowledge, skill and experience, was ascertainable'.

In *Re Purpoint Ltd* (1991)[79] Vinelott J held a director of the company liable under s 214 where it should have been plain to him that the company could not avoid going into insolvent liquidation. The purpose of an order under s 214 is to ensure that any depletion of the company's assets which occurs after a time when there is no reasonable prospect of the company's avoiding an insolvent winding up is made good. The company's business is being conducted at such a time at the risk of creditors.

As well as the potential liability of directors for matters occurring before the liquidation commences, there are various offences of fraud and deception which may be committed during a liquidation. These include:

- fraud etc in anticipation of a winding up[80];
- past or present officers making gifts or transfers of or charges on company property[81];

---

78  [1989] BCLC 520.
79  [1991] BCLC 491.
80  Ibid., s 206.
81  Ibid., s 207.

- misconduct by past or present officers during the course of the winding up[82];
- falsification, destruction, mutilation etc of the company's books, papers etc[83];
- material omission from the statement relating to company's affairs[84].

82  Ibid., s 208.
83  Ibid., s 209.
84  Ibid., s 210.

# CHAPTER 25

# TAXATION 1 – SOLE TRADER

This chapter considers the taxation implications of setting up as a sole trader, partnership or company.

## SOLE TRADERS

Income tax is charged in respect of a 'year of assessment' (6 April to 5 April).

Section 18(1) of the Income and Corporation Taxes Act 1988 provides for tax to be charged under Sched D in respect of the annual profits or gains arising or accruing:

> 'to inter alios any person residing in the United Kingdom from any trade, profession or vocation, whether carried on in the United Kingdom or elsewhere.'

Tax under Sched D is charged under various cases.

Case I provides for tax to be charged in respect of any trade carried on in the United Kingdom or elsewhere (other than trades carried on wholly outside the United Kingdom, which come within Case V).

Case II provides for tax of any profession or vocation to be charged.

Section 18(1) thus provides for the taxation of annual profits or gains.

In decided cases there is some guidance offered in interpreting the term 'profits'.

In *Re Spanish Prospecting Co Ltd* (1911)[1] in speaking of trading profits Fletcher Moulton LJ said:

> 'The word "profits" has in my opinion a well-defined legal meaning, and this meaning coincides with the fundamental conception of profits in general parlance, although in mercantile phraseology the word may at times bear meanings indicated by the special context which deviate in some respects from this fundamental signification. "Profits" implies a comparison between the state of a business at two specific dates usually separated by an interval of a year. The fundamental meaning is the amount of gain made by the business

---

1    [1911] 1 Ch 92 at p 98.

during the year. This can only be ascertained by a comparison of the assets of the business at the two dates.

For practical purposes these assets in calculating profits must be valued and not merely enumerated. An enumeration might be of little value. Even if the assets were identical at the two periods it would by no means follow that there had been neither gain nor loss, because the market value - the value in exchange - of these assets might have altered greatly in the meanwhile. A stock of fashionable goods is worth much more than the same stock when the fashion has changed. And to a less degree but no less certainly the same considerations must apply to buildings, plant and other fixed assets used in the business, because one form of business risk against which business gains must protect the trader is the varying value of the fixed assets used in the business. A depreciation in value, whether from physical or commercial causes, which affects their realisable value is in truth a business loss.'

Profits are to be computed in accordance with proper accounting principles.

There are obviously detailed rules for the computation of profits which apply for sole traders and for partnerships. It is not proposed to consider these rules in detail but some general points may be made:

- stock and work-in-progress should be valued at cost price or market value whichever is the lower;

- receipts of an income nature are taxable; those of a capital nature are in principle not taken into account in computing trading profits under Sched D. Income payments would include deposit payments and compensation payments made in lieu of trading revenue;

- payments made for 'know how' (as statutorily defined) where a trader is licensing others to use it are treated as income, as in certain cases are payments received on disposal of 'know-how';

- expenditure that is not wholly and exclusively incurred for business purposes is not deductible from profits. There is a considerable body of case law on this area of law, and the decisions are quite restrictive of what is allowable. For example, in *Mallalieu v Drummond* (1983)[2], Ann Mallalieu, the taxpayer, was not allowed to deduct the cost of her court clothes and cleaning bills in computing her profits as a barrister on the basis that the expenditure fulfilled a dual purpose;

- capital expenditure is in principle disallowable but capital allowances are available in respect of certain items of capital expenditure, for example that incurred on construction of an

2    [1983] STC 665.

'industrial building or structure' as statutorily defined or on the provision of plant and machinery to be used in the trade.

In relation to industrial buildings there is a writing down allowance of 4% of the construction cost per annum. The cost of an industrial building would therefore be spread over 25 years. In relation to plant and machinery the taxpayer may enjoy a 25% writing down allowance on a reducing balance basis.

To promote economic recovery between 1 November 1992 and 31 October 1993 in the first year the amount of allowances was temporarily increased to 40% for plant and machinery and 20% for industrial buildings.

Designated 'enterprise zones' are afforded favourable treatment for capital allowance purposes.

Income tax is payable on all of the profits of the trader under Sched D (subject to any allowances to which he is entitled in computing his total income for tax purposes). The lowest rate is 20% going up to 40% at the top rate with an intermediate rate of 25%.

A trader will therefore produce accounts to demonstrate his profit and loss for the year.

Section 60(3) of the Income and Corporation Taxes Act 1988 provides for assessment on a preceding year basis:

Section 60(3) states:

'if -

(a)    an account was made up to a date within the year preceding the year of assessment; and

(b)    that account was the only account made up to a date in that year; and

(c)    it was for a period of one year beginning either -

    (i)    at the commencement of the trade, profession or vocation; or

    (ii)    at the end of the period on the profits or gains of which the assessment for the last preceding year of assessment was to be computed, the profits or gains of the year ending on that date shall be taken to be the profit or gains of the year preceding the year of assessment.'

# COMMENCEMENT

Section 61(1) of the Income and Corporation Taxes Act 1988 provides that where the trade, profession or vocation has been set up and commenced within the year of assessment the computation of the profits or gains chargeable to income tax under Case I or Case II of Sched D is to be made either on the full amount of the profits or gains arising in the year of assessment or according to the average of such period, not being greater than one year, as the case may require and as may be directed by the inspector.

In relation to the second year of assessment, s 61(3) provides that where the trade, profession or vocation has been set up and commenced within the year preceding the year of assessment, the computation of the profits or gains chargeable to income tax under Case I or Case II of Sched D shall be made on the profits or gains for one year from its first being set up.

In the third year of assessment the normal preceding year rule will generally apply[3].

Generally speaking, these commencement rules will not work against a trader setting up in business - certainly not where the profits are rising. However, if profits are falling the commencement rules can work unjustly. For this reason the taxpayer can elect to be assessed for the second and third year of assessment, but not one without the other, on the profits that he makes in these years - on a current year basis. The option is exercisable within six years of the end of the third year of assessment.

# DISCONTINUANCE

If the business ceases, the trader is assessed in the last year of assessment on the actual profits of that year (ie from 6 April to the date of cessation)[4].

The previous two years of assessment will have previously been assessed in the normal way on the preceding year rule. The inspector of taxes may, however, elect to assess on a current year basis for these two years.

Post-cessation receipts, ie monies received after the business has ceased are chargeable to tax under ss 103 and 104 of the Income and Corporation Taxes Act 1988.

---

3    Income and Corporation Taxes Act 1988, s 60(3).
4    Ibid., s 63(1)(a).

These are chargeable under a different Case, namely Sched D Case VI.

*Note*: The Finance Bill, published on 11 January 1994, contains provisions to substitute a current year basis of charging for the preceding year basis. The change is scheduled to have immediate effect for businesses starting after 4 April 1994; existing businesses will move to the new basis as from the tax year 1997-98.

# RELIEF FOR TRADING LOSSES

If the trader makes losses there are various provisions which may help the trader:

- start-up loss relief under s 381 of the Income and Corporation Taxes Act 1988. If a loss is made in the year of assessment in which a business commences or any of the next three years the loss can generally be carried back and deducted from *any other* income of the taxpayer in the preceding three years;

- carry across relief for trading losses under s 380 of the Income and Corporation Taxes Act 1988 and s 72 of the Finance Act 1991. If a taxpayer makes a trading loss in any year it can be carried across to be deducted from *any income or chargeable gains of the taxpayer* of the tax year in which the accounting year of the loss ends;

- carry forward relief of trading losses under s 385 of the Income and Corporation Taxes Act 1988. A trading loss in any year can be carried forward to be set against any subsequent profits of *the same trade*;

- carry-back of a terminal trading loss under s 388 of the Income and Corporation Taxes Act 1988. If a taxpayer suffers a trading loss in the year of assessment in which the trade is discontinued, or a loss in that part of the previous year of assessment beginning 12 months before the discontinuance, the loss can be carried back and deducted from profits of the same trade for the three years of assessment prior to that of discontinuance.

*Note:* Where a taxpayer suffers trading losses as a sole trader and these losses remain unrelieved where he transfers the business to a company wholly or mainly in exchange for shares he may offset the losses against his income from the company provided the company continues to carry on the business[5].

---

5    Ibid., s 386.

# CAPITAL GAINS TAX

If a sole trader disposes of an asset, or indeed of his business, this may have implications in the field of capital gains tax.

Section 1(1) of the Taxation of Chargeable Gains Act 1992 provides:

'Tax shall be charged in accordance with this Act in respect of capital gains, that is to say chargeable gains computed in accordance with this Act and accruing to a person on the disposal of assets.'

Section 21(1) of the Taxation of Chargeable Gains Act 1992 defines assets. It provides:

'All forms of property shall be assets for the purposes of this Act, whether situated in the United Kingdom or not, including:

(a)     options, debts and incorporeal property generally;

and

(b)     any currency other than sterling; and

(c)     any form of property created by the person disposing of it, or otherwise coming to be owned without being acquired.'

Section 22(1) of the Taxation of Chargeable Gains Act 1992 provides that where a capital sum is derived from an asset then there is a disposal of that asset, notwithstanding that no asset is acquired by the payee, eg compensation for loss of, or damage to, assets. There is though an exemption on a person's death when assets are deemed not to have been disposed of but are deemed to be acquired by the personal representatives at market value. Here there will generally be a charge to inheritance tax, though even if there is no charge to inheritance tax there will be no charge to capital gains tax.

The gain is calculated by taking the acquisition cost of the asset or for an asset acquired before March 1982 its market value at that date if higher and adding incidental acquisition and disposal costs and certain costs expended on the asset. This sum is then deducted from the sale price and the difference arrived at is the gain. Indexation by reference to the RPI removes the purely inflationary part of the gain from charge.

If a sale is made at below the price reasonably obtainable there may be a charge to capital gains tax based on the market value of the asset at the date of disposal. This will not apply if there is a genuine sale at below market value - a bad bargain. A disposal between 'connected persons'[6] such as between close relatives is deemed to be made at market value .

---

6     Taxation of Chargeable Gains Act 1992, s 286.

There are certain reliefs which may reduce the tax bill for the taxpayer disposing of his business:

## Retirement relief

This is not confined to retirement and its appellation is therefore misleading. The taxpayer must be at least 55 years of age or alternatively must be retiring before that age because of ill health. There is a minimum qualifying period of one year for which the business must have been owned and maximum relief depends on 10 years' ownership. The maximum relief is:

- full exemption on gains of £150,000, (£250,000 under the Finance Bill 1994 for disposals on and after 30 November 1993); and
- 50% exemption on gains between £150,000 (£250,000 per Finance Bill 1994) and £600,000 (£1,000,000 under Finance Bill 1994 for disposals on and after 30 November 1993).

## Roll-over relief

Roll-over relief is available in a variety of circumstances:

- Relief on replacement of business assets falling into specified categories - eg land and buildings used and only occupied for the purposes of the trade[7].

The new asset does not have to be a replacement asset in the literal sense, provided that it is on the list of qualifying assets. An unconditional contract for the acquisition of the replacement must be entered into within a period commencing 12 months before the disposal and ending three years after it.

- Relief on transfer of a business to a company[8].

If a business is transferred to a company relief is available.

Section 162 applies where a person who is not a company transfers to a company a business as a going concern, together with the whole assets of the business or together with the whole of the assets other than cash, and the business is so transferred wholly or partly in exchange for shares issued by the company to the person transferring the business.

The net gain on disposal of the business assets to the company (ie gains less any losses) is first ascertained. Tax on the whole of the new gain may in principle be deferred until disposal of the consideration

---

7    Ibid., ss 152-158.
8    Ibid., s 162.

shares if the consideration consists exclusively of shares; the proportion of the net gain on which tax may be deferred is proportionately reduced if the consideration includes cash eg if the taxpayer has transferred his business to a company in return for shares with £50,000 and cash of £50,000 the amount of the net gain immediately chargeable is reduced by £50,000 (ie by half of £50,000 + £50,000).

## Relief on re-investment in shares.

This is available from 16 March 1993 where an individual disposes of securities in a qualifying company and then reinvests the proceeds under certain conditions. The relief is subject to a number of conditions. Generally speaking, the companies concerned must be trading (or in some instances the holding companies of trading subsidiaries) and unquoted and must be personal to the individual, ie broadly he must hold or have held 5% or more of the shares and he must have been a full-time working officer or employee of the old company or another company in the same group. Companies carrying on certain trades are excluded. Subject to these restrictive conditions set out in the legislation provided the reinvestment is made within the period commencing 12 months before the sale of the shares and three years afterwards, the cost of the acquisition may be set against the proceeds of the sale[9].

*Note:* Relief is extended in the Finance Bill 1994 to gains on all disposals on or after 30 November 1993 by individuals where proceeds are reinvested in shares in a qualifying unquoted trading company.

# EXEMPTION

Currently the first £5,800 of an individual's net gains are exempt from capital gains tax. There is no facility to carry forward unused exemptions.

## Inheritance Tax

Inheritance Tax is charged on the value of a chargeable transfer, that is, a transfer of value made by an individual other than an exempt transfer. By s 3(1) of the Inheritance Taxes Act 1984:

'... a transfer of value is a disposition made by a person (the transferor) as a result of which the value of his estate (that is, all the

---

9    Ibid., ss 164A-164M.

property to which he is beneficially entitled) immediately after the disposition is less than it would be but for the disposition and the amount by which it is less is the value transferred by the transfer.'

This does not apply to bad bargains (s 10 - dispositions not intended to confer gratuitous benefit).

On the death of any person tax is charged as if immediately before death a transfer of value was made, the value transferred being equal to the value of his estate immediately before his death.

Chargeable transfers made within the seven years ending with the date of transfer are taken into account in computing the tax due. The rate depends on whether the transfer is a lifetime transfer or a deemed transfer on death and, in the former case, on the period which elapses between the transfer and death.

Certain transfers are designated 'potentially exempt transfers' (s 3A of the Inheritance Taxes Act 1984) and normally escape a charge to tax if the taxpayer survives for seven years; this applies to gifts to individuals or into certain types of trust.

Companies do not make 'chargeable transfers'; gifts or other transfers of value by companies therefore do not in principle produce an inheritance tax liability. However, if a close company (principally companies under the control of not more than five persons) make a transfer of value, the value transferred is apportioned among the 'participators' (principally shareholders) in accordance with their interests in the company who may be taxed accordingly. An amount apportioned to a participator which is itself a close company may be apportioned amongst that company's own participators.

However, these rules do not apply to dividends, or to benefits in kind provided for directors or employees brought into charge to income tax under Sched E.

There are certain reductions to the value transferred depending on the nature of the asset.

# CHAPTER 26

# TAXATION 2 – THE PARTNERSHIP

## TAXATION IMPLICATIONS

Partnerships are assessable under s 111 of the Income and Corporation Taxes Act 1988:

'Where a trade or profession is carried on by two or more persons jointly, income tax in respect thereof shall be computed and stated jointly, and in one sum, and shall be separate and distinct from any other tax chargeable on those persons or any of them, and a joint assessment shall be made in the partnership name.'

In other words, although in general schedular income tax is assessed against individuals, in relation to a partnership the assessment is made against the firm. The Finance Bill 1994 contains provisions whereby each partner's share of the profits will be assessed on him individually, rather than the total profits being assessed on the partnership. This applies immediately to any new partnership starting after 5 April 1994. The new rule will apply to existing partnerships with effect from 1997-98. The income of the firm is allocated to each partner in the proportion in which each partner is entitled to share in the profits. If there is no agreement on the point, s 24(1) of the Partnership Act 1890 provides that profits and losses are shared equally.

Income Tax is payable on all of the profits of the partnership under Sched D. The rules for determining profits are as discussed above in relation to sole traders.

## COMMENCEMENT

Section 60 of the Income and Corporation Taxes Act 1988 provides for the preceding year basis as the normal yardstick where a business is carried on in partnership. Section 61 provides that in the first year of assessment the taxpayer is generally assessed on the profits which he actually makes in that year. Then in the second year he is assessed on the profits which he has made in the first 12 months. In the third year the normal preceding year basis generally applies. There is an option for the partners to adopt the current year basis for years two and three (but not for one without the other). This option is exercisable within six years of the end of the third year of assessment.

It may be seen that these commencement rules operate in the same way as the rules for sole traders *mutatis mutandis.*

# CHANGES OF PARTNERS

When there is a change in the firm's membership this will be treated as the discontinuance of one business and the commencement of another[1]. This includes a change from sole trader to partnership and vice versa (as does the election). Where there is a change of partners the old and new partners may, however, elect to be treated as if there had been no discontinuance. The availability of this election is subject to conditions; in particular, there must be one partner common to both periods. If the election is exercised, the profits for the year of change are apportioned between the old firm and the new[2].

On a change of partners if an election could be, but is not, made for continuance of the preceding year basis then the current year basis is to be used for the first four years of assessment[3].

The Finance Bill 1994 contains a provision that a change in partners is not to be treated as giving rise to a discontinuance unless there is an actual cessation.

# PERMANENT DISCONTINUANCE

Where the firm ceases business permanently the normal rules of discontinuance apply. These are that in the actual year when business ceases the firm is assessed on the actual profits of that year. In the penultimate and pre-penultimate years the firm is taxed in the normal way, ie the preceding year basis.

However, the Inspector of Taxes may opt to use the actual profits of the penultimate and pre-penultimate years as the basis of assessment.

The rules on post-cessation receipts apply in the same way as for sole traders (p 252).

---

1   Income and Corporation Taxes Act 1988, s 113(1).
2   Ibid., s 113.
3   Ibid., s 61.

# CAPITAL GAINS, INHERITANCE TAX AND THE PARTNERSHIP

The usual capital gains tax rules apply if the firm makes a disposal of a chargeable asset - such as a gift or more usually a sale.

The disposal is treated as if it were separate disposals by the partners of their interests in the asset. The consideration (or deemed consideration) is then attributed to the partners according to their entitlement. The tax on the gains accruing to each partner is then payable by that partner[4].

Each individual partner will, of course, have his annual exemption of £5,800 to utilise.

Roll-over reliefs may be available if the asset that is sold is an asset falling within certain specified categories, such as land occupied and used only for the purposes of the business, and if the sale proceeds are reinvested in another such asset[5].

Retirement relief on disposals of partnership interests may also be available, subject to certain conditions and roll-over relief may be applicable where a business is transferred to a company (p 156).

Inheritance tax rules apply to the partnership in the same way that they apply to the sole trader *mutatis mutandis*.

---

4    Taxation of Chargeable Gains Act 1992, s 59, Statement of Practice D11.
5    Ibid., ss 152-158.

# CHAPTER 27

# TAXATION 3 – THE COMPANY

Companies, as has been noted, are separate entities. They are taxed as such. Corporation tax is charged on a current year basis on a company's profits (income and chargeable gains).

Section 8(3) of the Income and Corporation Taxes Act 1988 provides:

'Corporation tax for any financial year (1 April to 31 March) shall be charged on profits arising in that year, but corporation tax shall be computed and chargeable (and any assessments shall accordingly be made) by reference to accounting periods and the amount chargeable (after making all proper deductions) of the profits arising in an accounting period shall, where necessary, be apportioned between the financial years in which the accounting period falls (for the definition of an accounting period see s 12 of the Income and Corporation Taxes Act 1988).

The rate of corporation tax for small companies is 25%, otherwise the rate is 33%. A small company is a company with profits not exceeding £250,000 in the accounting period[1]. Marginal relief is available for companies whose profits exceed £250,000 but do not exceed £1,250,000[2].'

## INCOME AND GAINS OF COMPANIES

The rules for assessing liability involve application of the income tax and capital gains tax principles considered above in relation to sole traders and partnerships.

Dividends are not allowable against profits but rather are payable out of taxed profits as will be seen below.

## DIVIDENDS AND OTHER DISTRIBUTIONS

As has been noted, when dividends are to be paid by a company these are not deductible in calculating the company's profits.

---

1    Income and Corporation Taxes Act 1988, s 13.
2    Ibid., s 13.

Indeed when the company pays a dividend it must pay Advance Corporation Tax (ACT) to the Inland Revenue. For the financial year 1994 (year beginning 1 April 1994) the ACT is equal to 25% of the dividend payment. Thus, if a shareholder receives £80 as dividend from the company, ACT of £20.00 is payable to the Inland Revenue. The ACT is credited against the company's corporation tax on its profits for the accounting period in which the dividend is paid. A UK resident shareholder receives a tax credit, generally equal to the ACT on the dividend paid to him, and (unless a company) is treated as receiving taxable income equal to the dividend plus the tax credit (£100 in the above example). An individual shareholder's tax liability in respect of the dividend is satisfied by the credit unless he is liable to higher rate tax (currently 40%).

# CLOSE COMPANIES – TAXATION RULES

## Definition

A close company is defined by s 414 of the Income and Corporation Taxes Act 1988 as (subject to specified exceptions):

- a company which is under the control of;
  - (a) five or fewer participators; or
  - (b) any number of participators who are directors; or
- a company in which five or fewer participators; or participators who are directors, together possess or are entitled to acquire such rights as would, in the event of winding up, entitle them to receive the greater part of the assets available for distribution among the participators, or such rights as would in that event so entitle them if any rights they have as loan creditors (of that or any other company) were disregarded.

The rights of 'associates' are attributed to participators by ss 416(6) and 414(2D) of the Income and Corporation Taxes Act 1988. An associate is defined as:

- the participator's spouse, parent, grandparent or remoter ancestor, child, grandchild or remoter issue, brother or sister;
- the participator's partner;
- the trustee or trustees of any settlement in relation to which the participator or any relative of his within (i) either living or dead is or was a settlor; and
- where the participator is interested, (whether or not beneficially) in any shares or obligations of the company which are subject to any

trust, or are the estate of a deceased person, the trustees of the settlement, the personal representatives of the deceased, or, if the participator is a company, any other company interested in the shares or obligation[3].

Where a close company incurs expense in providing any benefit or facility for a participator or associate of a participator, it is treated as making a distribution (unless the whole expense is made good) and must account for ACT accordingly. There are exceptions to this rule; in particular where the benefit is provided for a director or employee chargeable in respect of it under the 'benefits in kind' legislation (see below), the rule does not apply[4].

Where a close company lends money to an individual who is a participator or an associate of a participator, there is to be assessed on the company an amount equal to such proportion of the loan as corresponds to the rate of ACT for the financial year in which the loan is made. This amount is not actually ACT and therefore cannot be set off in computing the company's corporation tax liability. However, relief by discharge or repayment of tax is available if the loan is repaid.

There are exceptions to this rule in relation to loans made in the ordinary course of a money lending business, and also for loans to directors or employees of the company for not more than £15,000 and if the borrower works full time for the company or an associated company and has no material interest in the company or any associated company. Any other loans made by the company or an associated company must be taken into account in determining whether the £15,000 limit has been exceeded. 'Material interest' principally denotes a holding of more than 5% of the company's ordinary share capital, holdings of associates must be taken into account[5].

## Taxation of directors

The company, particularly if it is a small private family run company, will probably be paying a large proportion of its profits out as salary to its directors and senior employees.

Salaries and benefits received by directors and employees are taxable under Sched E which taxes the emoluments of an office or employment. The rules of taxation make a distinction between, on the one hand directors and employees whose emoluments (including taxable benefits) are at least £8,500 per annum and other employees on the other hand.

---

3   Ibid., s 417(3) and (4).
4   Ibid., s 418.
5   Ibid., ss 419 and 420.

Generally speaking, the former category is taxed on the cost to the employer of providing a benefit, whereas, save where the benefit is covered by some specific rule, the latter are taxed only if the benefit can be converted into cash and on the amount into which it can be converted. Special provisions apply to certain types of benefit, for example, cars and living accommodation.

Employees, in calculating their tax under Sched E, are able only to deduct those expenses incurred wholly, exclusively and necessarily in the performance of their duties. Expenses incurred to enable the employee to perform his duties, such as the cost of travelling from home to his work base, are not deductible.

## System of collection

Schedule E tax is collected at source by the PAYE system (Pay As You Earn system). The Inland Revenue allocates a code number to each employee based on the employee's emoluments and information gleaned from the annual tax return, and the employer deducts tax accordingly which is paid directly to the Inland Revenue. If the employer fails to make the appropriate deductions the Revenue can require him nonetheless to pay the tax.

## Taxation of shareholders

Section 20 of the Income and Corporation Taxes Act 1988 provides for the charge to income tax under Sched F as follows:

'Income tax under this Schedule shall be chargeable for any year of assessment in respect of all dividends and other distributions in that year of a company resident in the United Kingdom which are not specially excluded from income tax, and for the purposes of income tax all such distributions shall be regarded as income, however they fall to be dealt with in the hands of the recipient.'

As stated above, a UK resident shareholder receives a tax credit against his income tax liability which satisfies his liability to tax on the dividend unless he is a higher rate (currently 40%) taxpayer. If the taxpayer is not liable to pay tax he may reclaim the tax from the Inland Revenue.

## Relief on loan to acquire interest in a close company

If a taxpayer is liable to pay interest on a loan taken to acquire ordinary shares in or to lend money for business purposes to a close company which is a trading company then he may, subject to conditions, obtain relief on that interest. The taxpayer must either hold part of the ordinary share capital of the company and have worked for most of his time in the actual management or conduct of the company or an associated company or have a material interest in the company[6]. (Material interest is defined in s 360A(1) of the Income and Corporation Taxes Act 1988.) There is a similar relief where interest is paid on a loan to acquire shares in an employee-controlled company[7]. (An employee controlled company is defined in s 361(5) of the Income and Corporation Taxes Act 1988.)

## Other tax implications for shareholders

### Loans

If the company is a close company and has made a loan to an individual who is a participator in the company and that loan is later waived, he is treated as receiving income equal to the amount waived grossed up by income tax at the lower rate (currently 20%). The gross amount is taxable subject to a credit for the notional lower rate tax. No repayments in respect of this notional tax is made where the individual has insufficient income to be liable for tax (contrast the position with regard to tax credits attaching to dividends).

### Disposal of Shares

If shares are disposed of by a taxpayer then capital gains tax rules on losses and gains are generally applicable (pp 254-255). If shares are sold back to the company, the excess of the sale proceeds over the amount subscribed for the shares is in principle taxed in the same way as a dividend, although there are exceptions to this rule which may apply where the company is an unquoted trading company or the unquoted holding company of a trading group.

If an individual dies leaving shares or if he gives them away or deliberately transfers them at an undervalue, there may be a charge to inheritance tax. Certain lifetime transfers, for example gifts to individuals, do not attract a charge provided the donor survives for seven years. Lifetime gifts will be disposals for capital gains tax purposes (though holdover relief may be available to prevent any immediate charge).

---

6    Ibid., s 360(2) and (3).
7    Ibid., s 361.

## Taxation of debenture holders

Section 18(3) of the Income and Corporation Taxes Act 1988 provides for Sched D Case III tax to be paid in relation to:

'(a)  any interest of money, whether yearly or otherwise,or any annuity or other annual payment, whether such payment is payable within or out of the United Kingdom, either as a charge on any property of the person paying the same by virtue of any deed or will or otherwise, or as a reservation out of it, or as a personal debt or obligation by virtue of any contract or whether the same is received and payable half-yearly or at any shorter or more distant periods, but not including any payment chargeable under Sched A; and

(b)  all discounts; and

(c)  income, except income charged under Sched C, from securities bearing interest payable out of the public revenue.'

This therefore includes payments of interest to debenture holders. Payments to which Sched D Case III applies are taxed on a preceding year basis. (The Finance Bill 1994 provides for a current year basis, subject to transitional rules. There is an obligation on the paying company to deduct basic rate tax - s 349 of the Income and Corporation Taxes Act 1988.)

# CHAPTER 28

# CONTRACTUAL ASPECTS

It is anticipated that students pursuing the business law and practice course have a knowledge of contract law. Here there will be a brief review of the law relating to exemption clauses and then treatment of certain aspects of contracts relating to the sale of goods and relating to the provision of services.

## EXEMPTION CLAUSES

### The common law position

At common law before a person could be bound by an exemption clause, the exemption clause had to be incorporated into the contract. This could be done in various ways:

- The exemption clause could be incorporated into the contract by a written document. The written document, however, had to be a part of the contract. In *Chapelton v Barry Urban District Council* (1940)[1], a ticket was given for the hire of deckchairs. The ticket contained a provision exempting the Council from liability for accident or damage. It was held that the ticket was merely a receipt for the money and was not a part of the contract.

  Sometimes problems arise in relation to machines which 'give' tickets. In *Thornton v Shoe Lane Parking Ltd* (1971)[2], the ticket was dispensed by an automatic machine. It referred to conditions which were set out inside the car park. The Court of Appeal held that the exemption clause could not be a term of the contract. The contract was concluded when the motorist placed his money in the slot and the ticket came too late.

- The party who is bound by the exemption clause might be required to sign a document containing the exemption clause. This is what occurred in *L'Estrange v F Graucob Ltd* (1934)[3]. In such instances, the

---

1   [1940] 1 KB 532.
2   [1971] 2 QB 163.
3   [1934] 2 KB 394.

exemption clause will bind the party signing at common law provided that the exemption clause is not misrepresented to him, see *Curtis v Chemical Cleaning & Dyeing Co* (1951)[4].

- An exemption clause may be made part of the contract by notice. It is important that the notice should be seen before or at the time that the contract is concluded, see *Olley v Marlborough Court Ltd* (1949)[5].

At common law, exemption clauses are applied strictly and if there is any ambiguity, this ambiguity is applied against the person seeking to rely upon the exemption clause, see *Houghton v Trafalgar Insurance Co Ltd* (1954)[6].

## The Unfair Contract Terms Act 1977

The Unfair Contract Terms Act 1977 entered into force on the 1 February 1978. The aim of the Act is principally to limit the scope of exemption clauses in cases involving businesses.

Certain areas are outside the scope of the Act. Such matters as contracts of insurance, commercial charterparties, contracts for the carriage of goods by sea, international supply contracts, contracts of employment and contracts for the transfer of any interest in land are outside the scope of the Unfair Contract Terms Act 1977.

In cases of liability arising from negligence, s 2(1) of the Act provides that liability arising in the course of business or from the occupation of premises used for business purposes for a person's death or personal injury resulting from negligence cannot be excluded or restricted.

Business liability for loss or damage other than for death or personal injury may be excluded or restricted by the person responsible in so far as such exclusion is reasonable[7].

Where a person deals as a consumer or on the other's standard written terms of contract (a person deals as a consumer if he deals as a private individual with a business), then any exclusion or restriction of liability in respect of a breach or a claim to be entitled to render a contractual performance substantially different from that which was reasonably expected or a claim to be entitled to render no performance at all is only valid in so far as it is reasonable[8]. Section 4 of the Act provides that where a person deals as a consumer, he cannot be

---

4   [1951] 1 KB 805.
5   [1949] 1 KB 532.
6   [1954] 1 QB 247.
7   Unfair Contract Terms Act 1977, ss 1(3) and 2(2).
8   Ibid., s 3.

compelled to indemnify another person in respect of the latter's business liability for negligence or breach of contract except in so far as such a term satisfies the test of reasonableness.

Section 6 of the Act restricts the ability of a party to exempt himself from liability for breach of the implied terms in contracts for sale and hire purchase (discussed below). In relation to exclusions of the implied terms to title - these are outlawed completely. In relation to other implied terms - conformity to sample, conformity to description, quality or fitness for purpose - the exclusion is prohibited where the purchaser deals as a consumer and in other situations is only valid if reasonable. Section 7 of the Act provides similarly in relation to contracts of hire and contracts for work and materials.

The question of reasonableness is to be assessed at the time when the contract is concluded[9]. Guidelines are set out in Sched 2 to the Act. These refer to certain factors such as the strength of the bargaining position of the parties, whether the consumer received an inducement to agree to the term or had the opportunity of dealing without such a term, whether the customer knew of the term or ought reasonably to have done so etc.

There is a considerable body of case law in relation to the issue of reasonableness as well as in relation to exemption clauses generally.

# SALE OF GOODS, CONSUMER CREDIT, SUPPLY OF GOODS AND SERVICES

The Sale of Goods Act 1979, the Consumer Credit Act 1974 and the Supply of Goods and Services Act 1982 make provision respectively for these three types of contract. One aim of the statutes is to imply certain conditions into the relevant contracts. Furthermore, the Acts are designed to protect consumers in their dealings with businesses.

## The Sale of Goods Act 1979

The Sale of Goods Act 1979 is a consolidation of the Sale of Goods Act 1893 and the Supply of Goods (Implied Terms) Act 1973. This Act should be read together with the Unfair Contract Terms Act 1977 discussed above. It is proposed here to look at certain key features of the Act.

A contract for the sale of goods is a contract by which the seller transfers or agrees to transfer the property in goods to the buyer for a

---

9    Ibid., s 11.

money consideration called the price. This definition distinguishes a contract of sale from other transactions such as a gift, a contract of barter or exchange, or a contract for the supply of services.

## Implied terms

Certain key conditions are implied into contracts for the sale of goods. Thus s 12 of the Act implies a condition as to title. It has already been seen that this condition cannot be excluded from a contract.

Section 13(1) of the Act implies a term as to description, namely that where there is a contract for the sale of goods by description, there is an implied condition that the goods will correspond to the description. Section 13(2) provides that if the sale is by sample as well as by description, it is not sufficient that the bulk of the goods correspond to the sample if the goods do not also correspond with the description.

Section 14(2) of the Act relates to the implied term as to quality. It is provided that where the seller sells goods in the course of a business, there is an implied condition that the goods supplied under the contract are of merchantable quality except that there is no such condition:

(a) as regards defects specifically drawn to the buyer's attention before the contract is made; or

(b) if the buyer examines the goods before the contract is made as regards defects which that examination ought to reveal.

Section 14(3) of the Act implies a term as to fitness for purpose. Where the seller sells goods in the course of a business and the buyer, expressly or by implication, makes known (a) to the seller, or (b) where the purchase price or part of it is payable by instalments and the goods were previously sold by a credit broker to the seller, to that credit broker any particular purpose for which the goods are being bought, there is an implied condition that the goods supplied under the contract are reasonably fit for that purpose, whether or not that is a purpose for which such goods are commonly supplied, except where the circumstances show that the buyer does not rely, or that it is unreasonable for him to rely, on the skill or judgment of the seller or credit broker.

Section 15 of the Act provides that a contract of sale is a contract for sale by sample where there is an express or implied term to that effect in the contract (s 15(2)). In the case of a contract for sale by sample, there is an implied condition:

(a) that the bulk will correspond with the sample in quality;

(b) that the buyer will have a reasonable opportunity of comparing the bulk with the sample;

(c) that the goods will be free from any defect, rendering them unmerchantable, which would not be apparent on reasonable examination of the sample.

### Passing of property

Where there is a contract for the sale of specific or ascertained goods, the property in them is transferred to the buyer at such time as the parties to the contract intend it to be transferred[10]. There are certain rules set out as to how this intention is to be inferred. These rules are set out in s 18 of the Sale of Goods Act 1979.

- Where there is an unconditional contract for the sale of specific goods in a deliverable state, the property in the goods passes to the buyer when the contract is made.

- Where there is a contract for the sale of specific goods and the seller is bound to do something to them for the purpose of putting them into a deliverable state, the property does not pass until that thing is done and the buyer has notice that it has been done.

- Where there is a contract for the sale of specific goods in a deliverable state and the seller is bound to weigh, measure, test or do some other act or thing with reference to the goods for the purpose of ascertaining the price, the property does not pass until that act is done and the buyer has notice that it has been done.

- When goods are delivered to the buyer on approval or on sale or return or other similar terms, the property in the goods passes to the buyer:

  (a) when he signifies his approval or acceptance to the seller or does any other act adopting that transaction;

  (b) if he does not signify his approval or acceptance to the seller but retains the goods without giving notice of rejection, then if a time has been fixed for the return of the goods on the expiry of that time and if no time has been fixed on the expiration of a reasonable time.

- Where there is a contract for the sale of unascertained or future goods by description and goods of that description and in a deliverable state are unconditionally appropriated to the contract either by the seller with the assent of the buyer or by the buyer with the assent of the seller, the property then passes to the buyer; and the assent may be express or implied, and may be given either before or after the appropriation is made.

---

10  Sale of Goods Act 1979, s 17.

Where in pursuance of the contract the seller delivers the goods to the buyer or to a carrier or other bailee or custodian (whether named by the buyer or not) for the purpose of transmission to the buyer, and does not reserve the right to disposal, he is to be taken to have unconditionally appropriated the goods to the contract.

Section 19 of the Sale of Goods Act 1979 provides for situations of retention of title. Such situations often arise in relation to commercial contracts.

## Retention of title

Sometimes property will not pass in goods even though physical possession of the goods has passed. In *Aluminium Industrie Vaassen BV v Romalpa Aluminium Ltd* (1976)[11], we have a classic exposition of the law in relation to reservation of title. The supplier of aluminium foil in the Netherlands supplied aluminium foil to the company in the United Kingdom. The aluminium foil was supplied on credit terms. The supplier expressly reserved title in the goods until they were paid for. The supplier required the purchaser to store the aluminium foil separately and imposed fiduciary obligations upon the purchaser in relation to the property. Mocatta J held that there was an effective reservation of title. He was upheld unanimously by the Court of Appeal. The relevant clause of the contract of sale provided:

'The ownership of the material to be delivered by [AIV] will only be transferred to [Romalpa] when [it has] met all that is owing to [AIV]. Until the date of payment [Romalpa could be required] to store the material in such a way that it is clearly the property of [AIV].'

Three particular features were stressed in the case:

- there must be a clear and unambiguous reservation of the title in the property;
- the goods must not be inextricably linked with other goods and must be capable of being separated from other people's property;
- a fiduciary obligation must be placed on the purchaser by the supplier. In *Romalpa*, agency and bailment relationships had been created.

The principles in the *Romalpa* case (interestingly Romalpa was the company suffering from the so-called Romalpa clause which was actually a clause in the supplier's terms and conditions) have been applied and refined in subsequent cases.

Section 20 of the Sale of Goods Act 1979 provides that risk passes unless otherwise agreed at the same time as property passes.

---

11   [1976] 2 All ER 552.

## Where the seller has no right to sell

Section 12 of the Sale of Goods Act 1979, as has been mentioned, makes it an implied condition that title should be passed to the purchaser. Where the seller has no title to pass, then in general title cannot pass to the purchaser[12]. This is subject to certain exceptions:

- Apparent authority. The true owner of the goods may be estopped from denying the authority of the seller to pass title[13].

- Sales by factors are not subject to this provision. The power of a factor to pass good title is unaffected[14]. This means that a mercantile agent who is with the consent of the owner in possession of goods or the documents of title when acting in the ordinary course of business may pass title to the goods[15].

- Sales under certain special common law or statutory powers are unaffected. Section 21(2)(b) of the Sale of Goods Act 1979 so provides. Thus, persons who have specific powers such as sheriffs in respect of executions and landlords for goods distrained upon have the power to pass good title.

- In market overt. If goods are sold in market overt according to the usage of the market, the buyer acquires good title to them, if he buys in good faith and without notice of any defect or want of title[16]. Within the City of London, every shop or market constitutes market overt except on a Sunday, whereas elsewhere market overt depends on charter or custom or statute.

- Sale by voidable title. If a seller of goods has a voidable title to the goods and his title has not been avoided at the time of the sale, the buyer acquires good title to the goods if he buys in good faith and without notice of the defect[17].

- Sale by a seller in possession. If a person after selling goods continues to have possession of the goods or of the documents of title, the delivery or transfer by him of goods or documents of title to any person receiving the same in good faith and without notice of the previous sale confers good title upon that person[18].

- A sale by a buyer in possession. Section 25(1) of the Sale of Goods Act 1979 provides for the converse case. Where a person, having

---

12  Sale of Goods Act 1979, s 21.
13  Ibid., s 21.
14  Ibid., s 21(2)(a).
15  Factors Act 1889, s 2(1).
16  Sale of Goods Act 1979, s 22(1).
17  Ibid., s 23.
18  Ibid., s 24 .

bought or agreed to buy goods, obtains, with the consent of the seller, possession of the goods or documents of title to the goods, the delivery or transfer of the goods or documents of title will pass good title in respect of those goods to another person.

- A hirer of goods under a hire purchase agreement is not normally in possession as a person who has agreed to buy so is unable to pass good title under the above exception. However, if the subject matter is a motor vehicle and the hirer sells to a private purchaser who takes in good faith without notice of the hire purchase agreement, title is passed under s 192(3)(a) of the Consumer Credit Act 1974 and Sched 4 para 22.

*Obligations*

## Price

It is the duty of the seller to deliver the goods and of the buyer to accept and pay for them in accordance with the terms of the contract of sale. Section 28 of the Sale of Goods Act 1979 provides that, unless otherwise agreed, delivery and payment are concurrent conditions. If the wrong quantity of goods is delivered, then the buyer may reject them, but if the buyer accepts the goods so delivered, he must pay for them at the contract rate. If the seller delivers a larger quantity of goods than is contracted for, the buyer may accept the goods included in the contract and reject the rest or he may reject the whole[19]. If the seller delivers a larger quantity than is contracted for and the buyer accepts them all, the goods so delivered must be paid for at the contract rate[20].

Notwithstanding the property in the goods may have passed to the buyer, the unpaid seller has a lien over the goods for the purchase price. The seller has the right of stopping goods in transit where the buyer of the goods becomes insolvent[21].

If the buyer fails to pay for the goods that have been passed to him, then the seller may maintain an action for the price of the goods[22].

If the buyer refuses the goods, then the seller may maintain an action for non-acceptance[23].

---

19  Ibid., s 30(2).
20  Ibid., s 30(3).
21  Ibid., s 44.
22  Ibid., s 49.
23  Ibid., s 50.

If the seller wrongfully neglects or refuses to deliver the goods, the buyer may maintain an action against the seller for damages for non-delivery[24].

## The Consumer Credit Act 1974

The Consumer Credit Act 1974 is a complex statute dealing with different situations where money is lent. Previously such situations were covered by many Acts such as the Hire Purchase Act 1965 and the Pawnbrokers Acts 1872 to 1960.

It is not proposed to go into such contracts in detail here. Suffice it to say that implied conditions that apply to contracts for the sale of goods apply in a similar way to contracts relating to consumer credit. Thus there is an implied condition that the owner or seller has the right to sell the goods at the time when the property is to pass. There is an implied condition that where goods are let by description, the goods will correspond with that description. There is an implied condition under a hire purchase agreement that the goods are of merchantable quality and that they are reasonably fit for the purpose for which they are let. Where goods are let by reference to a sample, there is an implied condition that the bulk will correspond to the sample, that the hirer will have a reasonable opportunity of comparing the bulk of the sample and that the goods will be free from any defect rendering them unmerchantable which would not be apparent on reasonable examination of the sample.

A term attempting to exclude the implied condition as to title is void. A term attempting to exclude any of the other provisions is void in the case of consumer agreements and in other situations only valid if fair and reasonable. (*Note:* A 'consumer agreement' is in reality the same as a 'consumer sale'.)

## The Supply of Goods and Services Act 1982

The 1982 Act applies to situations of exchange or barter, contracts for work and materials and contracts for hire and contracts for the supply of services.

With regard to contracts for work and materials where there is a transfer of property, terms are implied in the same way as under the Sale of Goods Act 1979. In relation to contracts for the hire of goods, again similar terms are implied.

---

24  Ibid., s 51.

There is an outright ban on the exclusion of the condition as to title in the context of contracts of exchange and barter and for work and materials but the condition can be excluded if reasonable in contracts of hire.

In the case of other implied conditions an exclusion is not possible if the other party deals as consumer but may be excluded in a pure business deal if reasonable.

With regard to contracts for the supply of services, implied terms are as follows:

- Section 13 provides in a contract for the supply of a service that where the supplier is acting in the course of a business, there is an implied term that the supplier will carry out the service with reasonable care and skill.

- Section 14 provides that where under a contract for the supply of a service by a supplier acting in the course of a business, and the time for the service to be carried out is not fixed by the contract, but is left to be fixed in manner agreed by the contract or determined by the course of dealings between the parties, there is an implied term that the supplier will carry out the service within a reasonable time.

- Section 15 provides where under a contract for the supply of a service, the consideration for the service is not determined by the contract, but left to be determined in the manner agreed by the contract or determined by the course of dealings between the parties, there is an implied term that the party contracting with the supplier will pay a reasonable charge.

The Unfair Contract Terms Act 1977 provides restrictions in relation to exclusion clauses of these terms in contracts for the supply of services in a similar way as for contracts for the sale of goods (s 16).

# CHAPTER 29

# AGENCY

## INTRODUCTION

One element of the syllabus set out by the Law Society for the Business Law and Practice paper requires students to be able to advise on drafting agency agreements. Therefore an outline of some of the principles of agency law is appropriate here.

In its simplest form, an agency exists where there is a 'middle man' (the agent) between the principal and the third party. When A asks B to represent him in dealing with C, then A is the principal, B the agent and C the third party.

Agency may thus be defined as the relationship that exists when one is appointed to act as the representative of another.

The important point to note about agents in the context of business law is that they are in a position to make contracts which bind someone else.

## TYPES OF AGENCY

### Express

Where an agency is created expressly with the consent and wish of both the principal and the agent. Just as a contract can be made orally, an agency requires no formality. However as an intention to create legal relations exists in most situations, agencies are formally created by contract or deed.

### Implied

An agency may be implied from the terms of an agreement. In certain cases the agency itself might be implied. In deciding whether agency by implication exists, all aspects of the relationship between the parties must be looked at. Implied agency derives from the supposed consent of principal and agent.

## Necessity

This arises in emergency situations when a person who acts for another is said to become the latter's agent. Consequently, it may enable the agent to make a contract between the principal and a third party. Agency by necessity arises where an agent is entrusted with another person's property and some emergency arises making it necessary for the agent to act. An example of this arose in *Great Northern Railway Co v Swaffield* (1874)[1] where a horse was sent by railway and on arrival at its destination there was nobody there to collect it. The railway company was an agent of necessity, obliged to store the horse and it could charge for the storage of the animal.

## Apparent/ostensible authority

These are situations where the principal makes representations to the third party, endorsing the agent's authority to act on his behalf. The principal will be estopped from denying responsibility for acts of his agent. It follows that for ostensible authority to exist, three conditions must be satisfied:

- the principal must have made a representation;
- that representation must be relied on;
- the third party dealing with the agent must not know that the agent is acting without authority.

The analysis of the requisite features of agency by estoppel is set out in the company law case of *Freeman & Lockyer v Buckhurst Park Properties (Mangal)* (1964)[2]. Diplock LJ said in that case in the Court of Appeal that there must have been a representation that a person had authority and that representation must have been made by those who had authority within the company. The other party must have relied on the representations in entering into the contract.

## Usual authority

Some jobs carry with them ancillary powers and if an agent carries out such a job, he is deemed to have all the usual authority which goes with the job.

---

1    (1874) LR 9 Exch 132.
2    [1964] 2 QB 480.

# RATIFICATION

If a person acts with no prior authority or alternatively acts outside of the authority given to him, the person on whose behalf he purports to act may *ratify* what he has done. Where this occurs the contract becomes binding on the principal and upon the third party.

# DISCLOSED/UNDISCLOSED PRINCIPALS

A disclosed principal is one whose existence the third party was aware of at the time of contracting.

The disclosed principal is called a named principal if the third party also knew his name, and an unnamed principal if the third party knew of his existence but did not know his name. A principal is undisclosed if at the time of contracting, the third party was unaware of his existence.

# CAN THE PRINCIPAL SUE THE THIRD PARTY?

As a general rule, the principal is entitled to enforce the contract against the third party. This will, however, depend on whether the principal was disclosed or undisclosed. With regard to a disclosed principal, the general rule is that he can sue the third party.

If when dealing with the agent the principal is undisclosed, then if the agent absconds, the third party is free of liability for monies paid to the agent for that is the only creditor of whose existence he was aware.

However, the undisclosed principal can generally claim against the third party provided that the agent had authority to act for the principal and provided that the third party did not wish to deal exclusively with the agent and with nobody else.

# CAN THE THIRD PARTY SUE THE AGENT?

The general rule is that the principal is liable to the third party under the contract. However, where the principal is undisclosed, so that the agent gives the impression of acting on his own behalf, the third party has the option of suing either the agent (with whom he thought he was contracting) or the principal.

He can seek recompense from both but if he receives no recompense, he must choose which to sue, and if the one whom he sues cannot pay, he cannot then sue the other.

# CAN THE AGENT SUE THE THIRD PARTY?

The general rule is that the agent is neither liable nor entitled to enforce a contract which he makes on behalf of his principal. The agent simply disappears as soon as the contract comes into existence between principal and third party.

# TERMINATION OF AGENCY

Termination normally brings to an end an agent's authority to act on behalf of the principal.

If the agency is non-contractual, then either party would be able to withdraw at any time without legal liability. If on the other hand, the agency is contractual, it may be for a fixed term or it might specify a period of notice. If no notice is given in breach of the agreement, the innocent party is entitled to damages.

When either the principal or agent dies, the agency agreement is frustrated as one will not be able to perform without the other. Insanity of either the agent or principal is also likely to end the agency although it seems that a power of attorney may not be terminated by the insanity of the donor[3].

Bankruptcy of the principal or of the agent if central to the performance of the agency will terminate the agency.

# DUTIES IN AN AGENCY SITUATION

Agency may be contractual as has been seen but there may be non-contractual situations governed by general principles of agency. In any event, general agency principles may well be relevant in interpreting an agency agreement. Some of these are set out below.

## Duties of the agent to the principal

- An agent should act in good faith. Thus he must not make a secret profit.
- An agent should obey lawful instructions of the principal.
- An agent should show appropriate care and skill.

---

3   The Enduring Powers of Attorney Act 1985.

- An agent should supply an account when required to do so.
- An agent should act personally and not delegate his tasks unless this is customary or agreed expressly or impliedly with the principal.

## Duties of a principal to the agent

- The principal should pay any agreed remuneration or fee to the agent.
- The principal should indemnify the agent for any expenses incurred in the proper performance of his duties as agent.

# CHAPTER 30

# COMPETITION LAW

## INTRODUCTION

Before examining the substance of Competition Law, it is appropriate, by way of introduction, to have some mention of the spirit and objective of the European Community (now technically the European Union) and its workings vis-a-vis competition law.

European Community law has brought significant changes in the way businesses operate in the Community.

With the ratification of the Maastricht Treaty in all 12 Member States, the Treaty of European Union has come into force with effect from 1 November 1993. The European Community is now officially known as the *European Union*.

European Competition Law is made up of provisions of the Treaty of Rome 1957, regulations made under the authority of the Treaty, decisions of the Commission, the European Court, the Court of First Instance and national courts and notices issued by the Commission.

## RELEVANT ARTICLES OF THE TREATY OF ROME 1957 – GENERAL

There are certain provisions of the Treaty of Rome which have a general impact on Competition Law:

### Article 2

The Community shall have as its task, by establishing a common market and progressively approximating the economic policies of Member States, to promote throughout the Community a harmonious development of economic activities, a continuous and balanced expansion, an increase in stability, an accelerated raising of the standard of living and closer relations between the States belonging to it.

## Article 3

For the purposes set out in Art 2, the activities of the community shall include:

'(g) the institution of a system ensuring that competition in the common market is not distorted.'

# THE PRINCIPLE OF DIRECT EFFECT

The Court of Justice has made it clear that 'as the prohibitions of Articles 85(1) and 86 tend by their very nature to produce direct effects in relations between individuals, the Articles create direct rights in respect of the individuals concerned which national courts must safeguard' (*BRT v SABAM* (1974)[1]).

As Lord Denning MR said in *H P Bulmer Ltd v J Bollinger SA* (1974)[2]:

'Any rights or obligations created by the Treaty are to be given legal effect in England without more ado.'

Accordingly, 'direct effect' is a term used to denote provisions of Community Law which give rise to rights or obligations which individuals may enforce before their national courts.

# RELEVANT ARTICLES OF THE TREATY OF ROME – SPECIFIC

There are certain provisions of the Treaty of Rome which have a specific bearing on the area:

## 1 Free movement of goods

### Article 30

Quantitative restrictions on imports and all measures having equivalent effect shall, without prejudice to the following provisions, be prohibited between Member States.

---

1   (Case 127/73) [1974] ECR 51.
2   [1974] 2 All ER 1226.

## *Article 34*

(1) Quantitative restrictions on exports, and all measures having equivalent effect shall be prohibited between Member States.

(2) Member States shall, by the end of the first stage at the latest, abolish all quantitative restrictions on exports and any measures having equivalent effect which are in existence when this Treaty enters into force.

## *Article 36*

The provisions of Articles 30-34 shall not preclude prohibitions or restrictions on imports, exports or goods in transit justified on grounds of public morality, public policy or public security, the protection of health and life of humans, animals or plants, the protection of national treasures, possessing artistic, historic or archaeological value; or the protection of industrial and commercial property. Such prohibition or restriction shall not, however, constitute a means of arbitrary discrimination or a disguised restriction on trade between Member States.

# 2 Competition policy

## *Article 85(1)*

The following shall be prohibited as incompatible with the common market: all agreements between undertakings, decisions by associations of undertakings and concerted practices which may affect trade between Member States and which have as their object or effect the prevention, restriction or distortion of competition within the common market, and in particular those which:

(a) directly or indirectly fix purchase or selling prices or any other trading conditions;

(b) limit or control production, markets, technical development or investment;

(c) share markets or sources of supply;

(d) apply dissimilar conditions to equivalent transactions with other trading parties, thereby placing them at a competitive disadvantage;

(e) make the conclusion of contracts subject to acceptance by the other parties of supplementary obligations which, by their nature or according to commercial usage, have no connection with the subject of such contracts.

## Article 85(2)

Any agreements or decisions prohibited pursuant to this Article shall be automatically void.

## Article 85(3)

The provisions of paragraph 1 may, however, be declared inapplicable in the case of:
- any agreement or category of agreements between undertakings;
- any decision or category of decisions by associations of undertakings;
- any concerted practice or category of concerted practices which contributes to improving the production or distribution of goods or to promoting technical or economic progress, while allowing consumers a fair share of the resulting benefit, and which does not:

   (a)   impose on the undertakings concerned restrictions which are not indispensable to the attainment of these objectives;

   (b)   afford such undertakings the possibility of eliminating competition in respect of a substantial part of the products in question.

## Article 86

Any abuse by one or more undertakings of a dominant position within the common market or in a substantial part of it shall be prohibited as incompatible with the common market in so far as it may affect trade between Member States.

Such abuse may, in particular, consist in:

(a) directly or indirectly imposing unfair purchase or selling prices or other unfair trading conditions;

(b) limiting production, markets or technical development to the prejudice of consumers;

(c) applying dissimilar conditions to equivalent transactions with other trading parties, thereby placing them at a competitive disadvantage;

(d) making the conclusion of contracts subject to acceptance by the other parties of supplementary obligations which, by their nature or according to commercial usage, have no connection with the subject of such contracts.

# THE ENFORCEMENT MECHANISM

The Commission, which is the Executive of the European Union, is primarily responsible for the enforcement of competition policy.

It is entrusted with the task of implementing and executing Council Decisions, the Council of Ministers being the legislative arm of the Union. The composition of the Council of Ministers changes according to the matter under consideration. If the matter relates for example to transport it would be made up of the transport ministers of the Member States. If the matter concerned agriculture the Council of Ministers would be made up of the ministers of agriculture of the Member States.

The Commission is also responsible for submitting proposals to the Council for legislative action. The Commission is organised into departments called 'Directorates General'. The Directorate General in charge of competition policy is DG IV.

The Court of Justice of the European Union is based in Luxembourg. Of equal importance to the wordings of the various articles of the Treaty is the interpretation made of it by the Court of Justice, and other courts where such matters are heard, in particular the Court of First Instance established in 1989 to consider matters of competition law.

The function of the Court of Justice as set out in Art 164 is to 'ensure that in the interpretation and application of the Treaty, the law is observed'.

Since no definition has been given to many of the terms, a liberal approach has been adopted in its interpretation, with the courts laying emphasis on the spirit and objective of the Community.

Under Art 177, the Court of Justice gives preliminary rulings on points of law, referred to it by Member States. It also hears appeals on Decisions of the Commission.

The Court of First Instance, established in 1989, is testimony to the growing importance of competition law. Its jurisdiction lies principally on matters of competition policy (excluding Art 177 References), but includes hearing disputes between the Community and its servants ('staff cases'). There is a right of appeal from this court to the Court of Justice.

# HORIZONTAL AND VERTICAL AGREEMENTS

European competition law is littered with references to horizontal and vertical agreements so it is worth noting the meaning of these phrases.

'Horizontal' agreements are those agreements between firms on the same level in the marketing chain, eg between competing manufacturers or competing wholesalers fixing prices etc.

'Vertical' agreements are those between firms on different levels in the chain, eg between manufacturer and distributor, or distributor and retailer, setting up an exclusive supply agreement etc.

In general, the Commission and court will look more favourably on vertical agreements than horizontal ones.

# UNDERSTANDING THE ELEMENTS OF ART 85(1)

The key elements of Art 85 should be analysed:

## Undertakings

Any enterprise of commercial activity, whether for profit or otherwise.

## Agreements

Of a general nature including formal or informal, written or oral ones. It ranges from binding contracts to a 'gentleman's agreement'.

## Decisions by association of undertakings

Decisions of groupings, eg trade associations, where members agree on a particular stand, perhaps the pricing of their products.

## Concerted practices

A loose term going further than 'agreements' and 'decisions' by associations of undertakings. It infers a common understanding amongst participants in an industry that one would not act to the detriment of the other as to do so would endanger one's own position, eg price undercutting.

## Affect trade between Member States

To contravene Art 85(1), trade between Member States must have been affected. Any agreement which will exercise a direct or indirect, actual or potential effect on the flow of trade between Member States will breach Art 85(1). It must be noted that the question of effect on trade between Member States is not concerned with the increase or decrease of trade which might result from an agreement but a change in the usual trading pattern between Member States.

## Have as their object or effect, the prevention, restriction or distortion of competition within the common market

Central to competition law is that there should not be a distortion of the normal competition that should exist in the Community. The words 'object or effect' cover agreements that either specifically set out with a practice that restricts competition (object), or those which while not having such an aim, have the effect of producing restrictive competition (effect).

### Block exemptions

There are certain block exemptions from Art 85 expressed in regulations if certain conditions are fulfilled. In addition Art 85(1) does not apply in some situations. It is unlikely to apply to agreements between parent and subsidiary companies, for example. By virtue of a Notice on Agreements of Minor Importance agreements where the effect on trade is *de minimis* are in practice ignored by the Commission.

# UNDERSTANDING THE ELEMENTS OF ART 86

Although the Art is generally perceived as one prohibiting the abuse of power by oligopolies, it includes independent undertakings which collectively hold a dominant position. There are three aspects to the understanding of Art 86:

- there must be a dominant position;
- there must be an abuse of that position;
- the abuse must affect trade between Member States.

Dominance was defined in *United Brands Co v Commission*[3] as:

'... a position of economic strength, enjoyed by an undertaking which enables it to prevent effective competition being maintained on the relevant market by giving it the power to behave to an appreciable extent independently of its competitors, customers and ultimately of its consumers'.

---

3   (Case 27/76) [1978] ECR 207.

## 1 The Relevant Product Market (RPM)

The relevant product market is one in which products are substantially interchangeable. This includes identical products, or products considered by consumers to be similar by reason of their characteristics, price or use.

The Commission and the Court is concerned in maintaining what is known as the cross-elasticity of demand and supply. Cross-elasticity of demand is when the customer, or importer, or wholesaler is able to buy goods similar to those supplied by the dominant firm, or acceptable as substitutes.

Cross-elasticity of supply is when other firms are able to supply or capable of producing acceptable substitutes.

## 2 The Relevant Geographical Market (RGM)

The relevant geographical market is one in which consumers are willing to shop around for substitute supplies, or in which manufacturers are willing to deliver. It may constitute the whole of the common market or a substantial part of it.

## 3 Abuse

Dominance in itself is not an infringement but it is an abuse of that dominance which Art 86 prohibits. The Art provides examples of what constitutes an abuse.

## SANCTIONS FOR BREACHES OF ARTICLES 85 AND 86

The Commission has the power to impose fines for breaches of Articles 85 and 86. The severity of the fine will depend on a number of considerations such as the nature of the infringement; the economic importance and their share of the relevant market; the duration of the infringements; whether the infringements are deliberate, ie intended to restrict competition, or inadvertent; whether the party has already been found to have infringed Articles 85 and 85; and whether the behaviour is open or underhand.

## EXEMPTIONS UNDER ART 85(3)

The prohibition contained in Art 85(1) may be avoided by means of satisfying the requirements for exemption under Art 85(3). Article 85(3), in conjunction with Regulation 17/62, provides that the Commission is able to declare the prohibition inapplicable if the benefits of the agreement, decision or concerted practice concerned outweigh the harm to competition caused by it.

In arriving at its decision, the Commission needs to satisfy itself that the four substantive conditions set out in Art 85(3) are satisfied. These four conditions may be broken into two positive and two negative ones.

## Positive conditions

- 'improving the production or distribution of goods or to promoting technical or economic progress';
- 'allowing consumers a fair share of the resulting benefit'.

## Negative conditions

- must not 'impose on the undertakings concerned, restrictions which are not indispensable to the attainment of these objectives';
- must not 'afford such undertakings the possibility of eliminating competition in respect of a substantial part of the products in question'.

The Commission's approach seems to be that the nature of the agreement and the position of the parties on the market tend to be the most important factors in determining whether an agreement qualifies for an exemption or not. If a party to an agreement wants the benefit of an individual exemption under Art 85(3) application must be made to the Commission giving full details of the agreement and of the parties' business.

# DECIDED CASES

Some exposition of decided cases may help understand the scope of Articles 85 and 86.

## 1 Case law - Art 85

### *Societé Technique Minière v Maschinenbau Ulm GmbH (1966)*[4]

Maschinenbau Ulm GmbH (MU) was a German manufacturer of earth-moving equipment which went into an exclusive distribution

---

4    (Case 56/65) [1966] ECR 235.

agreement with a French distributor, Societé Technique Minière (STM). It contained no restrictions on parallel imports or exports.

The Court of Justice held that in order to ascertain whether an agreement is capable of preventing, restricting or distorting competition, a number of factors must be examined:

- the nature and quantity of the products concerned - the greater the market share held by the parties, the more damaging its impact on competition;

- the position and size of the parties concerned - the bigger they are, in terms of turnover and relative market share, the more likely it is that competition will be restricted;

- the isolated nature of the agreement or its position in a series;

- the severity of the clauses - the more severe the clause, the more likely they will be found in breach of Art 85(1).

The agreement between STM and MU was found on the facts not to breach Art 85(1).

*Comment*: This question of size and scale of an agreement and its operation led to the development of the *de minimis* principle

### Voelk v Establissement Vervaecke Sprl (1969)[5]

This concerned an exclusive distribution agreement between a small German manufacturer of washing machines, Voelk, and a Dutch electrical goods distributor, Vervaecke. The agreement provided for exclusive territorial protection for Vervaecke against Voelk's washing machines in Luxembourg and Belgium. The parties fell out and the Court was asked to decide on the disputed agreement.

It ruled that the agreement was insignificant on the washing machine market in Luxembourg and Belgium. It therefore did not infringe Art 85(1).

### ICI v Commission (Re Aniline Dyes Cartel) (1972)[6]

The case concerned the activities of three leading producers of aniline dyes, one of which was ICI. The three of them had uniform price increases almost simultaneously in 1964, 1965 and 1967.

The Commission investigated the matter and held that they were engaged in concerted practices in the fixing of price increases and imposed heavy fines on them.

---

5   (Case 5/69) [1969] ECR 295.
6   (Case 48/69) [1972] CMLR 557.

ICI disputed this, arguing that this was common practice amongst oligopolies. The Court rejected this and held that whilst parallel behaviour does not in itself constitute a concerted practice, it provides strong evidence of such a practice if it leads to conditions of competition which do not correspond to the normal conditions of the market.

## 2 Case law - Art 86

### United Brands Co v Commission (1978)[7]

United Brands had traditionally sold its bananas to ripeners-distributors in Europe at different prices according to the Member States where the ripener-distributor was established.

The Commission found this practice to be an abuse of a dominant position falling under Art 86(c).

In its decision, the Commission stressed that the bananas in question were all freighted on the same ships, were unloaded at the same cost in Rotterdam and Bremerhaven and were sold under the same conditions of sale and terms of payment.

United Brands argued in its defence that its prices were not discriminatory since they only reflected differences in the anticipated resale price of the bananas among the various Member States due to factors beyond its control such as the weather, the different availability of competing seasonal fruit, holidays, strikes etc.

The Commission and the Court, however, refused to take into account differences in market conditions at the ripener-distributor's level as an 'objective justification' for price differences at the supplier's level.

The Commission and the Court took the view that the price difference fell under Art 86(c) because they put at a competitive disadvantage those of United Brand's customers who wished to sell the bananas in a Member State other than that in which they were established.

*Comment* This case should not be read as meaning that dominant undertakings are in all cases subject to an obligation to charge uniform prices for their products throughout the Union. One of the essential features of the *'Chiquita'* case was that, as the Commission stressed in its decision, the product was sold at the same place at different prices, depending upon the location of the buyer.

---

7    (Case 27/76) [1978] ECR 207.

### *Hoffmann-La Roche & Co AG v Commission (1979)*[8]

La Roche was the world's largest pharmaceutical company, with a dominant position in seven separate vitamin markets. It introduced 'requirements contracts', which made its customers buy all or most of their requirements from La Roche. In compliance with it, customers were given 'fidelity' discounts. This was a case of tying-in practices.

The agreements also provided that if customers found similar products at cheaper prices from other suppliers, they should ask La Roche to 'adjust' their prices.

Although the practice was not oppressive to La Roche's customers, the Commission found the practices to be abusive. This was upheld by the Court, deciding that the tying-in system limited their customers' freedom to buy from competing suppliers.

### *BBC v European Commission (1991)*[9]

Magill TV Guide Ltd, a company incorporated under Irish law, began publishing the weekly television listings for a number of television companies including the BBC, ITV, and RTE an Irish television company.

All three television companies claimed the copyright over the programme listings and argued that they were entitled to the protection of the copyright legislation under British and Irish laws.

The three companies brought injunctions against Magill, to stop publication of the weekly guides.

The Commission found that by withholding their weekly listings of programmes, each of these companies had been guilty of an abuse of a dominant position contrary to Art 86.

On appeal, the Court of First Instance upheld the findings of the Commission and held the companies in violation of Art 86.

## DOMESTIC COMPETITION LAW

The terminology 'domestic competition law' is somewhat misleading as, of course, European Competition Law is as much a part of UK law as domestic legislation but in this context the division into these two categories may assist an understanding of this area of law.

---

8   (Case 85/76) [1979] ECR 223.
9   (1991) *The Times*, 21 October.

There is a fairly complex interlocking web of legislation in the UK made up of the Fair Trading Act 1973, the Restrictive Trade Practices Act 1976 and the Competition Act 1980. Of these statutes, the Restrictive Trade Practices Act 1976 which applies to agreements between businesses which are restrictive of competition is of importance in this context. Where there is such an agreement it should be referred to the Director-General of Fair Trading for registration. If the agreement is not referred for registration the restrictions contained in the agreement are void.

# ANNEX

# REPRODUCTIONS OF FORMS
# REFERRED TO IN THE TEXT

Companies Form No. 6 (p 1)

# G

COMPANIES FORM No 6

## Notice of application to the Court for cancellation of alteration to the objects of a company

# 6

Pursuant to section 6 of the Companies Act 1985

Please do not write in this margin

Please complete legibly, preferably in black type, or bold block lettering

* insert full name of company

To the Registrar of Companies (Address overleaf)

For official use

Company number

Name of company

gives notice that an application was made to the Court on _____

for the cancellation of the alteration made to the objects of the company by a special resolution passed

on _____

‡ Insert Director, Secretary, Administrator, Administrative Receiver or Receiver (Scotland) as appropriate

Signed                    Designation‡                    Date

Presentor's name address and reference (if any):

For official Use

General Section          Post room

300

## Notes

The address for companies registered in England and Wales or Wales is:-

The Registrar of Companies
Companies House
Crown Way
Cardiff
CF4 3UZ

or, for companies registered in Scotland:-

The Registrar of Companies
Companies House
100-102 George Street
Edinburgh
EH2 3DJ

# Companies Form 10 (p 1)

**COMPANIES HOUSE**

# 10

**Statement of first directors and secretary and intended situation of registered office**

CN _____  For official use ☐

Company name *(in full)* _____
_____
_____

**Registered office** of the company on incorporation.

RO _____
_____
Post town _____
County/Region _____
Postcode _____

If the memorandum is delivered by an agent for the subscribers of the memorandum mark 'X' in the box opposite and give the agent's name and address.

☐

Name _____

RA _____
_____
Post town _____
County/Region _____
Postcode _____

Number of continuation sheets attached ☐

To whom should Companies House direct any enquiries about the information shown in this form?

_____
_____
_____  Postcode _____
Telephone _____  Extension _____

Page 1

**Company Secretary** *(See notes 1 - 5)*

| Name | *Style/Title | **CS** |
| | Forenames | |
| | Surname | |
| | *Honours etc | |
| | Previous forenames | |
| | Previous surname | |

**Address** **AD**

Usual residential address must be given. In the case of a corporation, give the registered or principal office address.

Post town

County/Region

Postcode _____ Country _____

I consent to act as secretary of the company named on page 1

**Consent signature** Signed _____ Date _____

**Directors** *(See notes 1 - 5)*
*Please list directors in alphabetical order.*

| Name | *Style/Title | **CD** |
| | Forenames | |
| | Surname | |
| | *Honours etc | |
| | Previous forenames | |
| | Previous surname | |

**Address** **AD**

Usual residential address must be given. In the case of a corporation, give the registered or principal office address.

Post town

County/Region

Postcode _____ Country _____

Date of birth **DO** | | | | | | Nationality **NA**

Business occupation **OC**

Other directorships **OD**

* Voluntary details

I consent to act as director of the company named on page 1

Page 2 **Consent signature** Signed _____ Date _____

303

## Companies Form 10 ( p 3)

**Directors** (continued)

*(See notes 1 - 5)*

**Name**

\*Style/Title `CD`

Forenames

Surname

\*Honours etc

Previous forenames

Previous surname

**Address** `AD`

Usual residential address must be given. In the case of a corporation, give the registered or principal office address.

Post town

County/Region

Postcode          Country

Date of birth `DO`          Nationality `NA`

Business occupation `OC`

Other directorships `OD`

\* Voluntary details

I consent to act as director of the company named on page 1

**Consent signature**          Signed                    Date

Delete if the form is signed by the subscribers.

Signature of agent on behalf of all subscribers    Date

Delete if the form is signed by an agent on behalf of all the subscribers.

Signed                    Date

Signed                    Date

All the subscribers must sign either personally or by a person or persons authorised to sign for them.

Signed                    Date

Signed                    Date

Signed                    Date

Page 3          Signed                    Date

# Notes

1 Show for an individual the full forenames NOT INITIALS and surname together with any previous forenames or surname(s).

If the director or secretary is a corporation or Scottish firm - show the corporate or firm name on the surname line.

Give previous forenames or surname except that:

- for a married woman, the name by which she was known before marriage need not be given,

- names not used since the age of 18 or for at least 20 years need not be given.

In the case of a peer, or an individual usually known by a British title, you may state the title instead of or in addition to the forenames and surname and you need not give the name by which that person was known before he or she adopted the title or succeeded to it.

Address:

Give the usual residential address.

In the case of a corporation or Scottish firm give the registered or principal office.

2 Directors known by another description:

A director includes any person who occupies that position even if called by a different name, for example, governor, member of council. It also includes a shadow director.

3 Directors details:

Show for each individual director their date of birth, business occupation and nationality.
**The date of birth must be given for every individual director.**

4 Other directorships:

Give the name of every company of which the individual concerned is a director or has been a director at any time in the past 5 years. You may exclude a company which either is or at all times during the past 5 years when the person was a director was:

- dormant,

- a parent company which wholly owned the company making the return,

- a wholly owned subsidiary of the company making the return,

- another wholly owned subsidiary of the same parent company.

If there is insufficient space on the form for other directorships you may use a separate sheet of paper.

5 Use photocopies of page 2 to provide details of joint secretaries or additional directors and include the company's name.

6 The address for companies registered in England and Wales is:-

The Registrar of Companies
Companies House
Crown Way
Cardiff
CF4 3UZ

or, for companies registered in Scotland:-

The Registrar of Companies
Companies House
100-102 George Street
Edinburgh
EH2 3DJ

305

# Companies Form No. 12

**G**

COMPANIES FORM No. 12

## Statutory Declaration of compliance with requirements on application for registration of a company

**12**

Please do not write in this margin

Pursuant to section 12(3) of the Companies Act 1985

Please complete legibly, preferably in black type, or bold block lettering

To the Registrar of Companies
**(Address overleaf)**

For official use

For official use

Name of company

\* insert full name of Company

I, _____

of _____

_____

† delete as appropriate

do solemnly and sincerely declare that I am a [Solicitor engaged in the formation of the company]†

[person named as director or secretary of the company in the statement delivered to the registrar

under section 10(2)]† and that all the requirements of the above Act in respect of the registration of the

above company and of matters precedent and incidental to it have been complied with,

And I make this solemn declaration conscientiously believing the same to be true and by virtue of the

provisions of the Statutory Declarations Act 1835

Declared at _____

_____

_____

**Declarant to sign below**

the _____ day of _____

One thousand nine hundred and _____

before me _____

A Commissioner for Oaths or Notary Public or Justice of the Peace or Solicitor having the powers conferred on a Commissioner for Oaths.

Presentor's name address and reference (if any):

For official Use
New Companies Section

Post room

306

COMPANIES FORM No. 30(5)(a)

**Declaration on application for the registration of a company exempt from the requirement to use the word "limited" or its Welsh equivalent**

Pursuant to section 30(5)(a) of the Companies Act 1985

Please do not write in this margin

Please complete legibly, preferably in black type, or bold block lettering

**Note**
This declaration should accompany the application for the registration of the company

* insert full name of company

† delete as appropriate

To the Registrar of Cmpanies
(Address overleaf)

Name of company

For official use

Company number

I, _____

of _____

a [Solicitor engaged in the formation of the above-named company][person named as director or secretary of the above company in the statement delivered under section 10 of the above Act]† do solemnly and sincerely declare that the company complies with the requirements of section 30(3) of the above Act.

And I make this solemn Declaration conscientiously believing the same to be true and by virtue of the Statutory Declarations Act 1835.

Declared at _____

Declarant to sign below

the _____ day of _____

One thousand nine hundred and _____

before me _____

A Commissioner for Oaths or Notary Public or Justice of the Peace or Solicitor having the powers conferred on a Commissioner for Oaths

Presentor's name address and reference (if any):

For official Use
New Companies Section | Post room

**Notes**

The address for companies registered in England and Wales or Wales is:-

The Registrar of Companies
Companies House
Crown Way
Cardiff
CF4 3UZ

or, for companies registered in Scotland:-

The Registrar of Companies
Companies House
100-102 George Street
Edinburgh
EH2 3DJ

# G

COMPANIES FORM No. 30(5)(b)

**Declaration on application for registration under section 680 of the Companies Act 1985 of a company exempt from the requirement to use the word "limited" or its Welsh equivalent**

Please do not write in this margin

Pursuant to section 30(5)(b) of the Companies Act 1985

Please complete legibly, preferably in black type or, bold block lettering

To the Registrar of Companies (Address overleaf)

For official use

Company number

Name of company

* insert full name of company

\* _____

I _____

of _____

and I _____

of _____

† state whether directors or other principal officers of the company

† _____

of the company

do solemnly and sincerely declare that the company complies with the requirements of section 30(3) of the above Act.

And we make this solemn Declaration conscientiously believing the same to be true and by virtue of the provisions of the Statutory Declarations Act 1835.

Declared at _____

Declarants to sign below

_____

_____

the _____ day of _____

One thousand nine hundred and _____

before me _____

A Commisioner for Oaths or Notary Public or Justice of the Peace or Solicitor having the powers conferred on a Commissioner for Oaths.

Presentor's name address and reference (if any):

For official Use

General Section

Post room

309

## Notes

The address for companies registered in England and Wales or Wales is:-

The Registrar of Companies
Companies House
Crown Way
Cardiff
CF4 3UZ

or, for companies registered in Scotland:-

The Registrar of Companies
Companies House
100-102 George Street
Edinburgh
EH2 3DJ

COMPANIES FORM No. 30(5)(c)

# Declaration on change of name omitting "limited" or its Welsh equivalent

Pursuant to section 30(5)(c) of the Companies Act 1985

To the Registrar of Companies
(Address overleaf)

For official use

Company number

Name of company

*

I, _____

of _____

[a director][the secretary]† of_____

do solemnly and sincerely declare that the company complies with the requirements of section 30(3) of the above Act.
And I make this solemn Declaration conscientiously believing the same to be true and by virtue of the Statutory Declarations Act 1835.

Declared at _____

Declarant to sign below

the _____ day of _____

One thousand nine hundred and _____

before me _____

A Commissioner for Oaths or Notary Public or Justice of the Peace or Solicitor having the powers conferred on a Commissioner for Oaths.

Presentor's name address and reference (if any):

For official Use

General Section

Post room

311

Companies Form No. 30(5)(c) (p 2)

**Notes**

The address for companies registered in England and Wales or Wales is:-

The Registrar of Companies
Companies House
Crown Way
Cardiff
CF4 3UZ

or, for companies registered in Scotland:-

The Registrar of Companies
Companies House
100-102 George Street
Edinburgh
EH2 3DJ

COMPANIES FORM No. 43(3)

## Application by a private company for re-registration as a public company

Pursuant to section 43(3) of the Companies Act 1985

**Please do not write in this margin**

**Please complete legibly, preferably in black type, or bold block lettering**

To the Registrar of Companies
**(Address overleaf)**

For official use

Company number

Name of company

\* insert existing full name of company

*

applies to be re-registered as a public company by the name of ø _____

ø insert full name of company amended to make it appropriate for this company as a public limited company

and for that purpose delivers the following documents for registration:

1  Declaration made by a director or the secretary in accordance with section 43(3)(e) of the above Act (on Form No 43(3)(e) )

2  Printed copy of memorandum and articles as altered in pursuance of the special resolution under section 43(1)(a) of the above Act.

3  Copy of auditors written statement in accordance with section 43(3)(b) of the above Act

4  Copy of relevant balance sheet and of auditors unqualified report on it

§ delete if section 44 of the Act does not apply

[5  Copy of any valuation report.]§

† delete as appropriate

Signed                                                    [Director][Secretary]† Date

Presentor's name address and reference (if any):

For official Use

General Section                          |  Post room

313

Companies Form No. 43(3) (p 2)

## Notes

The address for companies registered in England and Wales or Wales is:-

The Registrar of Companies
Companies House
Crown Way
Cardiff
CF4 3UZ


or, for companies registered in Scotland:-

The Registrar of Companies
Companies House
100-102 George Street
Edinburgh
EH2 3DJ

COMPANIES FORM No. 43(3)(e)

## Declaration of compliance with requirements by a private company on application for re-registration as a public company

Pursuant to section 43(3)(e) of the Companies Act 1985

**Please do not write in this margin**

**Please complete legibly, preferably in black type, or bold block lettering**

To the Registrar of Companies
(Address overleaf)

For official use

Company number

Name of company

**\* insert full name of company**

\*

I, _____

of _____

_____

_____

**† delete as appropriate**

**§ insert date**

[the secretary][a director]† of the company, do solemnly and sincerely declare that:

1 the company, on _____ §, passed a special resolution that the company should be re-registered as a public company;

2 the conditions of sections 44 and 45 of the above Act (so far as applicable) have been satisfied;

3 between the balance sheet date and the application for re-registration, there has been no change in the company's financial position that has resulted in the amount of its net assets becoming less than the aggregate of its called-up share capital and undistributable reserves.

And I make this solemn declaration conscientiously believing the same to be true and by virtue of the provisions of the Statutory Declarations Act 1835.

Declared at _____

Declarant to sign below

_____

the _____ day of _____

One thousand nine hundred and _____

before me _____

A Commissioner for Oaths or Notary Public or Justice of the Peace or Solicitor having the powers conferred on a Commissioner for Oaths.

Presentor's name address and reference (if any):

For official Use

General Section

Post room

## Notes

The address for companies registered in England and Wales or Wales is:-

The Registrar of Companies
Companies House
Crown Way
Cardiff
CF4 3UZ


or, for companies registered in Scotland:-

The Registrar of Companies
Companies House
100-102 George Street
Edinburgh
EH2 3DJ

COMPANIES FORM No. 49(1)

# G

## Application by a limited company to be re-registered as unlimited

# 49(1)

Pursuant to section 49(1) of the Companies Act 1985

To the Registrar of Companies
(Address overleaf)

For official use

Company number

Name of company

*

applies to be re-registered as unlimited.

The following documents are attached in support of this application for the company to be re-registered as unlimited:

1. Signed assents by or on behalf of all the members of the company (Form No. 49(8)(a) )

2. A statutory declaration made by the directors of the company in compliance with section 49(8)(b) of the above Act§

3. A printed copy of the company's memorandum incorporating the alterations set out overleaf

4. [A printed copy of the company's articles incorporating the alterations set out overleaf]†[Printed articles for registration, the company not having previously registered articles].†

Nominal share capital (if any) provided for in the articles as altered

£

Signed                                         [Director][Secretary]† Date

Presentor's name address and reference (if any):

For official Use

General Section                 Post room

Page 1

# Companies Form No. 49(1) (p 2)

Alterations in the memorandum

Alterations in the articles

NOTE

The address for companies registered in England and Wales or Wales is:-
The Registrar of Companies, Companies House, Crown Way, Maindy, Cardiff CF4 3UZ

or, for companies registered in Scotland:-
The Registrar of Companies, Companies Registration Office, 102 George Street, Edinburgh EH2 3DJ

Page 2

318

COMPANIES FORM No. 51

## Application by an unlimited company to be re-registered as limited

Please do not
write in
this margin

Pursuant to section 51(4) of the Companies Act 1985

Please complete
legibly, preferably
in black type or,
bold block lettering

To the Registrar of Companies
**(Address overleaf)**

For official use

Company number

Name of company

\*

\* insert full name
of company

applies to be re-registered as limited.

A Special Resolution authorising the re-registration of the company as limited was

passed on _____ .The

following documents are attached in support of this application for the company to be re-registered as

limited

1 A copy of the Special Resolution (unless previously presented for registration)

2 A printed copy of the memorandum as altered in pursuance of the Special Resolution

3 A printed copy of the articles as altered in pursuance of the Special Resolution

Nominal share capital (if any) provided for
in the memorandum as altered

£

† delete as
appropriate

Signed

[Director][Secretary]†Date

Presentor's name address and
reference (if any):

For official Use

General Section

Post room

319

# Companies Form No. 51 (p 2)

## Notes

The address for companies registered in England and Wales or Wales is:-

The Registrar of Companies
Companies House
Crown Way
Cardiff
CF4 3UZ


or, for companies registered in Scotland:-

The Registrar of Companies
Companies House
100-102 George Street
Edinburgh
EH2 3DJ

COMPANIES FORM No.53

## Application by a public company for re-registration as a private company

Please do not write in this margin

Pursuant to section 53 of the Companies Act 1985

**Please complete legibly, preferably in black type, or bold block lettering**

To the Registrar of Companies
(Address overleaf)

For official use

Company number

Name of company

* insert existing full name of company

* 

§ insert full name of company amended to make it appropriate for this company as a private limited company

applies to be re-registered as a private company by the name of§

_____

_____

ø delete if previously presented for registration

and, for that purpose, delivers the following document(s) for registration:

[1 Copy of the special resolution that the company be re-registered as a private company.]ø

2 Printed copy of the memorandum and articles of association as altered by the special resolution that the company be re-registered

† delete as appropriate

Signed

[Director][Secretary]† Date

Presentor's name address and reference (if any):

For official Use
General Section

Post room

# Companies Form No. 53 (p 1)

## Notes

The address for companies registered in England and Wales or Wales is:-

The Registrar of Companies
Companies House
Crown Way
Cardiff
CF4 3UZ


or, for companies registered in Scotland:-

The Registrar of Companies
Companies House
100-102 George Street
Edinburgh
EH2 3DJ

COMPANIES FORM No. 54

## Notice of application made to the Court for the cancellation of a special resolution regarding re-registration

**54**

Please do not write in this margin

Pursuant to section 54(4) of the Companies Act 1985

Please complete legibly, preferably in black type, or bold block lettering

To the Registrar of Companies
**(Address overleaf)**

For official use

Company number

Name of company

\* insert full name of company

*

gives notice that an application has been made to the Court under section 54(1) of the above Act for the cancellation of the special resolution dated _____ that the company be re-registered under section 53(1) as a private company.

‡ Insert
Director,
Secretary,
Administrator,
Administrative
Receiver or
Receiver
(Scotland) as
appropriate

Signed

Designation‡

Date

Presentor's name address and reference (if any):

For official Use
General Section | Post room

Companies Form No. 54 (p 2)

**Notes**

The address for companies registered in England and Wales or Wales is:-

The Registrar of Companies
Companies House
Crown Way
Cardiff
CF4 3UZ


or, for companies registered in Scotland:-

The Registrar of Companies
Companies House
100-102 George Street
Edinburgh
EH2 3DJ

**COMPANIES FORM No. 88(2)(Rev 1988)**

## Return of allotments of shares

Pursuant to section 88(2) of the Companies Act 1985 (the Act)

**88(2)**

To the Registrar of Companies (address overleaf)
(see note 1)

**(REVISED 1988)**

This form replaces forms
PUC2, PUC3 and 88(2)

Please do not write in this margin

Please complete legibly, preferably in black type, or bold block lettering

\* insert full name of company

† distinguish between ordinary preference, etc.

§ complete (a) or (b) as appropriate

Company number

1. Name of company

\*

2. This section must be completed for all allotments

| Description of shares † | | | |
|---|---|---|---|
| A Number allotted | | | |
| B Nominal value of each | £ | £ | £ |
| C Total amount (if any) paid or due and payable on each share (including premium if any) | £ | £ | £ |

Date(s) on which the shares were allotted

(a) [on _____ 19 _____ ] §, or

(b) [from _____ 19 _____ to _____ 19 _____ ] §

The names and addresses of the allottees and the number of shares allotted to each should be given overleaf

3. If the allotment is wholly or partly other than for cash the following information must be given
(see notes 2 & 3)

| D Extent to which each share is to be treated as paid up. Please use percentage. | | | |
|---|---|---|---|

E Consideration for which the shares were allotted _____

**NOTES**

1. This form should be delivered to the Registrar of Companies within one month of the (first) date of allotment.

2. If the allotment is wholly or partly other than for cash, the company must deliver to the registrar a return containing the information at D & E. The company may deliver this information by completing D & E and the delivery of the information must be accompanied by the duly stamped contract required by section 88(2)(b) of the Act or by the duly stamped prescribed particulars required by section 88(3) (Form No 88(3)).

3. Details of bonus issues should be included only in section 2.

Presentor's name address, telephone number and reference (if any):

For official use

Post room

Page 1

# Companies Form No. 88(2) (p 2)

4. Names and addresses of the allottees

| Names and Addresses | Number of shares allotted | | |
| --- | --- | --- | --- |
| | Ordinary | Preference | Other |
| | | | |
| | | | |
| | | | |
| | | | |
| | | | |
| | | | |
| | | | |
| | | | |
| | | | |
| | | | |
| | | | |
| | | | |
| | | | |
| | | | |
| | | | |
| | | | |
| | | | |
| | | | |
| | | | |
| | | | |
| | | | |
| | | | |
| | | | |
| | | | |
| | | | |
| | | | |
| | | | |
| | | | |
| | | | |
| Total | | | |

Where the space given on this form is inadequate, continuation sheets should be used and the number of sheets attached should be indicated in the box opposite:

‡ Insert Director, Secretary, Administrator, Administrative Receiver or Receiver (Scotland) as appropriate

Signed_____Designation‡ _____Date_____

Companies registered in England and Wales or Wales should deliver this form to:-

The Registrar of Companies
Companies House
Crown Way
Cardiff
CF4 3UZ

Companies registered in Scotland should deliver this form to:-

The Registrar of Companies
Companies House
100-102 George Street
Edinburgh
EH2 3DJ

Page 2

COMPANIES FORM No. 88(3)

# Particulars of a contract relating to shares allotted as fully or partly paid up otherwise than in cash

# 88(3)

Pursuant to section 88(3) of the Companies Act 1985

**Please do not write in this margin**

**Note: This form is only for use when the contract has not been reduced to writing**

**Please complete legibly, preferably in black type, or bold block lettering**

To the Registrar of Companies
(Address overleaf)

For official use

Company number

**Please do not write in the space below. For Inland Revenue use only**

The particulars must be stamped with the same stamp duty as would have been payable if the contract had been reduced to writing. A reduced rate of ad valorem duty may be available if this form is properly certified at the appropriate amount.

Name of company

**\* insert full name of company**

*

gives the following particulars of a contract which has not been reduced to writing

| 1 The number of shares allotted as fully or partly paid up otherwise than in cash | |
|---|---|

| 2 The nominal value of each such share | £ |
|---|---|

| 3a The amount of such nominal value to be considered as paid up on each share otherwise than in cash | £ |
|---|---|
| b The value of each share allotted i.e. the nominal value and any premium | £ |
| c The amount to be considered as paid up in respect of b | £ |

| 4 If the consideration for the allotment of such shares is services, or any consideration other than that mentioned below in 8, state the nature and amount of such consideration, and the number of shares allotted | |
|---|---|

Presentor's name address and reference (if any):

For official Use

Capital Section

Post room

Page 1

## Companies Form No. 88(3) (p 2)

**5** If the allotment is a bonus issue, state the amount of reserves capitalised in respect of this issue

£

**6** If the allotment is made in consideration of the release of a debt, e.g., a director's loan account, state the amount released

£

**7** If the allotment is made in connection with the conversion of loan stock, state the amount of stock converted in respect of this issue

£

**8** If the allotment is made in satisfaction or part satisfaction of the purchase price of property, give below:

**a** brief description of property:

| **b** full particulars of the manner in which the purchase price is to be satisfied | £ | p |
|---|---|---|
| Amount of consideration payable in cash or bills ........... | | |
| Amount of consideration payable in debentures, etc...... | | |
| Amount of consideration payable in shares .................... | | |
| | | |
| Liabilities of the vendor assumed by the purchaser: | | |
| Amounts due on mortgages of freeholds and/or | | |
| leaseholds including interest to date of sale .................. | | |
| Hire purchase etc debts in respect of goods acquired ... | | |
| Other liabilities of the vendor,............................................ | | |
| Any other consideration ................................................. | | |

9 Give full particulars in the form of the following table, of the property which is the subject of the sale, showing in detail how the total purchase price is apportioned between the respective heads:

£

Legal estates in freehold property and fixed plant and machinery and other fixtures thereon* .......................................

Legal estates in leasehold property* .........................................

Fixed plant and machinery on leasehold property (including

tenants', trade and other fixtures) ...........................................

Equitable interests in freehold or leasehold property* ...........

Loose plant and machinery, stock-in-trade and other chattels

(plant and machinery should not be included under this head

unless it was in actual state of severance on the date of the

sale) ........................................................................................

Goods, wares and merchandise subject to hire purchase or

other agreements (written down value) ...................................

Goodwill and benefit of contracts ............................................

Patents, designs, trademarks, licences, copyrights, etc.

Book and other debts .................................................................

Cash in hand and at bank on current account, bills, notes,

etc ............................................................................................

Cash on deposit at bank or elsewhere ......................................

Shares, debentures and other investments ............................

Other property ..........................................................................

Signed                                   Designation‡                          Date

Certificate of value§

It is certified that the transaction effected by the contract does not form part of a larger transaction or series of transactions in respect of which the amount or value, or aggregate amount or value, of the consideration exceeds £

Signed                                                                                   Date

Signed                                                                                   Date

Companies Form No. 88(3) (p 4)

## Notes

The address for companies registered in England and Wales or Wales is:-

The Registrar of Companies
Companies House
Crown Way
Cardiff
CF4 3UZ

or, for companies registered in Scotland:-

The Registrar of Companies
Companies House
100-102 George Street
Edinburgh
EH2 3DJ

# G

COMPANIES FORM No. 97

## Statement of the amount or rate per cent of any commission payable in connection with the subscription of shares

**97**

Note: This form is not required in the case of shares offered to the public for subscription

Pursuant to section 97 of the Companies Act 1985

Please do not
write in
this margin

Please complete
legibly, preferably
in black type, or
bold block lettering

* insert full name
of company

† the commission
paid or agreed to
be paid must not
exceed ten per
cent of the price
at which the
shares are
issued or the
amount or rate
authorised by
the Articles
whichever is the
less

**Note**
This statement must
be delivered to the
Registrar of
Companies before
the payment of
commission

To the Registrar of Companies
(Address overleaf)

For official use

Company number

Name of company

*

Amount payable as commission for subscribing, whether

absolutely or conditionally, or agreeing to subscribe, or for

procuring or agreeing to procure, subscriptions, whether

absolute or conditional, for any shares in the company†   £ _____

or

Rate per cent of such commission † _____

Number of shares for which persons have agreed for

a commission to subscribe absolutely _____

Signatures of all the directors
or of their agents authorised in
writing

Date

Presentor's name address and
reference (if any):

For official Use

General Section

Post room

331

Companies Form No. 97 (p 2)

**Notes**

The address for companies registered in England and Wales or Wales is:-

The Registrar of Companies
Companies House
Crown Way
Cardiff
CF4 3UZ

or, for companies registered in Scotland:-

The Registrar of Companies
Companies House
100-102 George Street
Edinburgh
EH2 3DJ

COMPANIES FORM No. 117

# Application by a public company for certificate to commence business and statutory declaration in support

Please do not write in this margin

Pursuant to section 117 of the Companies Act 1985

Please complete legibly, preferably in black type, or bold block lettering

To the Registrar of Companies (Address overleaf)

For official use

Company number

Name of company

* insert full name of company

*

applies for a certificate that it is entitled to do business and exercise borrowing powers.

For that purpose I, _____

of _____

† delete as appropriate

[the secretary][a director]† of the above company,

do solemnly and sincerely declare that;

1  the nominal value of the company's allotted share capital is not less than the authorised minimum

2  the amount paid up on the allotted share capital of the company at the time of this application is

£

3  the [estimated]† amount of the preliminary expenses of the company is

£

and [has been paid][is payable]† by

§ insert name of person(s) by whom expenses paid or payable

§

Presentor's name address and reference (if any):

For official Use

General Section

Post room

Page 1

333

# Companies Form No. 117 (p 2)

COMPANIES FORM No. 117

## Application by a public company for certificate to commence business and statutory declaration in support

# 117

Pursuant to section 117 of the Companies Act 1985

**Please do not write in this margin**

**Please complete legibly, preferably in black type, or bold block lettering**

To the Registrar of Companies
(Address overleaf)

For official use

Company number

Name of company

\* **insert full name of company**

*

applies for a certificate that it is entitled to do business and exercise borrowing powers.

For that purpose I, _____

of _____

_____

_____

† **delete as appropriate**

[the secretary][a director]† of the above company,

do solemnly and sincerely declare that;

1    the nominal value of the company's allotted share capital is not less than the authorised minimum

2    the amount paid up on the allotted share capital of the company at the time of this application is

£

3    the [estimated]† amount of the preliminary expenses of the company is

£

and [has been paid][is payable]† by

§ **insert name of person(s) by whom expenses paid or payable**

§

Presentor's name address and reference (if any):

For official Use

General Section

Post room

Page 1

**COMPANIES FORM No. 122**

# Notice of consolidation, division, sub-division, redemption or cancellation of shares, or conversion, re-conversion of stock into shares

**122**

Please do not
write in
this margin

Pursuant to section 122 of the Companies Act 1985

Please complete
legibly, preferably
in black type, or
bold block lettering

To the Registrar of Companies
(Address overleaf)

Name of company

For official use     Company number

\* insert full name
of company

gives notice that:

‡ Insert
Director,
Secretary,
Administrator,
Administrative
Receiver or
Receiver
(Scotland) as
appropriate

Signed                    Designation‡              Date

Presentor's name address and
reference (if any):

For official Use
General Section          Post room

Companies Form No. 122 (p 2)

# G

**COMPANIES FORM No. 123**

## Notice of increase in nominal capital

# 123

Please do not write in this margin

Pursuant to section 123 of the Companies Act 1985

Please complete legibly, preferably in black type, or bold block lettering

To the Registrar of Companies
(Address overleaf)

For official use

Company number

Name of company

* insert full name of company

gives notice in accordance with section 123 of the above Act that by resolution of the company

dated _____the nominal capital of the company has been

§ the copy must be printed or in some other form approved by the registrar

increased by £ _____ beyond the registered capital of £ _____.

A copy of the resolution authorising the increase is attached.§

The conditions (eg. voting rights, dividend rights, winding-up rights etc.) subject to which the new

shares have been or are to be issued are as follow:

Please tick here if continued overleaf

‡ Insert Director, Secretary, Administrator, Administrative Receiver or Receiver (Scotland) as appropriate

Signed

Designation‡

Date

Presentor's name address and reference (if any):

For official Use
General Section

Post room

337

Companies Form No. 123 (p 2)

**Notes**

The address for companies registered in England and Wales or Wales is:-

The Registrar of Companies
Companies House
Crown Way
Cardiff
CF4 3UZ

or, for companies registered in Scotland:-

The Registrar of Companies
Companies House
100-102 George Street
Edinburgh
EH2 3DJ

# G

**COMPANIES FORM No. 128(3)**

## Statement of particulars of variation of rights attached to shares

# 128(3)

Please do not write in this margin

Pursuant to section 128(3) of the Companies Act 1985

Please complete legibly, preferably in block type, or bold block lettering

To the Registrar of Companies
(Address overleaf)

For official use

Company number

Name of company

* insert full name of company

\*

§ insert date

On §_____ the rights attached to

| Number of Shares | Class(es) of share |
|------------------|---------------------|
|                  |                     |
|                  |                     |
|                  |                     |

were varied as set out below (otherwise than by amendment of the company's memorandum or articles or by any resolution or agreement to which section 380 of the above Act applies)

‡ Insert Director, Secretary, Administrator, Administrative Receiver or Receiver (Scotland) as appropriate

Signed                    Designation‡                    Date

Presentor's name address and reference (if any):

For official Use

General Section          Post room

339

Companies Form No. 128(3) (p 2)

COMPANIES FORM No. 139

## Application by a public company for re-registration as a private company following a Court Order reducing capital

# 139

**Please do not write in this margin**

Pursuant to section 139 of the Companies Act 1985

**Please complete legibly, preferably in block type, or bold block lettering**

To the Registrar of Companies
**(Address overleaf)**

For official use

Company number

Name of company

* insert full name of company

•

a insert full name of company amended to make it appropriate for this company as a private limited company

makes application as authorised by the Court to be re-registered as a private company by the name of

a _____

_____ Limited

and, for that purpose, delivers the following document(s).

§ delete if previously presented for registration

[1. Office copy of Order of Court ]§ —

2. Printed copy of the company's memorandum and articles, as altered by the Order of Court.

† delete as appropriate

Signed

[Director][Secretary]† Date

Presentor's name address and reference (if any):

For official Use
General Section

Post room

Companies Form No. 139 (p 2)

# G

**COMPANIES FORM No.155(6)a**

## Declaration in relation to assistance for the acquisition of shares.

# 155(6)a

Pursuant to section 155(6) of the Companies Act 1985

Please do not write in this margin

Please complete legibly, preferably in block type, or bold block lettering

**Note**
Please read the notes on page 3 before completing this form.

\* insert full name of company

ø insert name(s) and address(es) of all the directors

To the Registrar of Companies
(Address overleaf- Note 5)

**For official use**

**Company number**

Name of company

\*

I/We ø

† delete as appropriate

§ delete whichever is inappropriate

[the sole director][all the directors]† of the above company do solemnly and sincerely declare that:

The business of the company is:

(a) that of a [recognised bank][licensed institution]† within the meaning of the Banking Act 1979§

(b) that of a person authorised under section 3 or 4 of the Insurance Companies Act 1982 to carry on insurance business in the United Kingdom§

(c) something other than the above§

The company is proposing to give financial assistance in connection with the acquisition of shares in the [company] [company's holding company _____

_____ Limited]†

The assistance is for the purpose of [that acquisition][reducing or discharging a liability incurred for the purpose of that acquisition].†

The number and class of the shares acquired or to be acquired is: _____

_____

| Presentor's name address and reference (if any): | For official Use | |
|---|---|---|
| | General Section | Post room |

Page 1

343

# Companies Form No. 155(6)(a) (p 2)

The assistance is to be given to: (note 2) _____

_____

_____

_____

Please do not write in this margin

Please complete legibly, preferably in block type, or bold block lettering

The assistance will take the form of:

The person who [has acquired][will acquire]† the shares is:

_____

_____

† delete as appropriate

The principal terms on which the assistance will be given are:

The amount of cash to be transferred to the person assisted is £_____

The value of any asset to be transferred to the person assisted is £_____

The date on which the assistance is to be given is _____ 19 _____

Page 2

344

I/We have formed the opinion, as regards the company's initial situation immediately following the date on which the assistance is proposed to be given, that there will be no ground on which it could then be found to be unable to pay its debts.(note 3)

(a)[I/We have formed the opinion that the company will be able to pay its debts as they fall due during the year immediately following that date]*(note 3)

(b)[It is intended to commence the winding-up of the company within 12 months of that date, and I/we have formed the opinion that the company will be able to pay its debts in full within 12 months of the commencement of the winding up.]*(note 3)

And I/we make this solemn declaration conscientiously believing the same to be true and by virtue of the provisions of the Statutory Declarations Act 1835.

Declared at _____          Declarants to sign below

_____

_____

the_____ day of _____

one thousand nine hundred and _____

_____

before me _____

A Comissioner for Oaths or Notary Public or Justice of
the Peace or a Solicitor having the powers conferred on
a Comissioner for Oaths.

## NOTES

1   For the meaning of "a person incurring a
    liability" and "reducing or discharging a
    liability" see section 152(3) of the Companies
    Act 1985.

2   Insert full name(s) and address(es) of the
    person(s) to whom assistance is to be given; if
    a recipient is a company the registered office
    address should be shown.

3   Contingent and prospective liabilities of the
    company are to be taken into account - see
    section 156(3) of the Companies Act 1985.

4   The auditors report required by section 156(4)
    of the Companies Act 1985 must be annexed
    to this form.

5   The address for companies registered in
    England and Wales or Wales is:-

    The Registrar of Companies
    Companies House
    Crown Way
    Cardiff
    CF4 3UZ

    or, for companies registered in Scotland:-

    The Registrar of Companies
    Companies House
    100-102 George Street
    Edinburgh
    EH2 3DJ

Page 3

**Companies Form No. 157 (p 1)**

COMPANIES FORM No. 157

## Notice of application made to the Court for the cancellation of a special resolution regarding financial assistance for the acquisition of shares

**157**

Please do not write in this margin

Pursuant to section 157(3) of the Companies Act 1985

Please complete legibly, preferably in black type, or bold block lettering

To the Registrar of Companies (Address overleaf)

For official use

Company number

Name of company

* insert full name of company

*

gives notice that an application has been made to the Court on _____

for the cancellation of the special resolution passed by the company on _____

approving the giving of financial assistance by

† delete as appropriate

   [the company]†

ø insert full name of the subsidiary company proposing to give the financial assistance

   [the company's subsidiary ø _____

   _____ ]†

for the purchase of shares :—

   (a) [in the company]†

§ insert full name of the holding company in relation to the acquisition of whose shares financial assistance is proposed to be given

   (b) [in § _____

   _____ , the company's holding company].†

‡ Insert Director, Secretary, Administrator, Administrative Receiver or Receiver (Scotland) as appropriate

Signed                Designation‡                Date

Presentor's name address and reference (if any):

For official Use

General Section               Post room

## Notes

The address for companies registered in England and Wales or Wales is:-

The Registrar of Companies
Companies House
Crown Way
Cardiff
CF4 3UZ

or, for companies registered in Scotland:-

The Registrar of Companies
Companies House
100-102 George Street
Edinburgh
EH2 3DJ

# Companies Form No. 169 (p 1)

**G**

COMPANIES FORM No. 169

## Return by a company purchasing its own shares

**169**

Pursuant to section 169 of the Companies Act 1985

Please do not write in this margin

Please complete legibly, preferably in black type, or bold block lettering

* insert full name of company

**Note**
This return must be delivered to the Registrar within a period of 28 days beginning with the first date on which shares to which it relates were delivered to the company

§ A private company is not required to give this information

‡ Insert Director, Secretary, Receiver, Administrator, Administrative Receiver or Receiver (Scotland) as appropriate

To the Registrar of Companies
(Address overleaf)

For official use

Company number

Please do not write in the space below. For Inland Revenue use only.

Name of company

*

Shares were purchased by the company under section 162 of the above Act as follows:

| Class of shares | | | |
|---|---|---|---|
| Number of shares purchased | | | |
| Nominal value of each share | | | |
| Date(s) on which the shares were delivered to the company | | | |
| Maximum prices paid § for each share | | | |
| Minimum prices paid § for each share | | | |

The aggregate amount paid by the company for the shares to which this return relates was: £

Stamp duty payable pursuant to section 66 of the Finance Act 1986 on the aggregate amount at 50p per £100 or part of £100 £

Signed                    Designation‡                    Date

Presentor's name address and reference (if any):

For official Use
General Section                    Post room

348

## Notes

The address for companies registered in England and Wales or Wales is:-

The Registrar of Companies
Companies House
Crown Way
Cardiff
CF4 3UZ

or, for companies registered in Scotland:-

The Registrar of Companies
Companies House
100-102 George Street
Edinburgh
EH2 3DJ

# Companies Form No. 173 (p 1)

**G**

COMPANIES FORM No.173

## Declaration in relation to the redemption or purchase of shares out of capital

**173**

Pursuant to section 173 of the Companies Act 1985

To the Registrar of Companies
(Address overleaf - Note 4)

For official use

Company number

Name of company

*

I/We ø

[the sole director][all the directors]† of the above company do solemnly and sincerely declare that:

The business of the company is:

(a) that of a [recognised bank][licensed institution]† within the meaning of the Banking Act 1979§

(b) that of a person authorised under section 3 or 4 of the Insurance Companies Act 1982 to carry on insurance business in the United Kingdom§

(c) that of something other than the above§

The company is proposing to make a payment out of capital for the redemption or purchase of its own shares

The amount of the permissible capital payment for the shares in question is £_____
(note 1)

Continued overleaf

Presentor's name address and reference (if any):

For official Use
General Section

Post room

Page 1

I/We have made full enquiry into the affairs and prospects of the company, and I/we have formed the opinion:

(a)  as regards its initial situation immediately following the date on which the payment out of capital is proposed to be made, that there will be no grounds on which the company could then be found unable to pay its debts (note 2), and

(b)  as regards its prospects for the year immediately following that date, that, having regard to my/our intentions with respect to the management of the company's business during that year and to the amount and character of the financial resources which will in my/our view be available during that year, the company will be able to continue to carry on business as a going concern (and will accordingly be able to pay its debts as they fall due) throughout that year.(note 2)

And I/we make this solemn declaration conscientiously believing the same to be true and by virtue of the provisions of the Statutory Declarations Act 1835.

Declared at _____     Declarant(s) to sign below

_____

the_____ day of _____

one thousand nine hundred and _____

before me _____
A Comissioner for Oaths or Notary Public or Justice of
the Peace or a Solicitor having the powers conferred on
a Comissioner for Oaths.

## Notes

1  'Permissible capital payment' means an amount which, taken together with
   (i) any available profits of the company; and
   (ii) the proceeds of any fresh issue of shares made for the purposes of the redemption or purchase;
   is equal to the price of redemption or purchase.
   'Available profits' means the company's profits which are available for distribution (within the meaning of section 172 and 263 of the Companies Act 1985).
   The question whether the company has any profits so available and the amount of any such profits is to be determined in accordance with section 172 of the Companies Act 1985.

2  Contingent and prospective liabilities of the company must be taken into account, see sections 173(4) & 517 of the Companies Act 1985.

3  A copy of this declaration together with a copy of the auditors report required by section 173 of the Companies Act 1985, must be delivered to the Registrar of Companies not later than the day on which the company publishes the notice required by section 175(1) of the Companies Act 1985, or first publishes or gives the notice required by section 175(2), whichever is the earlier.

4  The address for companies registered in England and Wales or Wales is:-

   The Registrar of Companies
   Companies House
   Crown Way
   Cardiff
   CF4 3UZ

   or, for companies registered in Scotland:-

   The Registrar of Companies
   Companies House
   100-102 George Street
   Edinburgh
   EH2 3DJ

Page 2

351

Companies Form No. 176 (p 1)

# G

**COMPANIES FORM No. 176**

## Notice of application to the Court for the cancellation of a resolution for the redemption or purchase of shares out of capital

**176**

Pursuant to section 176 of the Companies Act 1985


Please do not write in this margin

Please complete legibly, preferably in block type, or bold block lettering

* insert full name of company

To the Registrar of Companies
(Address overleaf)

For official use

Company number

Name of company

*

gives notice that an application has been made to the Court for the cancellation of the special resolution

dated _____ approving payment out of capital for

the redemption or purchase of some of the company's shares.

‡ Insert Director, Secretary, Administrator, Administrative Receiver or Receiver (Scotland) as appropriate

Signed                    Designation‡                    Date

Presentor's name address and reference (if any):

For official Use
General Section            Post room

352

## Notes

The address for companies registered in England and Wales or Wales is:-

The Registrar of Companies
Companies House
Crown Way
Cardiff
CF4 3UZ

or, for companies registered in Scotland:-

The Registrar of Companies
Companies House
100-102 George Street
Edinburgh
EH2 3DJ

Companies Form No. 190 (p 1)

# G

**COMPANIES FORM No. 190**

## Notice of place where a register of holders of debentures or a duplicate is kept or of any change in that place

**190**

Note: This notice is not required where the register is, and has always been, kept at the Registered Office

Pursuant to section 190 of the Companies Act 1985

To the Registrar of Companies
(Address overleaf)

For official use

Company number

Name of company

*

gives notice that [a register][registers]† [in duplicate form]† of holders of debentures of the company of

the classes mentioned below[is][are]† now kept at:

Postcode

Brief description of class of debentures

Signed

Designation‡

Date

Presentor's name address and reference (if any):

For official Use

General Section

Post room

354

## Notes

The address for companies registered in England and Wales or Wales is:-

The Registrar of Companies
Companies House
Crown Way
Cardiff
CF4 3UZ

or, for companies registered in Scotland:-

The Registrar of Companies
Companies House
100-102 George Street
Edinburgh
EH2 3DJ

# Companies Form No. 224 (p 1)

**COMPANIES FORM No. 224**

## Notice of accounting reference date
## (to be delivered within 9 months of
## incorporation)

**224**

Pursuant to section 224 of the Companies Act 1985
as inserted by section 3 of the Companies Act 1989

To the Registrar of Companies
(Address overleaf)

Company number

Name of company

*

gives notice that the date on which the company's accounting reference period is to be treated as

coming to an end in each successive year is as shown below:

Day    Month

Signed

Designation‡

Date

Presentor's name address
telephone number and reference (if any):

For official use
D.E.B.

Post room

356

## Notes

The address for companies registered in England and Wales or Wales is:-

The Registrar of Companies
Companies House
Crown Way
Cardiff
CF4 3UZ

or, for companies registered in Scotland:-

The Registrar of Companies
Companies House
100-102 George Street
Edinburgh
EH2 3DJ

Companies Form No. 287 (p 1)

**G**

COMPANIES FORM No. 287

## Notice of change in situation of registered office

**287**

Pursuant to section 287 of the Companies Act 1985
as substituted by section 136 of the Companies Act 1989

To the Registrar of Companies
(Address overleaf)

Company number

Name of company

* 

gives notice of a change in the situation of the registered office of the company to:

Postcode

Signed                    Designation‡                    Date

Presentor's name address
telephone number and reference (if any):

For official use
D.E.B.                              Post room

358

## Notes

The address for companies registered in England and Wales or Wales is:-

The Registrar of Companies
Companies House
Crown Way
Cardiff
CF4 3UZ


or, for companies registered in Scotland:-

The Registrar of Companies
Companies House
100-102 George Street
Edinburgh
EH2 3DJ

**COMPANIES HOUSE**

**288**

## Change of director or secretary or change of particulars.

Please complete in black using typescript or block lettering

Company number    CN

Company name

### Appointment

(Turn over page for resignation and change of particulars).

Date of appointment    DA    Day Month Year

Appointment of director    CD

Appointment of secretary    CS

Please mark the appropriate box.
If appointment is as a director and secretary mark both boxes.

**NOTES**

Show the full forenames. NOT INITIALS
If the director or secretary is a Corporation or Scottish firm, show the name on surname line and registered or principal office on the usual residential address line.

Give previous forenames or surname except:
- for a married woman the name before marriage need not be given.
- for names not used since the age of 18 or for at least 20 years.
A peer or individual known by a title may state the title instead of or in addition to the forenames and surname.

Name    *Style/title

Forenames

Surname

*Honours etc

Previous forenames

Previous surname

Usual residential address    AD

Post town

County/region

Postcode _____ Country _____

Date of birth†    DO    Nationality†    NA

Other directorships.

Give the name of every company incorporated in Great Britain of which the person concerned is a director or has been a director at any time in the past 5 years. Exclude a company which either is, or at all times during the past 5 years when the person was a director, was
- dormant
- a parent company which wholly owned the company making the return
- a wholly owned subsidiary of the company making the return
- another wholly owned subsidiary of the same parent company

Business occupation†    OC

Other directorships†

I consent to act as director/secretary of the above named company

Consent signature    Signed _____ Date _____

*Voluntary details    †Directors only

**A serving director etc must also sign the form overleaf.**

# Companies Form No. 288 (p 2)

## Resignation

(This includes any form of ceasing to hold office e.g. death or removal from office).

Date of resignation etc — **DR** | | | |

Resignation etc, as director — **XD**

Resignation etc, as secretary — **XS**

> *Please mark the appropriate box.*
> *If resignation etc is as a director and secretary mark both boxes.*

Forenames

Surname

Date of birth *(directors only)* — **DO** | | | |

If cessation is other than resignation, please state reason *(eg death)*

## Change of particulars *(this section is not for appointments or resignations).*

*Complete this section in all cases where particulars of a serving director/ secretary, have changed and then the appropriate section below.*

Date of change of particulars — **DC** | | | |

Change of particulars, as director — **ZD**

Change of particulars, as secretary — **ZS**

> *Please mark the appropriate box.*
> *If change of particulars is as a director and secretary mark both boxes.*

Forenames ⎤ *(name previously notified to Companies House)*
Surname ⎦

Date of birth *(directors only)* — **DO** | | | |

## Change of name *(enter new name)*

Forenames — **NN**

Surname

## Change of usual residential address *(enter new address)*

**AD**

Post town

County/region

Postcode _____ Country

## Other change

*(please specify)*

---

A serving director, secretary etc must sign the form below.

**Signature**

Signed _____ Date _____

(by a serving director/secretary/administrator/ administrative receiver/receiver). *(Delete as appropriate)*

After signing please return the form to the Registrar of Companies at

or

**Companies House, Crown Way, Cardiff CF4 3UZ** for companies registered in England and Wales

**Companies House, 100-102 George Street, Edinburgh EH2 3DJ** for companies registered in Scotland.

To whom should Companies House direct any enquiries about the information on this form?

_____

_____

_____ Tel: _____

# Companies Form No. 318 (p 1)

**G**

COMPANIES FORM No. 318

## Notice of place where copies of directors' service contracts and any memoranda are kept or of any change in that place

**318**

Note: This notice is not required where the relevant documents are and have always been kept at the Registered Office

Pursuant to section 318 of the Companies Act 1985

Please do not write in this margin

To the Registrar of Companies
(Address overleaf)

For official use

Company number

Please complete legibly, preferably in block type, or bold block lettering

Name of company

* insert full name of company

gives notice that copies of such of the directors' service contracts (or where they are not in writing written memoranda setting out the terms of such contracts) as are required to be kept by the company

† delete as appropriate

and to be open to the inspection of the members of the company are [now]† kept at:

Postcode

‡ Insert Director, Secretary, Administrator, Administrative Receiver or Receiver (Scotland) as appropriate

Signed                    Designation‡                    Date

Presentor's name address and reference (if any):

For official Use
General Section                    Post room

362

## Notes

The address for companies registered in England and Wales or Wales is:-

The Registrar of Companies
Companies House
Crown Way
Cardiff
CF4 3UZ


or, for companies registered in Scotland:-

The Registrar of Companies
Companies House
100-102 George Street
Edinburgh
EH2 3DJ

Companies Form No. 325 (p 1)

**G**

COMPANIES FORM No. 325

## Notice of place where register of directors' interests in shares etc. is kept or of any change in that place

Note: This notice is not required where the register is and has always been kept at the Registered Office

**325**

Pursuant to section 325 of and Schedule 13 paragraph 27 to the Companies Act 1985

Please do not write in this margin

Please complete legibly, preferably in black type, or bold block lettering

To the Registrar of Companies (Address overleaf)

For official use

Company number

Name of company

* insert full name of company

•

gives notice that the register of directors' interests in shares and/or debentures, which is kept by the

† delete as appropriate

company pursuant to section 325 of the above Act, is [now] † kept at:

Postcode

‡ Insert Director, Secretary, Administrator, Administrative Receiver or Receiver (Scotland) as appropriate

Signed

Designation‡

Date

Presentor's name address and reference (if any):

For official Use
General Section

Post room

364

## Notes

The address for companies registered in England and Wales or Wales is:-

The Registrar of Companies
Companies House
Crown Way
Cardiff
CF4 3UZ


or, for companies registered in Scotland:-

The Registrar of Companies
Companies House
100-102 George Street
Edinburgh
EH2 3DJ

# Companies Form No. 353 (p 1)

**G**

COMPANIES FORM No. 353

## Notice of place where register of members is kept or of any change in that place

**353**

Note: This notice is not required where the register is and has, since 1 July 1948, always been kept at the Registered Office

Pursuant to section 353 of the Companies Act 1985

To the Registrar of Companies
(Address overleaf)

For official use

Company number

Name of company

*

gives notice that the register of members is [now]† kept at:

Postcode

Signed

Designation‡

Date

Presentor's name address and reference (if any):

For official Use
General Section

Post room

366

## Notes

The address for companies registered in England and Wales or Wales is:-

The Registrar of Companies
Companies House
Crown Way
Cardiff
CF4 3UZ

or, for companies registered in Scotland:-

The Registrar of Companies
Companies House
100-102 George Street
Edinburgh
EH2 3DJ

# Companies Form No. 363a/bp (p 1)

**Company Name and Number**

Name: _____

No: _____

**Directors** (continued)

| Name | *Style/Title | CD |
| | Forenames | |
| | Surname | |
| | *Honours etc | |
| | Previous forenames | |
| | Previous surname | |

**Address**

Usual residential address must be given. In the case of a corporation, give the registered or principal office address.

AD

Post town _____

County/Region _____

Postcode _____ Country _____

Date of birth  DO

Nationality  NA

Business occupation  OC

Other directorships  OD

| Name | *Style/Title | CD |
| | Forenames | |
| | Surname | |
| | *Honours etc | |
| | Previous forenames | |
| | Previous surname | |

**Address**

Usual residential address must be given. In the case of a corporation, give the registered or principal office address.

AD

Post town _____

County/Region _____

Postcode _____ Country _____

Date of birth  DO

Nationality  NA

Business occupation  OC

Other directorships  OD

* Voluntary details

**363a/b continuation sheet**

**Directors** (continued)

**Name**   *Style/Title   **CD**

Forenames

Surname

*Honours etc

Previous forenames

Previous surname

**Address**   **AD**

Usual residential address must be given.
In the case of a corporation, give the
registered or principal office address.

Post town

County/Region

Postcode          Country

Date of birth   **DO**          Nationality   **NA**

Business occupation   **OC**

Other directorships   **OD**

**Name**   *Style/Title   **CD**

Forenames

Surname

*Honours etc

Previous forenames

Previous surname

**Address**   **AD**

Usual residential address must be given.
In the case of a corporation, give the
registered or principal office address.

Post town

County/Region

Postcode          Country

Date of birth   **DO**          Nationality   **NA**

Business occupation   **OC**

Other directorships   **OD**

* Voluntary details

# Companies Form No. 363a (p 1)

**COMPANIES HOUSE**

This form should be completed in black.

# 363a
# Annual Return

| | |
|---|---|
| Company number | **CN** |
| Company name | |

**Date of this return** *(See note 1)*
The information in this return is made up to

Day Month Year

**DA**    Show date

**Date of next return** *(See note 2)*
If you wish to make your next return to a date earlier than the anniversary of this return please show the date here. Companies House will then send a form at the appropriate time.

**DB**

**Registered Office** *(See note 3)*
Show here the address at the date of this return.

**RO**

Post town

County/Region

Any change of registered office **must** be notified on form 287.

Postcode

**Principal business activities**
*(See note 4)*
Show trade classification code number(s) for principal activity or activities.

**PA**

If the code number cannot be determined, give a brief description of principal activity.

1

**Directors** (continued)

**Name**

\*Style/Title | **CD**

Forenames

Surname

\*Honours etc

Previous forenames

Previous surname

**Address**

Usual residential address must be given. In the case of a corporation, give the registered or principal office address.

**AD**

Post town

County/Region

Postcode

Country

Date of birth | **DO**

Nationality | **NA**

Business occupation | **OC**

Other directorships | **OD**

**Name**

\*Style/Title | **CD**

Forenames

Surname

\*Honours etc

Previous forenames

Previous surname

**Address**

Usual residential address must be given. In the case of a corporation, give the registered or principal office address.

**AD**

Post town

County/Region

Postcode

Country

Date of birth | **DO**

Nationality | **NA**

Business occupation | **OC**

Other directorships | **OD**

\* Voluntary details

# Companies Form No. 363a (p 3)

**Directors** *(See note 8)*
*Please list directors in alphabetical order.*

Details of new directors **must** be notified on form 288.

**Name**

*Style/Title     **CD**

Forenames

Surname

*Honours etc

Previous forenames

Previous surname

**Address**   **AD**

Usual residential address must be given.
In the case of a corporation, give the
registered or principal office address.

Post town

County/Region

Postcode            Country

Date of birth   **DO**           Nationality  **NA**

Business occupation   **OC**

Other directorships   **OD**

---

**Name**

*Style/Title     **CD**

Forenames

Surname

*Honours etc

Previous forenames

Previous surname

**Address**   **AD**

Usual residential address must be given.
In the case of a corporation, give the
registered or principal office address.

Post town

County/Region

Postcode            Country

Date of birth   **DO**           Nationality  **NA**

Business occupation   **OC**

Other directorships   **OD**

* Voluntary details

3

372

**Issued share capital** *(See note 9)*
Enter details of all the shares in issue at the date of this return.

| Class | Number | Aggregate Nominal Value |
|-------|--------|-------------------------|
|  |  |  |
|  |  |  |
|  |  |  |
|  |  |  |
| Totals |  |  |

**List of past and present members**
*(Use attached schedule where appropriate)*

A full list is required if one was not included with either of the last two returns.
*(See note 10)*

*Please mark the appropriate box(es)*

There were no changes in the period ☐

|  | on paper | not on paper |
|--|----------|--------------|
| A list of changes is enclosed | ☐ | ☐ |
| A full list of members is enclosed | ☐ | ☐ |

**Elective resolutions** *(See note 11)*
*(Private companies only)*

If an election is in force at the date of this return to dispense with annual general meetings, *mark this box* ☐

If an election is in force at the date of this return to dispense with laying accounts in general meetings, *mark this box* ☐

**Certificate**
I certify that the information given in this return is true to the best of my knowledge and belief.

**Signed** ............................................................... Secretary/Director*
*(*delete as appropriate)*

Date ...........................................................

This return includes ........................... continuation sheets.
*(enter number)*

To whom should Companies House direct any enquiries about the information shown in this return?

_____

_____

_____

_____ Postcode _____

Telephone _____ Extension _____

When you have signed the return send it with the fee to the Registrar of Companies at

**Companies House, Crown Way, Cardiff CF4 3UZ**
for companies registered in England and Wales
**or**
**Companies House, 100-102 George Street, Edinburgh EH2 3DJ**
for companies registered in Scotland.

4

# Companies Form No. 363a (p 5)

**Directors** (continued)

**Name**

\*Style/Title **CD**

Forenames

Surname

\*Honours etc

Previous forenames

Previous surname

**Address** **AD**

Usual residential address must be given.
In the case of a corporation, give the
registered or principal office address.

Post town

County/Region

Postcode      Country

Date of birth **DO**      Nationality **NA**

Business occupation **OC**

Other directorships **OD**

---

**Name**

\*Style/Title **CD**

Forenames

Surname

\*Honours etc

Previous forenames

Previous surname

**Address** **AD**

Usual residential address must be given.
In the case of a corporation, give the
registered or principal office address.

Post town

County/Region

Postcode      Country

Date of birth **DO**      Nationality **NA**

Business occupation **OC**

Other directorships **OD**

\* Voluntary details

5

**Directors** (continued)

**Name**

*Style/Title    **CD**

Forenames

Surname

*Honours etc

Previous forenames

Previous surname

**Address**    **AD**

Usual residential address must be given.
In the case of a corporation, give the
registered or principal office address.

Post town

County/Region

Postcode      Country

Date of birth    **DO**      Nationality   **NA**

Business occupation    **OC**

Other directorships    **OD**

**Name**

*Style/Title    **CD**

Forenames

Surname

*Honours etc

Previous forenames

Previous surname

**Address**    **AD**

Usual residential address must be given.
In the case of a corporation, give the
registered or principal office address.

Post town

County/Region

Postcode      Country

Date of birth    **DO**      Nationality   **NA**

Business occupation    **OC**

Other directorships    **OD**

* Voluntary details

6

# Companies Form No. 363a Schedule (p 1)

**LIST OF PAST AND PRESENT MEMBERS**                    **SCHEDULE TO FORM 363**

| | | Account of Shares | | |
|---|---|---|---|---|
| Company Number:<br><br>Company Name: | Number of shares or amount of stock held by existing members at date of this return. | Particulars of shares transferred since the date of the last return, or, in the case of the first return, since the incorporation of the company, by<br>(a) persons who are still members, and<br>(b) persons who have ceased to be members. | | |
| Name and address | Number Currently Held | Number Transferred | Date of Registration of Transfer | Remarks |
| | | | | |
| | | | | |
| | | | | |
| | | | | |
| | | | | |
| | | | | |
| | | | | |
| | | | | |
| | | | | |
| | | | | |
| | | | | |
| | | | | |
| | | | | |
| | | | | |
| | | | | |
| | | | | |
| | | | | |
| | | | | |
| | | | | |
| | | | | |
| | | | | |
| | | | | |
| | | | | |
| | | | | |
| | | | | |
| | | | | |
| | | | | |
| | | | | |
| | | | | |
| | | | | |

**Continued overleaf**

**LIST OF PAST AND PRESENT MEMBERS (continued)**  SCHEDULE TO FORM 363

Company Number:

Company Name:

| Name and address | Number of shares or amount of stock held by existing members at date of this return. Number Currently Held | Particulars of shares transferred since the date of the last return, or, in the case of the first return, since the incorporation of the company, by (a) persons who are still members, and (b) persons who have ceased to be members. Number Transferred | Date of Registration of Transfer | Remarks |
|---|---|---|---|---|
|  |  |  |  |  |
|  |  |  |  |  |
|  |  |  |  |  |
|  |  |  |  |  |
|  |  |  |  |  |
|  |  |  |  |  |
|  |  |  |  |  |
|  |  |  |  |  |
|  |  |  |  |  |
|  |  |  |  |  |
|  |  |  |  |  |
|  |  |  |  |  |
|  |  |  |  |  |
|  |  |  |  |  |
|  |  |  |  |  |

Companies Form No. 386 (p 1)

# G

COMPANIES FORM No. 386

## Notice of passing of resolution removing an auditor

# 386

Pursuant to section 386 of the Companies Act 1985

Please do not write in this margin

To the Registrar of Companies
(Address overleaf)

For official use

Company number

Please complete legibly, preferably in black type, or bold block lettering

Name of company

* insert full name of company

*

gives notice that by a resolution passed at a general meeting of the company

on _____ 19 _____

§ insert name and address of removed auditor(s)

§_____

_____

of _____

_____

Postcode:

was removed as auditor before the expiration of his term of office, with effect from

ø delete or complete as appropriate

[the passing of the resolution]ø

[_____19_____ ]ø

‡ Insert Director, Secretary, Administrator, Administrative Receiver or Receiver (Scotland) as appropriate

Signed

Designation‡

Date

Presentor's name address and reference (if any):

For official Use
General Section

Post room

378

## Notes

The address for companies registered in England and Wales or Wales is:-

The Registrar of Companies
Companies House
Crown Way
Cardiff
CF4 3UZ

or, for companies registered in Scotland:-

The Registrar of Companies
Companies House
100-102 George Street
Edinburgh
EH2 3DJ

Companies Form No. 395 (p 1)

**M**

COMPANIES FORM No. 395

## Particulars of a mortgage or charge

**395**

Pursuant to section 395 of the Companies Act 1985

To the Registrar of Companies
(Address overleaf - Note 5)

For official use

Company number

Name of company

*

Date of creation of the charge

Description of the instrument (If any) creating or evidencing the charge (note 2)

Amount secured by the mortgage or charge

Names and addresses of the mortgagees or persons entitled to the charge

Postcode

Presentor's name address and
reference (if any):

For official Use

Mortgage Section

Post room

Page 1

Time critical reference

380

Short particulars of all the property mortgaged or charged

Particulars as to commission allowance or discount (note 3)

Signed                                          Date

On behalf of [company][mortgagee/chargee]†

## Notes

1 The original instrument (if any) creating or evidencing the charge, together with these prescribed particulars correctly completed must be delivered to the Registrar of Companies within 21 days after the date of creation of the charge (section 395). If the property is situated and the charge was created outside the United Kingdom delivery to the Registrar must be effected within 21 days after the date on which the instrument could in due course of post, and if dispatched with due diligence, have been received in the United Kingdom (section 398). A copy of the instrument creating the charge will be accepted where the property charged is situated and the charge was created outside the United Kingdom (section 398) and in such cases the copy must be verified to be a correct copy either by the company or by the person who has delivered or sent the copy to the registrar. The verification must be signed by or on behalf of the person giving the verification and where this is given by a body corporate it must be signed by an officer of that body. A verified copy will also be accepted where section 398(4) applies (property situate in Scotland or Northern Ireland) and Form No. 398 is submitted.

2 A description of the instrument, eg "Trust Deed", "Debenture", "Mortgage" or "Legal charge", etc, as the case may be, should be given.

3 In this section there should be inserted the amount or rate per cent. of the commission, allowance or discount (if any) paid or made either directly or indirectly by the company to any person in consideration of his;
    (a) subscribing or agreeing to subscribe, whether absolutely or conditionally, or
    (b) procuring or agreeing to procure subscriptions, whether absolute or conditional,
for any of the debentures included in this return. The rate of interest payable under the terms of the debentures should not be entered.

4 If any of the spaces in this form provide insufficient space the particulars must be entered on the prescribed continuation sheet.

5 The address of the Registrar of Companies is:-

Companies House, Crown Way, Cardiff CF4 3UZ

Page 2

Companies Form No. 400 (p 1)

**COMPANIES FORM No. 400**

**Particulars of a mortgage or
charge subject to which property
has been acquired**

Pursuant to section 400 of the Companies Act 1985

Please do not
write in
this margin

Please complete
legibly, preferably
in black type, or
bold block lettering

To the Registrar of Companies
(Address overleaf - Note 3)

For official use

Company number

Name of company

* insert full name
of company

Date and description of the instrument (if any) creating or evidencing the mortgage or charge (note 1)

Amount secured by the mortgage or charge _____

Names and addresses of the mortgagees or persons entitled to the mortgage or charge

Short particulars of the property mortgaged or charged

Continue overleaf as necessary

Presentor's name address and
reference (if any):

For official Use

Mortgage Section

Post room

Time critical reference

Page1

382

Short particulars of the property mortgaged or charged (continued)

Date of the acquisition of the property _____

Signed_____Designation‡_____Date_____

‡ Insert
Director,
Secretary,
Administrator
or
Administrative
Receiver as
appropriate

## NOTES

1 A description of the instrument, eg."Trust Deed","Debenture", etc, as the case may be, should be given.

2 A verified copy of the instrument must be delivered with these particulars correctly completed to the Registrar of Companies within 21 days after the date of the completion of the acquisition of the property which is subject to the charge. The copy must be verified to be a correct copy either by the company or by the person who has delivered or sent the copy to the registrar. The verification must be signed by or on behalf of the person giving the verification and where this is given by a body corporate it must be signed by an officer of that body. If the property is situated and the charge was created outside Great Britain, they must be delivered within 21 days after the date on which the copy of the instrument could in due course of post, and if despatched with due diligence have been received in the United Kingdom.

3 The address of the Registrar of Companies is:-

Companies House
Crown Way
Cardiff
CF4 3UZ

Page 2

Companies Form No. 405(1) (p 1)

**M**

COMPANIES FORM No.405(1)

**Notice of appointment of receiver or manager**

Pursuant to section 405(1) of the Companies Act 1985

**405(1)**

Please do not write in this binding margin

Please complete legibly, preferably in black type, or bold block lettering

To the Registrar of Companies
(Address overleaf)

For official use

Company number

Name of company

* insert full name of company

•

I/We

of

give notice that

ø insert name and address of receiver/manager

ø

† delete as appropriate

§ name of court making the order

‡ enter description and date of the instrument under which appointment is made, and state whether it is a debenture secured by a floating charge

was appointed as [receiver][manager][receiver and manager]† of [part of] the property of the company.

The appointment was made by

[an order of the §

made on                    ]†

[me/us on                    under the powers contained in‡

]†

Signed                                          Date

Presentor's name address and reference (if any):

For official Use
Liquidation Section          Post room

Time critical reference

384

## Notes

**The address of the Registrar of Companies is:-**

**Companies House
Crown Way
Cardiff
CF4 3UZ**

Companies Form No. 405(2) (p 1)

<table>
<tr><td>

**M**

</td><td>

COMPANIES FORM No. 405(2)

**Notice of ceasing to act as receiver or manager**

</td><td>

**405**(2)

</td></tr>
</table>

Please do not write in this margin

Pursuant to section 405(2) of the Companies Act 1985

Please complete legibly, preferably in black type, or bold block lettering

To the Registrar of Companies (Address overleaf)

For official use

Company number

Name of company

* insert full name of company

*

I/We _____

of _____

Postcode: _____

† delete as appropriate

give notice that I/we ceased to act as [receiver][manager][receiver and manager]†

of the above company on _____ 19 _____

Signed

Date

Presentor's name address and reference (if any):

For official Use

Liquidation Section

Post room

## Notes

The address of the Registrar of Companies is:-

Companies House
Crown Way
Maindy
Cardiff
CF4 3UZ

# INDEX